Flowers in the Crags

Ralph C. Walls

Ralph C. Walls
Betty Herr Walls

Flowers In The Crags
by Ralph C. Walls

Printed in the United States of America

ISBN 978-1-60266-082-3
LOC# TXu1-334-881

www.xulonpress.com

THIS BOOK IS DEDICATED TO THESE "FLOWERS" WHOM GOD PLACED ALONG MYJOURNEY:

For Jeanie, who taught me how to live; for Gid, who taught me how to laugh; for Betty, who thought she couldn't teach but from whom I have learned so much; for Stephanie and Rodney for their forgiveness; for Mom for putting up with me, for Evelyn's unceasing prayers, to Gene for his example; to Hal for being a true brother; to Karla and Mike for accepting me; to CJ, Kari, and Kalica for making me feel loved; to Maddie and Lexi, for being the treasures of my life; to Jeff for giving his all; to Alva and Laura for their faithfulness to their calling; to Elizabeth and Arie for making me feel like family; and last of all to Mike and Bonnie for standing at the fork in the road and pointing the way.

There are many many more as you will notice when you read this story. The amazing thing is that new flowers are popping up every day!

DISCLAIMER

The story contained in this book is true. Information was obtained through newspaper articles, magazine articles, logbooks, diaries, letters, and interviews with family and friends. Where information of early life was not obtainable, this author, with permission of family, was allowed to use his imagination to create the desired settings for the story. By request of some, a few names have been changed for personal reasons. In some instances, the dates are close approximations. In no way was this story ever meant to defraud or harm anyone.

CONTENTS

FLOWERS IN THE CRAGS

By Ralph C. Walls

FOREWORD

The idea to write a book came to me in May of 1997 as I was driving to Geisinger Medical Center in Danville, PA. My wife, who was in the vehicle with me, startled me when she shouted out, "Look, look at the flowers in the crags!" In the story you are about to read you will come to know why I chose this as the title for this book.

Webster defines a crag as: 1. A steep rugged rock or cliff; 2. A sharp detached fragment of rock. I've always been fascinated with the beauty of mountains. There is something about them that keeps drawing me to them. I guess it's the spirit of adventure that I have. I just need to know what is up there. As a child I would make many trips up the small mountain we had behind the farm where we lived. I learned my way around that mountain - where to step and where not to step. One false step and you could seriously hurt yourself. When you're young you take a few more chances because you don't really know about the consequences of a serious fall. I remember climbing out on a rock face in an effort to get to the top or to the other side. In order to do that you would have to look for cracks and crags in the rock in which to put your fingers or feet. This could be a dangerous thing to do, as you never knew what could be hiding in one of those crags, such as snakes! For my entire life, until the age of 50, thoughts of danger would flash through my mind whenever I would hear the word crag until there suddenly came a day when it took on an entirely new meaning for me.

I have always been proud of my ability to find my way, to not get lost when traveling to a location that I previously might have been to only once before. But in the journey of life the road we travel depends on the choices we make. Sometimes we are faced with a fork in the road, and the decision we make concerning which road to choose could drastically affect the rest of our lives. The easiest or best-looking route isn't always the right choice. In this fast-paced world we seldom slow down long enough to see what we are passing. We are in such a hurry to get to our next destination that we rarely notice anything of importance. The Bible tells us that *"the way is narrow that leads to life and few are those who find it."* The story I'm about to tell is about the lives of four people who traveled different roads, but the roads they traveled with all their twists and turns and ups and downs still brought them together. There are many other people in this story who have greatly influenced their lives and helped to make them who they are today. Is it just coincidence that we bump into certain people along the road of life, or were they purposely placed in our path to influence us or give us direction along the way? Could there be a higher power moving us around like little chess pieces, trying to point us in the right direction? As I reflected back on the past sixty years of my life, it became clear to me that I had spent over half my years in rebellion to my true purpose in life. Finally I have found true delight in my life. I was lost, but now I have been found. It is my prayer that you will enjoy *Flowers in the Crags.*

PREFACE

Let me begin with a small confession: by trade I am not a writer. I barely passed English class in high school. I was born in Morristown, New Jersey, and when I was three years old, my father and mother moved the family (my little brother and me) to a farm in Lebanon, New Jersey. The farm was located exactly in the center of what was called Round Valley. It was my father's job to work on the farm owned by two brothers named Alvah and Russell Haver. They provided us with a two-story home. On our lot, which was quite large, we had a large hay barn, three chicken houses, pear, plum, and apple trees, and lots of dogwood trees. There was a big tree in the yard that we always called the bean tree because of what looked to us like big beans hanging from the limbs. We had space to cultivate two gardens, and garden we did! We had our own springhouse and a little building we called the outhouse. Rolling pasture on one side surrounded the property. At the bottom of the pasture was Prescott Brook, great for trapping and fishing. Hay and cornfields surrounded the other sides of the property. All my life I've cherished the memories of my brother and me growing up on that farm. What we learned and saw couldn't be taught in a schoolroom. The adventures we shared in our valley still bring back many memories of great joy. But like all good things, it came to an end.

I remember one evening while sitting at the dinner table my father and mother were talking about moving. I found out that the state of New Jersey had decided to make our perfect Round Valley into a reservoir. It made sense because it was shaped just like a big bowl and thus they wouldn't need a lot of dams. That meant, though, that everyone had to move out and find new housing and employment. My father had purchased a piece of land in what we called Stanton, New Jersey, but it was still a Lebanon address. He built a ranch house on it and got a job working for a drywall contractor. I guess he was a quick learner, because in six months or so he started his own business. I remember one evening sitting at the dinner table finishing my meal. My father got up from his chair, reached over and grabbed me by the collar of my shirt and said, "Come on, you're going to work with me tonight. You can spot some nails." I had no idea what that meant, but I was excited to go and see what he was doing.

Little did I know that getting up from the dinner table that night and going to work with my father would change my life drastically. You see, I was just twelve years old. Up until then I had helped on the farm, but that was all I had done in the way of work. I knew how to drive tractors, load bales on hay wagons, and how to endure the dirtiest of jobs - riding on the back of the combine bagging grain. Now everything was about to change. We had always gone to church and Sunday school while living on the farm. As a matter of fact, I had perfect attendance bars that I wore proudly on my jacket. I knew the 100th and the 23rd Psalms by heart. But now I was working some evenings after school, every weekend, and almost every holiday including Easter and Christmas until I was out of high school. I was getting paid and paid well, not like the last summer that I worked on the farm (when I had earned $12.00 for the entire summer's work and it wasn't even given to me in cash. It was put in a savings account with my name on it and given to me at Christmas.) I graduated high school in 1964, and by then I had saved quite a bit of money and I had already mastered a trade. My father offered me a fulltime job at a salary as good as most experienced men were earning — an offer I couldn't refuse. But I would have to pay room and board to live at home. The offer sounded great and I accepted. I became just like my father — a workaholic. As long as he had the work, I would work. I remember getting my paychecks every week and rushing to the bank to make my deposit. My family would always tease me by saying that I just kept the change out and deposited the rest. They were practically right. I would round off the numbers. For example, if my check was $198.65, I would either deposit $190.00, keeping out the $8.65, or if I needed more cash that week, I might deposit only $175.00. It was fun watching my account grow, and then to get that extra bonus of earned interest was even better.

I didn't need much cash. I stayed home a lot, watched TV in the evenings and would watch old movies on Sunday afternoons with my mother. She would always have to get up and run for a box of tissues at some point in the picture. I didn't date very much; I'd had my fill of all the high school cliques, and that wasn't my style. Besides, every girl had three or four different boyfriends already, and the guys would tell of their conquests with the girls. I wanted a girl who hadn't been on the dating circuit, which to me seemed impossible to find – but more about that story later. When I think about my life and the road I've traveled, the people that I have met as our paths have crossed, I've often thought: *Just make one change and you have changed your entire life.* Once you've made a change in direction on the road you are traveling, nothing will be exactly the same again. But we know we can't go back and change what and where we have already walked. However, we don't have to walk alone. I traveled a long time alone and didn't even know I was alone. I was lost and didn't even know I was lost.

I pondered writing this book for about seven years. I could picture this whole story unfolding just like I was watching it happen right before my eyes. But when it came to putting it on paper I was totally lost. I just didn't know how to begin. Then just before Christmas my wife and I received the annual Christmas letter from one of our daughters, but instead of our daughter writing the letter, this time it had been written by our granddaughter, Kari, who was 15 at the time. We couldn't stop reading the letter, as she really had a gift for writing. I thought I should ask her to help me write this book, but then I thought, *There are some pretty serious and bad things that I will be writing about; would it be proper for a young girl her age to read and to write about those things?* So I let the idea simmer for a while. About six months later Kari approached me and asked if I would teach her how to drive. I was honored to do so and we got to spend many, many hours together that summer. I really got to know her and how mature she was beyond her years. While on vacation sometime later in Lake Tahoe, CA, while the ladies were busy shopping, I spotted some empty chairs and decided to sit and wait while they finished shopping. It wasn't too long before my granddaughter Kari came over and sat down beside me. We started to talk and I told her how I've wanted to write this book, but that I didn't know how to begin. I told her how I could see it all happening. Her comment to me was, "Just write it exactly how you told me." I protested that I couldn't write very well, and that I don't know proper punctuation, spelling, and grammar, and she said she would help me. She even bought me some books on writing. Well, after seven and a half years of procrastinating, this is my feeble attempt at writing a story to honor and remember those who've gone before us. It is my sincere prayer that as you read this book, you might find strength and courage to carry on in your journey of life.

FLOWERS IN THE CRAGS

1

THE SECRET

In the theater of my mind, I have watched this story unfold a thousand times. It's a true story and I'm sitting in a theater anticipating the opening scenes. The lights go dim and the screen widens. It's all gray now and there are strange sounds of something happening behind the screen. Then these words appear across the screen: In the Summer of 1954 on an Amish farm in Lancaster, Pa ... As the words start to fade out, an out-of-focus picture starts to fill the screen. The sounds are getting much louder now and the picture is becoming clearer. Finally you're aware that the sound was that of a wooden-wheeled wagon being pulled by a team of draft horses. There are voices of people talking and some laughter intermixed with the other sounds. But now you hear a sound that is not usually associated with such a rural scene: it sounds like an engine idling in the distance. The camera has now pulled back and the picture is in full view. There is a wagon, and it is almost completely filled with hay, and there are two Amish girls sitting on top laughing. There are Amish men and boys forking hay unto the wagon, and bits of hay are glistening in the sunlight as they float by in the air. Now you can see that there is a young Amish boy with his fork filled with hay and his head tilted back as he is looking skyward. The camera slowly turns to the sky and you can see a small plane flying overhead. The young boy is named Gideon Miller, and the wagon has passed him by. A voice suddenly penetrates the air.

"Gideon, Gideon, get your eyes out of the sky and back on the hay," his father shouts down at him from where he sits driving the team of horses. Gideon suddenly comes out of his trance and lifts the fork over his head only to miss the wagon. The two girls on top of the wagon, who are two of his sisters, are now hysterical with laughter. While missing the wagon with his fork the momentum of his swing had carried him forward, causing him to fall to the ground. But now that the wagon is fully loaded and headed for the barn, Gideon picks himself up and races to catch up so he can help with the unloading process.

Gideon B. Miller was born to Eli and Arie Miller on October 22, 1938. He was the oldest of their eight children and the only boy. His sisters were: Sarah, Katie, Mary, Nancy, Rachel, Emma, and Rebecca. Gideon was tall, slender, and good-looking with reddish brown hair, and he liked to be called "Gid." He was very inquisitive; he loved to read and was eager to learn. Gid was a hard-working teenager and always did his share of the chores. With the wagon unloaded and the chores completed, the ringing of the dinner bell sounded good to his ears. After gobbling down his food at a record pace, Gid asked to be excused from the table. Sarah and Katie yelled almost in unison, "We know where you're going! You're going to Mel Glick's." Mel Glick was the man who had flown the plane over the field earlier that afternoon. Mel's place was a couple of miles up the road from the Miller's farm.

Gid's father, Eli, interrupts, "Do you have all your chores done?"

"Yes sir," Gid replies.

Eli responds, "We have a long day ahead of us tomorrow; you need to be home and in bed early. We have to start early tomorrow."

"I know. Yes, sir. I will." Gid replies as he pushes himself away from the table and heads for the door.

The shortest way to Mel's was through the meadow, and with Gid's long legs he looked like a deer in full sprint. You see, there was a reason for his excitement. He had a secret that his family didn't know about, something that only a few of his friends knew - to be precise, the six Fisher boys. Last Thanksgiving while out hunting rabbits with Dan, Davey, Elmer, John, Levi, and Mike Fisher, they were at Boogersville near the hobo camp when Gid saw a plane coming in for a landing. Gid suggested that they all run up to the field where the plane had just landed and get a closer look. The field where the plane had landed belonged to Mel Glick. Mel had a plant farm and was the owner of the plane. When they reached the field where the plane sat, Gid said, "Let's go look at the plane." The others weren't quite sure they should, but Gid had already started over. When they reached the plane, Gid commented, "Nice plane, mister."

"Thanks," was the response from the man. "And who might you all be?"

"I'm Gid Miller and these are my friends, the Fishers," and he named them all.

"Nice to meet you all. My name is Mel Glick," was the man's response. "So what can I do for you young men today?"

Gid was never shy, and he knew you would never get anything unless you asked for it, so he said, "Well, for starters we could take a ride in your plane." Not only was Mel a little taken back by the request, but also, the Fisher boys were shocked that Gid would ask such a thing. First of all, their parents wouldn't allow it and secondly they didn't think it was a good idea.

Mel was always a kind and generous person, and seeing the fear on most of their faces, he replied, "Well, who wants to go?"

Gid had his "I do!" response out of his mouth before Mel had even finished his sentence and had turned to the Fisher boys to see who else would go.

"I will!" came the response from the youngest of the brothers, Levi, and just about in unison, "You are crazy!" from the rest. Well, on Thanksgiving Day, 1953, Gid and Levi took their first ride in an airplane. This was a secret they would all keep for a long time.

By the time Gid made it to the barn, he could hardly catch his breath. The barn door was a big sliding door, wide enough for Mel's plane to easily go in and out. There was a light on in the barn , which was shining through the opening in the door. Gid could see the nose of the plane and the legs of a person standing on the far side as he approached the door. Leaning against the doorway while catching his breath, Gid called out, "Mel, is that you?"

"Yes, Gid, I've been expecting you. Come on in."

By now Gid had gotten his breath back and asked, "So what are you doing tonight, Mel?" "Well, Gid, I'm just looking over the engine making sure everything is up to par." Mel loved to talk about his plane, and he was very skilled at teaching what he knew. This was the ideal setting for Gid because of his desire to learn. He always needed to know how everything worked and why it worked that way. So this became a pretty regular event, spending every free minute he had soaking up everything Mel could teach him.

His thirst for knowledge continued at home. While his family would be sleeping, Gid would keep the night candle burning while reading the books he had hidden under his mattress. Morning would soon be there. He never needed an alarm clock, as he always knew when it was time to get up by the sound of the rooster crowing and the clanging of the kettles as his mother prepared breakfast downstairs. The morning routine was pretty much the same every morning. Get dressed, run down the stairs, say good morning to Mother as he headed out the door towards the barn. Father was already out in the barn starting the milking process, so Gid would join him there as well as help tend to the chickens, horses, and the rest of the animals with the older sisters helping. The younger ones would have some easier chores in and around the house. Most of the girls were still in school. Gid had graduated the eighth grade and that's all that was required back then. He had skipped a grade, and so he had to repeat the eighth grade until he was fourteen, the age that Amish children could quit school. He now helped his father on the farm. Once the cows were milked he washed up and went in for breakfast. After breakfast it was back out to the barn, hitching up the horses for planting, tilling, or harvesting crops, depending on the season. There were always horses to shoe, manure to spread, trips to the market, and fences to mend. There was always plenty to do. Then evening would come when Gid could head back to Mel's place to learn more about planes. This was pretty much how the days went. There were days that the young Amish boys dreaded - the days of thrashing. Those were usually the hottest and longest days of the year, or so it seemed. The Millers and their neighbors helped each other with most of the fieldwork since everything was done by hand. So Gid and the Fisher boys would be doing lots of these tasks together. When it came to thrashing day, they would pray that the thrasher would break so they could all head up to their favorite swimming hole, which they called Mark Groff's swimming hole. So when the thrashing was completed it was a given where they were going. There was no need for bathing suits, and girls weren't allowed. They pretty much had the place to themselves except for an occasional fisherman who would wander by. Someone would holler, "Fisherman coming," and everyone would stay in the water. They always noticed that the fishermen were laughing as they walked by. Since the area attracted a lot of fisherman, Gid thought this was a golden opportunity to make some extra spending money. They all came up with the idea to sell worms to them. This meant going out at night and finding worms, so that's what they did. They had a good business going - one hundred worms for $1.00. They kept this up for awhile when one day Gid decided he was going to up his price, so he made a new sign selling one hundred worms for $2.00. When John Fisher saw it he said, "Gid, you're not going to be able to sell as many worms."

"That's the idea," was Gid's reply. He figured he could make as much money with half as much work! This was the beginning of many business ventures yet to come.

2

WHAT'S MY PRIZE?

By the summer of 1955, Gid was sixteen-and-a-half years old, and his desire to know more about the world outside of the Amish life had peaked. Staying on the farm with his family wasn't the life he envisioned for himself. Without his family's knowledge he had purchased a car and hid it in the Fisher's cornfield. Now with a car he could go anywhere he wanted to. Gid didn't have a driver's license until he and some friends were planning a trip to the beach, and so he decided the day before that he should go take his driver's test. It was fortunate that he did, because the next day he was stopped by the police and had to show his driver's license.

His seventeenth birthday was fast approaching, and he had to make some serious decisions. His decision to leave was a hard one to make. He loved his family very much and didn't want to hurt them in any way. He hadn't joined the church yet, but he knew if he did and then left he would be shunned. So he knew he had to leave soon before joining the church. Telling his father that his only son was leaving was weighing heavily on his heart. So after a lot of planning Gid finally broke the news to his family, and in the late autumn of 1955, Gid, sporting his new English haircut, left home and moved in with Mervin and Miriam Landis. Merv and Mim had three children, Janet, Joann, and Doug, and they owned a big dairy farm. Gid worked on the farm with Merv for about a year. Gid would often tell Merv and Mim of all the things he wanted to do in his life, and on one occasion Mim suggested that with all he intended to do, he should further his education. An eighth-grade education just wasn't enough. She offered to help him study to get his GED. So while living with the Landis's, Gid studied long and hard and acquired his GED.

In 1956 Gid was hired to work as a mechanic at the Lancaster Lincoln Mercury dealership, but he continued to help Merv with the milking of the cows. On the weekends Gid would go back home to visit with his family. His family was always anxious to see him and hear the stories he would tell. Gid had a gift of telling stories, and with his sense of humor and wit he could always keep them laughing. One of their favorite stories went something like this:

On one particular day before Gid left for school, he had taken a dead mouse out of a trap and thought he could have some fun with it at school. So he stuck it in his pocket and took off to school with a jaunty swagger. The school was a one-room schoolhouse with all eight grades in the same room. The desks were all in rows facing the teacher's desk in the front. Gid had made sure he was the first one in school that day so that no one would see what he was up to. Entering the building and noticing the schoolroom was empty, he placed the dead mouse on teacher Lydia's chair then pushed the chair back under the desk. He then ran back outside and joined all the other children who were playing. It wasn't long before the bell rang and everyone headed in and sat in their seats. Teacher Lydia was the last to enter the room making sure no one was still outside. She then headed straight for the front of the classroom. With her hand now on her chair ready to pull it back and sit down, she said, "Good morning, children." While the children were responding, "Good morning, Miss Lydia," she let out a scream that startled the entire class. Then reaching down and with two fingers lifting a dead mouse into view of the class, she exclaimed, "Who is responsible for this?" A chorus of "I didn't do it! I don't know!" erupted along with nervous laughter, and then silence descended as everyone could see Miss Lydia wasn't very happy. Stepping from behind her desk, she dropped the mouse into the waste container. It was evident by the look on her face that this was not going to end until someone was punished. Miss Lydia stood in front of the class and asked in a serious voice, "I'll ask again. Who is responsible for this?" By now everyone was looking around at each other to see if anyone was going to answer, but no one did. Miss Lydia always took pride in the fact that she could look at someone and tell whether or not that person was lying. When no one answered after the second demanding question, she got very serious. Now she was determined to find the culprit, so she moved to the first row, turned to face the child and asked, "Did you do this?" "No, Miss Lydia," would be the response. Then moving to the next student she would repeat the same question, and each time "No, Miss Lydia" was the answer. Gid could see that it wouldn't be long before Miss Lydia was face to face with him, and he knew it was wrong to lie. But he saw a way out - directly beside him was an empty desk, and all he would have to do was to wait until she passed the empty desk and had her back to him and then he'd jump over to the empty seat. So when Miss Lydia passed the empty desk beside him, he quietly moved to the row she had just passed. Most of the class had seen Gid's sneaky maneuver, but no one said a word. Completing her trips up and down the rows of desks without a confession was upsetting to Miss Lydia. Now she would have to use a different approach, one that would surely get results. She would offer a reward, a prize for the one who would tell who the guilty student was. So she exclaimed, "If you know who put the mouse on my chair, stand up and tell me and I will give you a prize." Without any hesitation, Gid jumped to his feet. "Yes, Gideon, who is it?" Gid answered, "It was me! What's my prize?" Needless to say his family laughed every time they heard this story. And about the prize, I don't ever remember him telling what the prize was or even what the punishment was.

Gid loved his family and never stayed out of touch with them for very long. But Gid had places to go and things to do, so even though his visits were regular, they were fairly short. Even though it was Sunday, cows still had to be milked, so he would soon leave and head back to the Landis's to help with the evening chores. Then Monday would come and Gid would head back to work at Lancaster Lincoln Mercury. Gid had joined Mellingers Mennonite Church, so during the evenings he would meet with friends for youth activities and on Sunday attend church services. Gid enjoyed the time he had with his friends, and those relationships held a great deal of value to him.

* * * * *

Twenty miles away on a farm in the Buck, the alarm was ringing. Five-thirty in the morning seemed to come so quickly for Betty. It seemed like she had just gone to bed and it was already time to get up. It was summer of 1957 and Betty had just graduated from Solanco High School a few weeks earlier. Betty was one of seven children of J. Elvin and Elizabeth Landis Herr. The children were: Henry, Lydia, Ruth, Betty, Carl, Mary, and Elvin (Pete). Betty's older brother and sister, Henry and Lydia, had already moved out on their own. Henry was married and in the Air Force, and Lydia was teaching school. So, along with her sister Ruth, Betty got up every morning and milked the thirty cows they owned. Their father had been suffering with heart problems and would sleep in a little later. The young children also helped with other various chores on the Herr farm. Their farm was located on top of the hill just south of the Buck. When Betty wasn't doing farm work, she was actively involved with the youth programs at Mechanics Grove Mennonite Church where her family were members.

Ruth worked at Sam Wenger's law office in Lancaster. One day while she was at work, Ruth found out from her friend, Dorothy, that she would be leaving her job at the dentist's office. Knowing that her sister Betty was looking for a job, Ruth told Dorothy she would tell Betty. Well, Betty applied for the job, and in the fall of 1957 started to work at Dr. Garvey's dental office in Lancaster, which she thoroughly enjoyed.

Betty was eighteen years old, very friendly and outgoing. She was five foot, two inches tall with brown hair and a smile that wouldn't quit. Betty was quick to learn, and with her pleasant attitude and charm was a perfect fit in the dental office. The dental office closed late each day so that by the time Betty got home, the evening milking had already been completed. That was a relief to Betty since it had already been a long day for her. Evening meals would always be filled with lots of conversation about everyone's activities that day. With seven people each having a story to tell, meals could last quite some time. Then there were dishes to do and homework for the younger ones before the day ended.

Betty still had time during the week, however, to participate in the youth activities at church. This was a time that Betty really enjoyed. Having lots of friends and doing things together made it even more fun. The Mechanic's Grove youth group, along with the New Providence youth group, always had a summer project to raise money for mission work. One particular project that took a lot of work was selling vegetables, but selling them was the easy part. First they had to till the ground, plant the seeds, water, and weed until harvest time. Of course, after the work was completed, it was time for refreshments and games. One of the games they played was called "The Flying Dutchmen." In this game you hold hands and make a circle. One couple would remain on the outside of the circle, but still holding hands, would run around and then smack the hands of a couple in the circle. Then the couple who got smacked would run around the outside of the circle in the opposite direction trying to beat the other couple back to the empty spot they had just created. The whole time you must remain holding hands. The game ends when it's time to go home or time for snacks. Of course they loved this game because they hoped to hold hands with someone who'd caught their interest, so all the work of running around the circle was worth it!

Being able to help in the work of the church and on the mission field meant a great deal to Betty and the rest of her friends. Betty was a hard worker and wasn't afraid to get dirty. Her sisters sometimes accused her of not always doing her share because she was out with her friends a lot and they often thought she was trying to win her mother's favor because she frequently did the housecleaning. However, the reason she cleaned the house was so that it would look good when her friends came over to visit. She always had a kind word for everyone and wasn't afraid to help someone in need. Work on the farm wasn't easy with their father having health problems and the two older ones gone. Everyone had to do his or her share. Their mother worked extremely hard, too.

There were, however, times for fun on the farm, but sometimes the games got dangerous, such as the time when Carl convinced Betty to hook him up to a rope on a pulley in the granary and lower him out the upstairs barn door to the ground below. This is what their older brother, Henry, did with the bags of grain. It sounded like a lot of fun, but no one took into consideration the weight difference. No sooner had they started than Betty was lifted up and dropped to the ground below, knocking her unconscious. Her father had heard the commotion and was there in seconds. As he carried her into the house, she regained consciousness. There were no broken bones or other injuries, but later on her brothers and sisters would say that she had suffered brain injuries!

Another time when fun and games turned serious was when Ruth and Carl were teasing and clowning around and Carl threw a pair of scissors and they stuck in Ruth's leg. There was a lot of blood, but no serious injury once again. Of course Carl turned out to be a great guy, and as you can see, there was never a dull moment on the Herr family farm!

* * * * *

The Landis home was really close to Mel's runway, but because of Gid's long hours at Lancaster Lincoln Mercury and helping with the milking, there wasn't much time to pursue his interest in flying. During his drive back and forth to work Gid was able to catch a glimpse every now and then of Mel taking off or landing his plane, which kept Gid's interest alive. He would think, *someday I'll have my own plane and fly wherever and whenever I want.* But right now he needed to keep working and save his money so his dream would come true. It was late in 1958 and Gid had some new interests now. He had started to test the dating waters, mostly with double dating and going to youth activities at church. Afterwards they'd hop in a couple of cars and head to someone's house for food and games. This time always seemed to go too quickly for Gid. He enjoyed being with his new friends but missed his old friends a lot. You see, when he left his home to go out on his own, he was leaving his Amish lifestyle behind, and he worried that he would be a bad influence on his family and his best friends even though he was still going to church, so he made a promise to himself that he wouldn't let that happen. This meant breaking the ties with his old friends, like the Fisher boys. Gid belonged to the workforce now so if it started to get late Gid would have to cut the evening activities short and head home to get some sleep so he could be back at work on time the next day.

* * * * *

Betty liked to have friends come over to the house a lot, but the preparation time was always hectic. Everything had to be just right which meant cleaning the house. Her little sister, Mary, would complain about this, saying, "Betty always gives me the dirty jobs because she doesn't want to mess up her nails." But in the end the house would be clean and the friends would arrive and everyone would have fun. Betty had now started to date. Along with her girlfriends, Lucy, Mim H., Anne, and Mim M., double-dating seemed to be the most fun. Getting a group together and going to Youth for Christ meetings and playing "Rook" was really popular with her gang of friends. On Sunday afternoons they would get a big group together and play softball back in the meadow. Between the dental job, milking, entertaining, and dating now in the mix, time was flying by for Betty.

* * * * *

Winter of 1959 came and Gid was still working at Lancaster Lincoln Mercury. Knowing that he had some vacation time coming up, Gid asked his friend, John Henry Groff, if he would like to drive down to Florida with him. John liked the idea, so they planned when it would suit both of them, checked with their respective employers, and the trip was on. They packed up the 1956 Mercury and headed south for Sarasota, Florida. Gid wanted to make the most of their time off, so he decided to drive straight through to save time and money. It sure felt good to reach those warmer temperatures in Florida. Since they drove straight through, they were a little overdressed for the seventy-degree temperatures and quickly began to shed clothing. With their jackets now off and sleeves rolled up, they drove into the Sarasota city limits. Gid wanted to check out the beach first of all. They pulled into a service station to fill the car with gas and John went inside and asked if they had a map of Sarasota. The attendant noticed their northern attire and asked where they were from. John said, "Lancaster, Pennsylvania."

"When did you get here?" asked the attendant,

"We just pulled in. Where is the beach?" John inquired.

"Well, it's about twenty-five minutes due west of here," the attendant replied, and then he gave John driving directions.

By then Gid had paid the boy who had pumped the gas and was about to join the conversation. "John, did you find the way to the beach?"

"Sure did, you ready?" asked John.

"I just want to ask this man a question."

"What can I help you with?" the man inquired.

"Do you have an airport close by?"

"Yes, we do, and as a matter of fact, you're closer to the airport than you are to the beach."

"How would I get there?" Gid asked, unable to hide the eagerness in his question.

"Well, it's about ten minutes north of here. Just go down to the next crossroad, turn right, go about three miles to University Parkway, then turn left. It will be down the road on your right. You can't miss it."

"That sounds easy; I'd like to watch some planes landing and taking off. Hey, John, let's go over there first and take a look."

"Sounds good to me, Gid, you're driving, go for it! Besides, the beach isn't going anywhere."

It didn't take long to drive there and before they knew it the airport was right ahead of them. There were lots of small planes tied down everywhere. Gid wanted to pull in and get a closer look. Just as they were about to pull into the entranceway they saw a big sign along the road.

"Hey, Gid, did you see that sign?"

"No, what sign?" Gid had been focused on all the different planes and not really paying attention to any signs. "What did it say? 'Keep Out' or something?"

"No, it said, 'See Sarasota by Air'."

"Really? Let's check it out!" After parking the car, they headed for the building where there was another sign saying, 'See Sarasota by Air.'

They entered the building and saw a man standing behind the counter. As they approached him he asked, "how can I help you young men today?'

Gid was the first to speak up. "We just got down here today from Pennsylvania and thought we might like to check out Sarasota. We saw your sign, so we pulled in. A friend of mine took me up in a plane some years back and I really enjoyed it." For the next ten minutes Gid must have asked a dozen questions about the planes.

When the man finally had a chance to speak, he said, "Tell you what. Why don't you just take a flying lesson; it won't cost you much more than a tourist flight would, just the cost of a logbook to enter your flight time in, and you'll get some real flight training at the same time."

"That sounds good to me. What do you think, John?"

"Let's do it!" John replied. So in December 1959 Gid took his first flying lesson. The rest of their time spent in Sarasota was a blur. The conversation was all about flying and nothing else. With logbook in hand Gid headed back to Pennsylvania. He had a goal now. He knew what he wanted to do. He had taken that first step. *Wait till the family hears about this*, he thought with anticipation.

Gid made up his mind that as soon as he arrived back in Pennsylvania and got settled in at work again, he was going to the local airport to find out how he could take some flying lessons. He was hooked now, and plus he had a logbook that needed to be filled with flight time. He hadn't been back for long when he got word that one of his cousins in Sarasota had an accident and needed his help. Gid quickly volunteered to go down and pick her up, and now that he had told his family about his adventures in Sarasota, he had plenty of volunteers to ride along with him. His mother and father decided to go along this time. After arriving in Sarasota and checking on his cousin's situation, he dropped his parents off at the place where some relatives were staying and headed for the airport, amazed at how things had fallen into place so perfectly to bring him back again so soon. During this visit Gid was able to get two more flying lessons in before he headed back north. Once back home Gid went to the New Holland Airport and signed up for lessons under Al Stover.

3

TWO WHOLE WEEKS

In the spring of 1960, Gid was with his girlfriend and another couple at the Rawlinsville Mennonite church for an evening service. A friend of Gid's, Elias Groff, had asked Betty and another couple to go to that same service that particular evening. Elias had planned on showing slides of his trip to Puerto Rico back at Betty's house after the service. When he saw Gid, he invited him and his friends to come along. Once at Betty's house the slide show began. Almost everybody was watching the slides except for Gid and Betty, who seemed to be more interested in stealing sideways glances at one another out of the corners of their eyes. The evening came to an end and everyone went his or her respective ways. After dropping his date off, Gid headed for home. All the way home Gid couldn't get Betty off his mind. He was wondering how he could "accidentally" run into her. Gid and his current girlfriend knew they weren't getting along very well, and recently they had talked about seeing other people. He was hoping now that Betty might just be that other person.

Back at the Herr house, Betty was tidying up the living room and washing up the dishes from the snacks the group had just finished, but she seemed absentminded as she went about her work because she couldn't stop thinking about that handsome guy named Gid Miller. She wanted to know more about him and couldn't wait to talk to some of her friends who could tell her more about Gid. A few days later Betty found out through a friend that Gid had been dating the girl he was with on and off for about a year. After hearing that Betty put him out of her mind as best she could. But within a couple of weeks that same friend came back and said, "You know that guy you were asking about? Well, he and his girlfriend just broke up." Now the only question was when and how would they meet again. About twenty miles away Gid was thinking almost the same thoughts, wondering, *How and when will I get to see that cute Betty Herr again?*

One Saturday evening at a Youth for Christ meeting in Lancaster, Betty, who was there with a girlfriend, saw Gid Miller walking towards her. They passed each other, both smiling and saying, "Hi!" She noticed, though, that he was alone, and she liked the big smile he had on his face. Little did she know that Gid had seen her first and had made a point of getting close enough for her to notice him. Neither initiated a conversation. The next day Betty was with some friends down at Black Rock just enjoying the day. Back at the Herr farm, a 1956 Mercury pulled into the driveway and a tall, red-haired young man got out, walked up to the porch, and knocked on the door. Betty's mom, Elizabeth, answered the door. "Hello, can I help you?"

"Oh, hi, is Betty home?" asked the stranger.

"No, I'm afraid she's out with some friends this afternoon."

"Oh, OK, thank you," Gid answered matter-of-factly, and then he got back into his car and drove straight away.

When Betty arrived home a little later, her mother told her, "A young man stopped by earlier asking for you."

"What color was his car?" Betty asked. "It was black and white," her mother replied. Betty now became very excited, because she remembered that Gid drove a black-and-white Mercury. *Oh, I hope he comes back*, she was thinking longingly. After the milking was finished, it was time for evening services at church, so Betty and her girlfriend Mim left for the church. It was dark when Betty returned home, and she hadn't been home very long when the flashing of car lights pulling in the driveway hit the wall in the living room. Betty, looking out the window and seeing it was Gid's car, hollered, "I'll get the door." With her heart racing, Betty walked to the door as Gid was knocking. She took a deep breath and opened the door with a smile.

"Hi, Betty," Gid spoke up right away.

"Hi, Gid. Come on in." Making sure her brothers and sisters weren't hiding just around the corner eavesdropping, Betty led Gid into the living room where they sat on the couch at a nervous distance.

"So what brings you to this neighborhood so late at night?" asked Betty.

"Well, to be honest, I came over to see you," replied Gid.

"You did? Why would you want to see me?"

"I thought maybe we should get to know each other a little better."

"Why did you think that?"

"Well, so when I ask you out you won't be going out with a stranger."

"So I guess that means you came over here to ask me out and you are assuming I'm going to say yes."

"That was my main thought."

"I guess then you better start telling me about yourself, so I will know how to answer when you ask me out."

They talked for about half an hour and Gid asked Betty out. Now, Betty, knowing that she didn't have an open day for about two weeks said,

"I would love to, but the earliest I can go out is the 25th of June, and I'm invited to a wedding. Would you like to go with me?"

Wow, two whole weeks?! Gid yelped in his thoughts. Of course Gid had hoped they could go out the very next day, but if he had to settle for a two-week delay, he knew he'd just have to survive until June 25th.

Despite his clamoring thoughts, Gid answered politely, "Sure, I guess I can wait till then. Well, I guess I better go now, Betty; I left John sitting in the car."

"You have someone waiting out there?" Betty exclaimed.

"It's OK, he doesn't mind. It was nice talking with you, and you will let me know about the details for the wedding?"

"I will; give me a call during the week," answered Betty reassuringly.

"Great, good night."

"Good night."

Gid loped to the car, jumped in, turned to John and said, "Sorry that took so long."

"That's OK, you'd do the same for me, right?"

"Sure would," Gid replied with a smile for his good friend.

"So, how did it go?" John asked.

"Well, she said she'll go out with me, but I have to wait two weeks and then I can take her to a wedding."

"A wedding?"

"You heard me right, a wedding. I don't care where it is as long as I can be with her!" Gid retorted with a joking shove to his buddy.

In Gid's mind it seemed like those two weeks were probably the longest two weeks on record. The only thing that made it bearable was that he was able to call Betty on the phone, enjoying every minute of talking with her. And with every phone call Gid and Betty were able to get to know each other a little better.

On Saturday, June 25, 1960, Gid picked Betty up and they went to the wedding of Bob and Judy Leaman. Bob was the one who had given Betty her first airplane ride a year or so earlier. Everyone had a great time at the wedding reception, and Betty and Gid found that they really enjoyed each other's company. When Gid brought Betty back home that evening, he asked her if she would like to ride to Scranton with him the next day, as he was taking his parents up to see some friends. "That would be nice," said Betty. They said their goodnights and parted.

Sunday morning came quickly, and before she knew it Gid was at her door to pick her up again. Once in the car Gid introduced Betty to his parents and they began the trip to Scranton. There was lots of conversation between Betty, Arie, and Eli — the usual talk about each other's family and who is related to whom. They were well into the trip when Gid reached across the seat and held Betty's hand. He was enjoying her hand so much that he didn't notice the flatbed truck slowing down in front of him, and he ran into the back of it knocking off the Mercury's hood ornament. Gid's mother let out a scream from the back seat, "Gideon!" When they saw that there was no other damage to either vehicle, they went on their way. When they arrived at their destination, they all went inside and visited for a while. Gid and Betty excused themselves shortly afterwards and left the house. They strolled through the town hand in hand, just talking and enjoying each other for the remainder of that day. This was the beginning of their courtship. They dated twice a week at first, and then it became three times a week.

While they were dating Gid also was squeezing in flying lessons. On August 25, 1960 he flew to Harrisburg and took his written test for his private pilots' license and passed with no problems. He just needed a few more hours of flying to meet all the required hours to take his check ride. In September the day finally came. Without any big fan fare Gid Miller became a private pilot. As he left the airport that day he was thinking back to how a little Amish boy asked a man for a ride in his plane. Now he wanted that man to be the first to know where that ride had led. He would have told Betty first, but it was Saturday morning and she was working till noon at the dental office, so his first stop was at Mel Glick's. Mel shook Gid's hand and congratulated him, and the two of them began to reminisce about how this all began. Gid then suggested to Mel that they start a flying club. He thought that they could purchase a plane and share the use of it. Mel liked the idea and suggested the names of two others he should ask. Mel had been considering purchasing a Piper Tri-pacer and thought this would be the perfect plane for their club, so he suggested they pursue it. Gid thought it sounded like a great idea because the Piper Tri-pacer would be an affordable plane for a group of them to purchase together. Gid was amazed at how this was coming together so perfectly. Not only had he just become a pilot, but now he would be part owner of a plane. Wow, did he have news to tell Betty now! When Gid met Betty that afternoon, he couldn't stop talking in his excitement. He wanted to take her up with him right away, but he wanted the first ride to be in the Piper Tri-pacer, so that first airplane ride with Betty would have to wait a bit. However, a few weeks later the purchase was complete, and on September 28th Gid got his wish and took Betty up for her first flight with him. They had been sharing their hopes and dreams with each other for the last few months. Now with his private pilots' license in hand, Gid was heading for his next goal, which was to become a flight instructor. He told

Betty what a great way to make a living that would be. "I'll get to do something I love and get paid for it!" But to get his instructors' rating Gid knew he needed to get his commercial pilots' license first, which meant a written test and a lot more hours of flying.

September was gone in a flash what with all the details of purchasing the plane, and suddenly October with its autumn beauty was upon them. On one particular October evening Betty and Gid had just returned from the service at church and were relaxing on the couch in the living room when Gid put his arm around Betty and looked into her eyes. After a brief pause he asked, "Betty, would you marry me?" Betty was taken by surprise. She had not expected this question so soon, but staring back into his eyes she could tell he was serious, and she knew they were truly in love. Without pause she answered, "Yes, I will." They spent the rest of the evening talking about the future, their plans and dreams, and of course, when this big day would happen. They were leaning toward June of 1961, but both agreed that this date could change. The evening came to a close and their lingering goodbyes now took a little longer to say.

During the ride back home that evening Gid's mind was spinning. Not only had he just asked the girl of his dreams to marry him, but also his love of flying was taking on a whole new meaning. He had a lot of work to do to get to that point. On December 13, 1960, Mel and Gid flew their Piper Tri-pacer to Harrisburg, Pennsylvania, where they both took and passed their commercial pilots' written test.

On Christmas Day, 1960, Gid and Betty announced their engagement to their families, and the wedding date was set for April 22, 1961. The months preceding the wedding were very busy. In January Betty purchased fabric to make the bridesmaids' dresses. They also met with Betty's cousin, Paul Landis, who was the local Director of Voluntary Service. They wanted to devote two years to voluntary service before setting up housekeeping. Since Gid was a conscientious objector, this would take the place of military service.

February continued to be busy with making a guest list and picking out wedding invitations and addressing them. One thing Gid soon learned about Betty was that she was a good organizer and planner and kept a very accurate calendar, so nothing would ever be missed.

In March they received the information detailing where they would be doing their voluntary service work. They were going to be sent to Immokalee, Florida, starting June 1, 1961.

On March 17th Betty wanted to take her good friend, Dotty Benner, out for her birthday dinner. Once they had arrived back at Dottie's house after enjoying a delicious dinner, she found the living room full of people gathered for a surprise bridal shower in her honor. There were a lot of beautiful gifts and an exceptionally big box on the floor. Betty's dad said, "Why don't you open the big box first." That sounded like a good idea, and as she was opening the top, her hand brushed against something hairy inside. Betty jumped back with a little scream just as she saw Gid's grinning face coming up out of the box as he stood and stepped out to give her a big hug. Everyone had such a good laugh over this prank that it was difficult to settle down to opening the "real" shower gifts surrounding them! In the month of March, Betty was asked to give a speech at the Mechanics' Grove Young Peoples Meeting. The topic was to be "What a Girl Expects of a Christian Boy." The following is the exact speech, written by Betty Herr:

What a Girl Expects of a Christian Boy

I think that the first and most important thing that a Christian girl looks for, or at least should look for in a boy, is that he is a Christian. In 2 Corinthians 6:14 it says; "Be ye not unequally yoked together with unbelievers." It is from the boys that we date that we will someday choose the boy that we will marry. Therefore, if we date only Christian boys, we will be sure to be yoked to a believer of Christ.

Another thing a girl expects is friendliness. Have a friendly smile. Also listen with interest when someone talks to you. Be able to carry a conversation. Conversation is very much like a game of catch. The game stops if you don't throw the ball back to your playing partner. Conversation stops too, if you say only the necessary "yes" or "no." So try to toss back a question or an idea.

Be thoughtful about the desires and needs of others. Have the Christian quality of honestly liking and being interested in all people. "A man that hath friends must shew himself friendly" (Proverbs 18:24).

What about "looks"? Dressing habits can make or break your dating opportunities. Be well-groomed. Use soap, deodorant, comb, and toothbrush often. Wear neat and clean clothes. It's not necessary to have the latest styles.

Have an appearance appropriate for a Christian. Many of the long hairdos that the boys have today make them look wild and tough, which is not appropriate for a Christian. Dress suitably for the occasion. It is always nice to know where you are going on a date, because it is no fun for either one if he arrives in sport clothes with a doggie roast in mind, and she's dressed in her Sunday best.

Being a consecrated Christian, having an honest interest in people around, being able to carry on a conversation, and having a neat appearance will all work together to make your personality attractive to others.

God has given us clear and definite directions, which help us to know how to live and work happily with those around us. He has said, "Be ye kind one to another, tenderhearted, forgiving one another .... And whatsoever ye do in word or deed, do all in the name of the Lord Jesus (Ephesians 4:32; Colossians 3:17). God gave these guides to living to help in everyday situations. Live by them and your personality will become so attractive that you will be liked by all who know you.

When asking a girl for a date, a boy should realize that he is just giving an invitation. He should act in a friendly manner and be exact and to the point, especially for the first date. Later dates can be planned together. For an example: a girl will like it when a boy says, "The Mennonite Acappella Chorus is giving a program at Lampeter-Strasburg School on Saturday evening. Would you like to go with me?" Instead of "What are you doing Saturday evening?" It helps her to decide whether she can accept the date. Maybe she isn't doing anything, but she hesitates to say no until she knows what the boy has in mind. This also gives her opportunity to dress for the occasion as I mentioned before.

If the girl accepts the date, the boy should let her know that he is pleased by giving a response like, "Good, I'm glad you can go." If the girl refuses the date, it's still the boy's responsibility to be pleasant. Maybe she wants to go with him, but can't explain why it is impossible. If he is pleasant, he stands a good chance of getting a date with her in the future.

Problems of what to do and where to go on dates are not so difficult if they're both Christians. Furthermore, no one has as much fun as a Christian. He enjoys himself while on a date with no regrets afterwards. To sincere believers there is little question about appropriate places to go and things to do. From God's Word we learn, "Whether therefore ye eat, or drink, or whatsoever ye do, do all to the glory of God" (1 Corinthians 10:31).

There are many church activities that we can attend on Sunday evenings. On Saturday evening there are Youth for Christ meetings. Also there is a lot of good, clean recreation that we can share like skating, hiking, doggie roasts, badmitten, croquet, and many games that can be played indoors. Enjoy and appreciate simple, everyday fun. Suggest and make plans for things to do and places to go. Popularity can be gotten by learning to enjoy what you are doing. A girl appreciates a treat from the boy once in a while, but most girls also enjoy preparing a treat that can be eaten at home, especially on a Sunday evening.

A couple can get the most out of every date if they sense the presence of Christ [who is] with them, remembering, "Trust in the Lord with all thine heart, and lean not on thine own understanding. In all thy ways acknowledge him, and he shall direct thy paths" (Proverbs 3:5, 6).

Heavy petting does not bring popularity, nor does it honor Christ. Such popularity is not lasting or desirable. Genuine popularity is based largely upon friendliness, sincerity, and good Christian character. A Christian girl likes to date a boy who encourages her spiritually, who can do things, who is interesting, who is sincerely friendly and fun to be with. Some verses that will help you are: Philippians 4:13 — "I can do all things through Christ which strengthened me;" 1 Corinthians 10:3 — "There hath no temptation taken you, but such as is common to man: but God is faithful, who will not suffer you to be tempted above that ye are able; but will with the temptation be able to bear it." And then, 2 timothy 2:19 — "Let everyone that nameth the name of Christ depart from iniquity."

At evangelistic meetings at Mellingers this winter, Glenn Sell said that the person we date should be someone who will bring out the best in us and not [bring out] the beast in us. Boys, this may sound as if we expect a lot of you, but we know that we aren't perfect, so we are willing to accept some of your faults, also. (All Scriptures are from the King James Version.)

* * * * *

On April 22, 1961, Betty wrote in her diary "Beautiful day! Our Wedding Day!!" Betty woke up early and went to the church at 8:45 to get dressed. Clayton Keener married Gid and Betty at 10:00 in the morning. After they were married they went to Lancaster to have their pictures taken. The reception was at Lancaster Mennonite School. After the reception they were to honeymoon in Colorado. They arrived at Mel Glick's airstrip in Smoketown and took off in the Piper Tri-pacer at around 4:00 pm. After checking the weather conditions, Gid decided to take the southern route. They landed in Winchester, Virginia at 6:00 and found a motel for the evening. The next day they were up at 5:30 am to get an early start, but the mountains were wrapped in fog so they had to land in Harrisonburg, Virginia, where they went to Parkview Mennonite Church for the morning service. By 2:00 pm the weather had cleared and they took off again. They made it to Portsmouth, Ohio, and spent the night there. The next stop was in Arthur, Illinois to visit some of Gid's relatives, Milt and Lucy Otto and Lucy's dad, Obed Diener. Gid took Milt and his son, Harold, for a ride in the Piper.

Once back in the plane Gid and Betty made a few more stops before landing at their destination in LaJunta, Colorado.

They visited with Fred and Mim Martin, who gave them a delicious meal. From there they flew to Colorado Springs and met with Betty's cousin, Edith, and her husband, Art Sensenig. The next day was Betty's birthday and Gid surprised her with a set of silverware in a beautiful, cherry wood box. They spent some time sightseeing, taking in Pike's Peak, Garden of the Gods, and Seven Falls. Gid and Betty had met some VSer's while there and took some of them for a ride in the Piper. All this flying would help Gid get the needed hours for his commercial pilots' license. But Betty was missing something from her dating days. You see, the Tri-pacer had only one door and it was on the right side of the plane and the pilot sits in the left seat. So every time they got in the plane, Betty had to let Gid in first, then she got in and had to close the door herself!

Some time later they started their trip back east. They went back home by way of Niagara Falls and also stopped at the Piper factory in Lockhaven, Pennsylvania. They arrived back home on May 2nd and opened their wedding gifts at Betty's parents' house where they were to spend the next three weeks before heading to Immokalee, Florida.

4

BORN TO FLY

On May 25th Gid and Betty loaded the Mercury and headed for Florida. . They had allowed themselves extra time so they could take in some sights on the way down. It rained really hard on Thursday the 26th, but that didn't slow them down. They drove through the Great Smokey Mountains National Park where they saw two bears and stopped at the Hillbilly Village and Cherokee Indian Village. They continued on to Atlanta where they spent the night.

They continued to enjoy the trip making many other stops along the way. Betty's sister, Lydia, was teaching school in Tampa, so they stopped at her house for a while. Lydia had some friends over and Gid and Betty showed slides of their wedding and honeymoon trip to Colorado. On May 30th they got up early, Gid washed the car, and they took off for their final destination, the town of Immokalee. Gid had wanted to show Betty where he took his first flying lessons so they stopped in Sarasota on the way. Twenty miles outside of Immokalee they had to stop once again to change a flat tire, but finally Gid and Betty pulled into Immokalee at 4:00 pm on May 30, 1961.

The first people they met were Harold and Ellen Shearer, who were to be their unit leaders. Harold showed them around the facility and introduced them to the others they would be working with. The unit house where they would be living was also the home for two young women volunteers. They had their own bedrooms but would share the living room and kitchen. The next day Gid got the tire fixed while Betty started the unpacking.

The mission work of the Voluntary Services unit in Immokalee consisted of providing child care for preschool children, running clubs and craft programs, visiting the homes of shut-ins, and providing worship services for the migrant workers and their families. Gid and Betty quickly settled into their routines. Betty did the laundry and cleaning, and she also taught Bible school. On Sundays she taught Sunday school and worked in the nursery. Gid did vehicle maintenance and property maintenance, which made use of his good mechanical skills. On Sunday he taught a 3rd grade Sunday school class. Another one of their duties would be leading the Girls' and Boys' Clubs in the fall after school each day.

On Saturday, June 10th, Gid got up at 6:30 am. He came back into the room fifteen minutes later to tell Betty that last evening, while they had been in Sarasota for a pizza party, a phone call came saying that her father had died. They had to make arrangements to fly back home to Pennsylvania. Harold drove them to Tampa Airport where they took an Eastern Airlines flight at 3:00 pm. Gid called home to find out what had happened and was told that Betty's father had been planting sweet potatoes when he became short of breath. Lydia and her mother got him into the car to take him to the doctor, but he was gone before they arrived. Gid and Betty arrived in Washington at 6:00 pm where Mel's brother, Norm Glick, picked them up in the Piper and flew them to New Holland, and from there Norm drove them to the Landis farm where Gid had left his old Dodge car. They arrived at the Herr farm late that evening.

The days leading up to the funeral were filled with activity. The whole family was there, except for Betty's sister, Ruth, who was in the hospital giving birth to her second child, Sandra Ann. (Ruth was married to Donald Moore and they also had a son named Kenny.) On June 12th Betty and her sisters, Lydia and Mary, went to Ruth's garden and picked twenty quarts of strawberries and froze them for her so they wouldn't go to waste rotting on the vine. Her brothers worked around the farm helping everywhere they could. Her brother, Carl, who was attending college at Penn State, decided he would stay home now to help with the work of the farm. They had the viewing that evening at Reynolds Funeral Home. The following day J. Elvin Herr was laid to rest in the cemetery at Mechanics Grove Church. That evening after their friends had all gone home, the family had a birthday cake for Pete, the youngest child of the Herr family. His father was buried on his 15th birthday.

On June 17th, Norm and Mabel Glick picked up Gid and Betty and took them to New Holland Airport so they could fly back to Florida. Once they returned to their new home, there was a lot to do. It seemed like there was always a house that needed painting, and even the church got painted. The many vehicles on the property were always in need of maintenance, and once school began in the fall, Gid and Betty were in charge of the after-school Girls' and Boys' Clubs, which were a lot of fun but required a lot of preparation.

In November, they had a series of tent meetings and many heard the Gospel and accepted Christ as their Savior. The days were long and hot. Gid often spent hours driving the youth and others to different activities. Whenever time permitted or the trip was near an airport, he would squeeze in a flight. In December, while dropping someone off at Miami Airport and waiting for their new cook to arrive, Gid took another lesson from a nearby flight school. Whenever he could fly, he would. His flying was becoming more frequent now, but he never forgot his responsibilities at the VS unit.

In February of 1962 Gid got his Instrument and Instructors' ratings. Now he could take on students and teach them to fly. But he still had an obligation to fulfill with his Voluntary Service duty in Immokalee. This limited the times when he could fly, but he still managed to teach a few people. One of his first students was a man named Bob Black, who owned a hardware store in Immokalee, and they became good friends. The lessons had to be done either very early in the morning or late in the evening. Gid was also able to give flight lessons on the Saturdays that he had off from work.

Tragedy struck in the summer of that year while Gid was driving a van full of young boys back from the beach. As they were heading to Immokalee, a slow-moving power-company truck didn't notice Gid passing and decided to turn into a dirt trail on the left side of the road. Gid hit the brake so hard that the brakes locked and the van rolled over the embankment on the side of the road, causing one of the boys to be hurled through the front windshield. He was killed instantly. It was determined that the driver of the truck didn't have a signal on. Careless driving charges were dropped, but Gid suffered a broken sternum from hitting the steering wheel. Gid agonized over the loss of a child who had been in his care. Word spread quickly about the death and injuries suffered to those in the accident. Bob and Louise Black came forward and offered to take Gid and Betty to their cabin near Crystal Lake for a week so that Gid could rest and recover from his injuries. Betty took good care of Gid while they were there, but Gid didn't want her to just play nursemaid to him, so he told her to go have some fun on the lake. And Betty did just that – Crystal Lake was where Betty learned how to water-ski.

Because of the accident a lawsuit had been filed against the Mennonite Church and the Florida Power & Light Company who owned the truck. Gid and Betty had to make many trips to Naples for court appearances, but their unit leaders, Harold and Ellen Shearer, were always there to support them. The charges against both parties were eventually dropped.

Once Gid was fully recovered they were back at work in Immokalee. Betty was now the nursery director for the migrant workers' children. This was always the busy time of year, with a lot more workers and children to minister to, but they didn't complain because this voluntary service was their duty and an honor.

The two years of Voluntary Service went by quickly, and before they knew it, it was June of 1963. When Gid had been in Miami a few times he had made contact with SunLine Helicopters and had been offered a job working for them once he was finished with his Voluntary Service. He would be instructing on their small planes. So in June of 1963 he and Betty moved to Miami. Betty was six months pregnant and it seemed like it was going to be a long, hot Florida summer. Since the Miami Voluntary Service Unit needed some help for three months, they lived there. In the meantime they purchased a furnished house located in northwest Miami. They were able to make the purchase because of some money Betty received from the inheritance of her grandfather's estate. They moved in early September and loved having their own home. Gid loved his job teaching people to fly planes. It was what he had wanted to do as far back as he could remember. Now, not only was he instructing on planes, but he was learning how to fly helicopters as well.

On September 21, 1963, Betty gave birth to their first child, a little girl who they named Karla Sue. She was now the main focus in their lives.

Fall in Florida is right in the middle of hurricane season, and in October a hurricane named Flora slammed into Haiti and Cuba. Headlines read, "One of the strongest and deadliest hurricanes." A news crew had asked SunLine to fly a two-man team of a photographer and a reporter down to survey the damage. Gid was asked to fly in the right seat on the trip. Weather forecasters had said the hurricane had turned to the north, so they took off for Haiti around the southern band of the hurricane. After they were air borne the hurricane changed direction and was headed directly in their flight line. They had no choice but to fly the Aztec right through it. This was quite an experience for Gid. Since the strong winds had slowed them down so much, the gas tank gauges were reading empty. Gid said there were a lot of prayers being prayed and they arrived safely. The headlines in the next day's paper read, "We flew through a killer 'cane."

Gid was becoming quite a pilot. He had finished his training on the helicopters and was now instructing on them also. SunLine Helicopters was offering a $99.00 solo class on flying small planes and Gid thought it would be a good idea for Betty to learn how to land an airplane in case anything ever happened to him. Deciding that it was probably not a good idea to take her instruction from Gid, it was agreed that Jimmy Fox would be her instructor. Betty was a natural, and after completing all her lessons, she soloed in the spring of 1964.

One day a student of Gid's told him he had applied for a job with TWA and that Gid should apply also. Gid thought that sounded like a good idea and Betty agreed, so he sent in his application. In the meantime SunLine had purchased a new helicopter, which had to be flown from California to Miami, and Gid was asked to make the delivery. So they sent him to California to receive and deliver the helicopter. When he returned home he received notice that TWA had accepted his application; the acceptance letter informed Gid that should he choose to work for TWA, he would be required to move to Kansas City, Missouri, for six months of training. TWA frowned on students bringing their families along, thinking that it caused distractions, but Gid was not going to be away from his family for that long of a period, so arrangements were made for them to go along with him. He was to start his training on January 11, 1965. There was plenty to do in preparation for this big change in their lives, but first Gid needed to inform SunLine and his students of his intention to leave.

5

JABBERWOCK

Sunday was a warm fall day in Stanton, New Jersey. The year was 1964. Six young boys were finishing off the weekend just hanging around talking and joking with one another. The boys were Butch, John, and Mike Teets, Herb Rohrer, and Ralph and Glenn Walls. Their laughter trailed off when they saw a horse being walked up to them with two girls riding bareback together. "Hey, Butch," called out the girl sitting in back. "Do you have a towel or blanket I can sit on? My bottom is getting pretty sore."

"I'll see," Butch said as he ran to his dad's garage.

Not one to miss an opportunity for a good laugh, Ralph looked down and saw a burlap bag lying in the ditch, so he picked it up and held it out, dripping and muddy, shouting, "Will this do?" "Very funny," retorted the girl sitting in the front, trying to hide a little smile. By then Butch had returned carrying a towel from the garage. Handing it to the girls he said, "Here you go." They said, "Thank you," then put it in place and rode off.

Ralph had just graduated from high school in June, and he knew a lot of people in the area, but he had never before seen these two girls; being naturally curious, he asked his friends, "Anybody know who they are?"

Herb spoke up, "Yeah, the one in the front is named Debbie Luster, and the other one is my sister, Jeanie."

"Really?!?" was Ralph's remark. "I didn't know you had a sister." To be honest, Ralph didn't know too much about Herb at all. He had only met him a short time ago.

"Yeah, she's my sister," Herb continued. "She just graduated from the 8th grade and is going to North High now." North Hunterdon Regional High School was where Ralph had just graduated.

"So she is a freshman," Ralph said slowly, nodding appreciatively. "Is she dating anyone, yet?"

"You've got to be kidding!" Herb responded.

Butch then interrupted, "Ralph, they're Mennonites."

"What's *Mennonites*?" Ralph asked with a slight sneer in his voice.

"Well, they're pretty strict, and the girls wear things on their heads and they drive cars with their bumpers painted black," replied Butch, all in one long breath.

"You mean like Amish people?" asked Ralph.

Laughing at the Ralph's misinformation, Herb replied with a hint of friendly patience in his voice, "No, we're not Amish."

Getting down to what he was really interested in, Ralph asked with a bit of annoyance, "So does that mean I can't ask your sister out?"

"Mother wouldn't allow it," says Herb. "She just turned fourteen, and my mother says she can't date till she is at least sixteen."

"Wow! That's too bad. Your sister is really cute. Say, tell her I think she's cute and to give me a call when she is sixteen!"

"Don't worry, I will," Herb said, laughing and shaking his head a little.

The day was drawing to an end and each of the boys headed home reluctantly, not wanting to see the weekend come to a close. They all had to face getting up early for school the next day except for Ralph. It was back to work for him. Ralph was age eighteen-and-a–half, and he worked for his dad in the drywall business. He had worked for his dad during all four summers of his high school years, and now he was a full-time employee. Ralph enjoyed the work and was quite proficient in his dry walling skill. The thing he liked the most, though, was the pay. The Walls drywall company had a good reputation for quality work and was always busy. In fact, they had never gone a single day without work. Ralph's dad was also named Ralph, Ralph H. Walls. Ralph's middle initial was C, so one day Ralph C. told his dad he was going to start calling him RH with no disrespect intended, and before long, everywhere they went people referred to them as "RH" and "RC."

One of their employees was a young man named Charlie who had just gotten out of the navy. Ralph's dad would often send Ralph and Charlie on jobs to tape and second-coat while he would put a third coat on another job. On weekends Ralph's Uncle Leon and his brother, Glenn, would help, and they usually would go and hang a whole house of drywall. Ralph's favorite time of year was during wrestling season, and he could always be found rooting for his alma mater's wrestling team. Between work, basketball, going to wrestling matches, and catching an occasional movie, Ralph stayed really busy. Most of the guys Ralph hung out with were still in high school.

Ralph really wanted to find a nice girl to go out with, but just couldn't find the perfect one. He had tried the dating scene in high school, but he soon found that to be a game of everyone minding everybody else's business. If you talked or looked at the wrong person outside of the clique, you were avoided. Occasionally now he would go to the local dance which was held Friday nights at the Stanton Grange. They had different bands come in and play, but the band he liked best was the Harber Brothers. They seemed to draw a big crowd, and there were always plenty of girls there without dates. This was late 1964 when the Beatles were all the rage and everyone was dancing. Ralph usually met with a couple of his friends, Gary and Joe, and when they saw some girls who caught their interest, they would work up the courage to head out onto the dance floor to see if the girls wanted to dance with them. Back then there were very few "no" responses. Everyone just wanted to dance. But that was about all the contact he had with girls.

Christmas of 1964 had come and gone and the New Year was fast approaching, which meant Ralph would soon be nineteen. It seemed like everywhere he went, the first question he was always asked was, "So, do you have a girlfriend?" and Ralph would always respond, "No, not yet."

Some of the men on the job would say, "So, don't you like girls?" and he would usually respond, "Oh, I like girls, I just haven't found the right one yet." There would always be some smart remarks, but Ralph would just ignore them for the most part. It might have been their constant teasing that made him start seriously thinking about finding the right girl to date. The one girl who had never left his thoughts, though, was the girl he had seen on horseback that Sunday afternoon last fall. *But, heck, she was only fourteen and her brother said their mom was strict about dating. Now she would be the perfect girl*, Ralph thought to himself, *because she hasn't been on the dating scene yet and no other guy has had the chance to corrupt her*. Well, after a few sleepless nights thinking about how to approach her, Ralph finally decided to give it a try. So in March of 1965, he worked up his nerve and called the Rohrer home.

* * * * *

It was a very cold winter in Kansas City that year. Gid, Betty and little Karla had arrived just two months earlier. They had made the trip from Florida driving two cars. Gid drove the 1956 black-and-white Mercury towing behind it a U-Haul trailer filled with all their valuable possessions, including the crib, Betty's hope chest and sewing machine, and Gid's tool box. Betty drove the VW Bug with their most precious possession, their baby Karla. The temperature had dropped 20 degrees in a few hours and the lightweight clothing they had on (being recent Floridians) wasn't enough. They had already found an apartment to live in not too far from where Gid would be training for the next six months. The days went by quickly. Gid would be training five days a week and sometimes have to go in on the weekends for flight simulator work. Betty kept busy taking care of Karla, as well as keeping up with the housework and sewing, and in the evenings, with the use of flash cards, she helped Gid study. Gid always felt he needed to work a little harder to catch up to the rest because of his lack of experience on larger aircraft. But because of his eagerness and ability to learn, he never fell behind at all. In fact, many of his fellow students said that Gid was born to fly.

Gid and Betty found time to have fun, and they had begun attending the Rainbow Mennonite Church where they quickly made many new friends. There were times of visiting and playing games (Mennonites love to play games). Their friends meant a lot to them and they cherished them. Just knowing that others were concerned and cared about you, meant a great deal.

One Sunday afternoon Gid asked Betty to drive him to simulator training. So with Karla in the car she drove Gid to school. After dropping him off, she turned and headed back home. As she approached a green light and headed through it, out of the corner of her eye she caught a glimpse of a car coming toward her. There was no time to react. The car broadsided her sending the Volkswagen slamming into the corner of one of TWA's buildings. It wasn't long before a man came running over to see if she was OK and found that Betty was bleeding from the head. He handed her a handkerchief to stop the bleeding. Feeling a little dazed, Betty then realized that this was the same man who had just run into her. Betty's first concern was not for herself but for her daughter in the back of the car. After getting to Karla and checking her over, they only found one slight scratch on her head. By then more people had shown up. It was determined that both should go to the hospital. Gid was called and their pastor and his wife were also called. One can only imagine Gid getting a call that his wife and daughter had just been in a car accident and were in the emergency room. By the time Gid got there, it had been determined that Karla was OK and that Betty needed six stitches on her head. The police investigation found the other driver to be at fault, as he had run a red light. Everyone recovered, but their little blue VW suffered $700.00 worth of damage.

Life got back to normal in the days ahead, and Gid's training would soon be done. Once training ended Gid would have his Flight Engineer rating on the Convair 880 and would have to choose a domicile (an airport that would be his home base). Gid and Betty had given this much thought. They had established close friendships with many couples there in Kansas City, but their families were in Pennsylvania. The day finally came when they had to write down their choices. Their first choice was Kansas City, their second was New York, and their third choice was Chicago. Now they just had to wait and see where the next chapter of their life would unfold.

* * * * *

The phone was ringing. Ralph's mind was racing, *what if her mother answers? What will I say?* Just then the ringing stopped. "Hello."

"Uh, hello, is Jeanie there?"

"This is Jeanne."

"Oh, hi! You probably don't remember me. I'm Ralph Walls. I saw you last fall while you were riding on a horse and…"

"Oh, I remember you," Jeanie interrupted. "You wanted me to sit on that muddy bag!"

"Yeah, that was me. I was just joking with you — you know, just trying to be funny!"

"I know," Jeanie said.

"Well, the reason I called," Ralph continued nervously, "was that I was talking with your brother, Herb, and I asked him if you were going out with anyone and he said you're not..."

"I know," Jeanie chimed in. "He told me all about it."

"He did?"

"Yes, he did."

"You mean he told you everything I said?"

"Yes, he did."

"Well, do you think your mom would make an exception to the rule and let you go out, and by the way, would you like to go out with me?"

"I don't know, and yes."

"So you don't know if she will let you go out, but, yes, you would go out with me?" Ralph repeated, wanting to make sure he didn't miss anything.

"If I can get my mother to say yes, then what do you have in mind?"

"Well, I guess we could go to a movie or a dance."

"We aren't allowed to dance, but I'll ask her about the movie when she gets home from work, but don't get your hopes up."

"OK, great, should I call you back?"

"No, you better let me call you."

"OK, let me give you my number."

"That's OK, I have it."

"You do?"

"Yeah, it's in the book."

"Oh, right. I'll wait to hear from you."

"OK, thanks for calling and be patient, this might take awhile."

"OK, bye."

"Bye." Now Ralph's mind was really racing. He just called a fourteen-year-old girl and asked her out. If it turned out that she was able to go out with him, he knew he would get ribbed by everybody. "Cradle robber" and all that, he could hear it already! Then Ralph's thoughts really got panicky as he wondered, *What if she asks her mom, and she is really mad that I asked her daughter out, and so her mom calls my house and what if my mom answers?? What have I done?*

* * * * *

Meanwhile at the Rohrer house Jeanie hadn't even thought about asking her mother yet; being a typical teen girl, her first thought was who to call first, Joyce or Carol Jo, her two best girlfriends. But before she could even dial the phone, she heard the sound of her mother's car coming down the driveway. Evelyn and her husband, Mervin Rohrer, had gotten divorced a few years earlier. There were five children in the family, and Herb and Merv helped with the chores of the farm to pay the rent. Jeanie knew that the whole family would be coming in soon to get cleaned up and to start on dinner preparations. She knew that any phone calls to her girlfriends would have to wait. Besides, she was hoping that her mother had a good day and wasn't too tired. It was

Monday night, and if she were hoping to go out this coming weekend she would need to have a plan. Helping to prepare the meal, as well as helping with the dishes and laundry would be a good start. Hoping her brothers didn't upset her by ruff-housing tonight would be a good idea also.

* * * * *

As soon as he had hung up the phone, Ralph was thinking, *what do I do now?* Do I just hang around the house all night waiting for the phone to ring, but not only that, should I answer the phone every time it rings? That would be a pain with all the business-related calls they got every night. That would be too much. Ralph wasn't a very patient person. He never liked waiting for anything. Now he had to wait on someone else to, first of all, ask her mother if she could go out and, second, to call him back. That could take days, maybe even weeks! *Why did I do this to myself?* Ralph thought with annoyance.

Tuesday was a typical day at work. Ralph was sent to do a spackling job by himself. Usually this was a lot of fun. Ralph loved working with his hands and creating things. And whenever he was sent to work on a job by himself, he always made it into a game. He'd count the number of rooms, including walk-in closets and hallways, and then multiply it by a number of minutes. Then he would add time for nailing on and spackling corner beads. This would give him an idea of when he would be done so he would race the clock. But this day he had other things on his mind. It was a day of wrangling with "what if" scenarios. *What if her mother is really mad and calls my father or mother? What if - what if?* By day's end Ralph was not only physically tired but also mentally exhausted. He pulled the truck back into the shop at 5:00 that afternoon. His father had already gotten back to the shop and was washing up tools and getting things ready for the next day's work. "How much did you get done?" asked RH.

"It's all taped and I got the beads nailed on and coated."

"Wow, that's good! Now you can go with me tomorrow morning to sand the Grefe job, then we can go back to your job and second coat it," continued RH.

"You need any help cleaning up?" Ralph asked.

"No, I'm almost done."

All Ralph wanted to do was get in the house and hope that Jeanie would call. As he neared the house he could smell the aroma of dinner penetrating the air. "Smells good, Mom. What's on the menu tonight?"

"Meat loaf," came his mother's reply. "I hope you're hungry!"

"Aren't I always? Where's Glenn?"

"He's down in the basement, but you had better get washed up before your Dad comes in and needs to use the bathroom. He has a township meeting tonight and has to leave right after dinner."

"OK, I'm on my way". That was great to hear. *If Jeanie calls tonight dad won't be home,* Ralph was thinking as he left the kitchen.

With dinner over Ralph's dad headed for the den where the days mail was waiting for him on his desk. He always looked to see if anyone had sent a check for a completed job, first, and if there were he would make out a deposit ticket so that his wife, Norma, could deposit it the next day. Norma was the type of person who was always busy. The house was always spotless, the lawn was always manicured, and the car was always clean. Ralph used to say she was always cooking, cleaning, canning, baking or mowing, and the mowing part she did mostly by hand! Norma loved to work in the garden, and RH took care of all the shrubbery and all the fruit trees. The only time Ralph ever saw his father and mother sit down together and relax was when they lived in Round Valley on the farm. When they purchased their first TV, a small black-and-white one, you needed binoculars so you could see it from where the couch was. They had about four shows they would watch. Ralph and Glenn were young then so they were upstairs in bed trying to sleep, but with the laughing downstairs, it was difficult. Their parents' favorite programs were "The Honeymooners," "I Love Lucy," "Dragnet," and "Run for Your Life."

But Ralph's dad really didn't have much time for TV. He basically stayed in his den reading or working on his stamp collection until bedtime every night. Sometimes he would go to a township meeting in Annandale. Glenn usually had some homework to finish, which was the case on this particular evening, so Ralph headed into the living room to see what was on TV. From the other room a voice called out saying, "I'm leaving now."

"OK, when do you think you'll be home?" Norma asked her husband.

"Hopefully by ten," and with that Ralph's dad headed out the door.

As Ralph walked pass the coffee table he noticed a Time magazine lying there with an interesting title on its cover, so he picked it up and said, "Has Pop seen this yet?" He always called his dad "Pop" at home.

"No, he hasn't," was his mother's response.

"Good, I can have some fun with this." The front cover had pictures of a bunch of men, just face shots, and the caption read, "Millionaires Under 40." Well, his family had always teased him about how he was saving all his money except for the change, so he thought, *I'll carefully cut out one of the faces and paste mine in its place*. His mom loved to have fun, too, so she got him the scissors and found one of his high school wallet-size pictures, but that's as far as she went. The rest he had to do. After completing the project, he placed it on his father's desk. His Dad got a good laugh out of that. Ralph was always up to something, but usually it was his mother who was the victim.

* * * * *

One day Ralph purchased a fake can of peanuts. Inside the can was a spring-loaded snake that would fly out when you opened it. Knowing his mother was on one of her many "diets," he sat it on the kitchen counter and left the room. By the way, his mother loved peanuts. When she came home and saw the can of nuts, she asked, "Who bought these nuts?" "I did," Ralph hollered from the other room. "Help yourself." "I'm not eating any nuts," came her response. Ralph and Glenn waited in the other room no longer than five minutes when there was a scream and the sound of a can hitting the floor. "You boys are going to be the death of me yet!" she yelled. They came into the room holding their sides and laughing. They got her so many times: One time with a fake ice cube that had a fly in it and they served it to company; then there was the fake rubbery vomit that looked like it had food in it lying on her clean kitchen floor. One of the best times was when he bought a rubber chocolate donut and served it to his grandfather. His grandfather tried in vain to bite a piece off that donut. Ralph's mom was a good sport. As a matter of fact, she might even have been responsible for Ralph's joke playing.

A few years earlier Norma had worked for a company in Lebanon, The Eclipse Mattress Factory, and would get out of work after the boys were already home from school. But one day she got out early and decided to have some fun, so she hid in the living room closet. Ralph and Glenn came home from school and had started making themselves some peanut butter crackers when they heard a moaning sound. Looking puzzled, as their hands froze with peanut butter-covered knives in mid-air, listening intently, they heard it again. They hollered, "Who's there?" No answer, and again they heard the noise. Thinking someone had broken into the house, they decided to search, but Ralph first grabbed his father's double–barrel, 12-gauge shotgun. They went from room to room and finally determined it was coming from the closet in the living room. Standing in front of the door with Glenn behind him, Ralph said, "We know you're in there, we have a gun, and you better come out." The door opened slowly. Ralph and Glenn's hearts could be seen beating through their shirts. As the door opened slowly, their mother's face in disbelief at having a shotgun pointed at her, Ralph hollered shrilly, "I could have killed you!" The gun, however, was not loaded. That was also the last time his mother ever hid in the closet!

* * * * *

It was now 9:00 pm and still there had been no phone call. Ralph figured that if Jeanie didn't call by nine, she probably wasn't going to call that night. He had just sat down in the living room when the phone rang. "I'll get it," he yelled as he jumped up off of the couch. Picking up the phone on the third ring, he answered urgently, "Hello."

"Hi, is this Ralph?"

"Yes, it is. "

"Hi, this is Jeanie."

He knew it was she as soon as she said hi, but he had to act surprised so as not to seem so desperate and eager. "Oh, hi!" Ralph responded, as if he hadn't been expecting her call. "So give me the bad news. What did your mother say?"

"Well after a three-hour conversation and a little help from my brother, Herb, she said I could go out with you."

"Really? She did?"

"Yes, but only to school functions."

"Wow! That's great!"

"Yeah, that's pretty good, kind of."

"What do you mean, kind of?" asked Ralph.

"Well, what she said exactly was that I could go out on a date twice a month, but only to school functions."

"You mean like basketball games or wrestling matches?" asked Ralph.

"Yes, anywhere there are large crowds of people. And she also said that I have to come home right after."

"When does this go into effect?" The wheels were already turning in Ralph's mind, making plans.

"What do you mean?" Jeanie replied.

"I mean, when can I ask you out?"

"Right now," Jeanie answered with a smile in her voice.

"Well, OK, would you like to go out this weekend?"

"Yes, and we could go to the Jabberwock. It's Friday and Saturday night."

"Which night is good for you?" Ralph asked.

"Friday's fine with me."

"OK, great, I'll pick you up at six o'clock."

"OK, I'll be ready. Bye."

"Good night, Jeanie."

Ralph went back to the couch and sank down on it in relief, folding his hands behind his head with a big smile on his face. Finally, a date with Jeanie this weekend!

* * * * *

This hadn't been a pleasant night at the Rohrer home. Jeanie's mother, Evelyn, wasn't at all happy about the idea of her fourteen-year-old daughter going out on dates. The questions flew back and forth between mother and daughter for three hours: Who is this Ralph Walls, anyway? She had heard of their family and that they were well respected in the community, but what is he like? And why would he want to date a fourteen-year-old girl? He had just graduated from high school. Why wasn't he dating girls his own age? And another thing — is he a Christian man? What are his beliefs? Where does he go to church?

Evelyn had lots of concerns and rightly so. She was trying to raise five children on her own. Evelyn was a good Mennonite woman and didn't want to have her daughter going out at such a young age and with a non-believer. She figured this was pretty safe, just letting her go to school functions that she would have gone to anyway. And besides, they lived only about ten minutes from the high school. The fact that there would be a couple hundred other people there also sounded safe. So, in Evelyn's mind, by saying OK to school functions it didn't seem like she was really letting Jeanie go out on a real date with someone alone.

* * * * *

Friday night was soon there. All day long at work, Ralph had been running scenarios through his head about tonight's date. He had purposely set the time for six o'clock because that allowed a whole hour to get to the school. He figured Jeanie's mother was probably going to grill him when he got there, so he would need the extra time. But now he was wishing he hadn't built in so much extra time, because if they had less time, they could say they had to leave or else they'd be late for the program. He was kicking himself now for allowing that extra time to be interrogated by Jeanie's mother. But then Ralph had this thought: he could call and say he was running a little late and allow just enough time to drive to the high school. But in the end Ralph pulled in the driveway on March 12, 1965, at two minutes to six. Walking to the door, he didn't know if his heart was pounding from fear of meeting the mother or the excitement of meeting Jeanie. They had never really met, as he had only seen her riding double with another girl on a horse and that had been just a glimpse. After knocking on the door, he could hear someone yell, "I'll get it!" and what sounded like a hundred people racing to the door. Then the door opened and there stood Herb. "Hey, Ralph," Herb said, with a few other little faces behind him trying to get a closer look.

"Hi, Herb," Ralph responded. "Is Jeanie ready?"

From the back of the crowd came Jeanie trying to push her way through and at the same time yelling, "Herbie, I said, I'll get it."

"Yeah, she's right here," Herb said with an impish grin on his face, because he had just beat his sister to the door.

As Jeanie squeezed past her brother and pulled the door shut behind her, she said, "Sorry about that." They exchanged "Hi's" and walked to the car. Ralph opened her door and let her in, and then went around to his side, jumped in, and started the car.

As they were backing around to leave, he asked, "So where is your mother? I figured she would be here tonight to meet me."

"Oh, on Friday nights she gets out of work at five o'clock, and by the time she cashes her check and buys groceries, it's usually six-thirty before she gets home."

"Oh, that's too bad; I was really looking forward to meeting her."

"Really?" Jeanie asked.

"No, I was just kidding. So who were all those other kids in the house?"

"Well, you know Herbie. The other two were Timmy and Joann and there is another brother, Merv, but I don't know where he is tonight."

It was a short ride to the high school, and since they were early, they sat in the car talking until a quarter to seven, and then they went in. The show seemed to end too quickly and it was time to go home. It just seemed too soon to head home, so knowing that he had been working on a few jobs not too far from the school, Ralph asked Jeanie if she would like to go for a short ride so he could show her some houses he was working on.

"That sounds like fun," Jeanie responded. Of course it was already dark out, so they weren't going to be able to see anything, but neither one of them thought about that. The "short ride" turned out to be about 15 miles one way. Ralph knew that he was already breaking the rules and this only being the first date, but he decided to take a chance. He just wanted to spend more time getting to know Jeanie. Besides the fact that he was driving 15 miles away at nighttime, the place he wanted to show her was on top of a mountain, called Hell Mountain. They talked all the way there, but when they got there they couldn't see the house through the trees, plus it was too dark. So they turned and headed down the mountain.

Halfway down the mountain, Ralph felt something going wrong with the steering; it kept pulling to one side. So he said he'd better pull over and take a look. There was a spot on the ninety-degree turn halfway down the mountain where he could pull off. After getting out and walking around the car, he realized his one tire was completely flat. *Great, now I'm in big trouble*, he thought. *I will really be getting her home late and her mother will be screaming*. What mother is going to believe a guy who gets her daughter home late and then says, "We had a flat tire and, oh, by the way, I just had your daughter up on Hell Mountain and we were just talking." *I know I would never believe that*, Ralph thought miserably. After standing and staring for a few long minutes at that flat tire, imagining all the worst-case scenarios that could happen once he got her back home, he opened the car door and told Jeanie the bad news and that she should stay in the car while he changed the tire since it was March and very cold outside. "OK…" Jeanie replied nervously. Ralph opened the trunk, got the tire out, and then went back to reach in the driver's door to turn on the radio for Jeanie to keep her company while he changed the tire. Finally, with the tire changed and trunk shut, Ralph opened the car door to get in and noticed that Jeanie was asleep. He started the car and drove quietly down the mountain so as not to wake her.

While he is driving back to Jeanie's house, Ralph couldn't stop thinking what a beautiful girl she was, not just in looks but in personality as well. In his opinion, she was the complete package of what he'd been looking for in a girl, but there was only one problem: she was fourteen years old. Ralph pondered as he drove, *She's got at least four years of school ahead of her, and I'm out of school. She is going to be around other guys in school. How can I compete with them, considering I can only see her twice a month?* Jeanie woke up after a couple of miles. "Sorry, I didn't mean to nod off on you," she said sleepily, sitting up and smoothing her hair.

"That's OK, it gave me a good chance to check you out."

"Oh, yeah, you did, huh? So what are you thinking?"

"Well, for starters, I'm wondering if you would go out with me again."

"Are you asking me out?"

"Yes, would you go out with me again?"

"Yes, I would," came her response as they pulled in her driveway.

"When's a good time for me to call?" Ralph asked.

"Call anytime, but not after eight-thirty. Mom goes to bed early and the phone would wake her."

"Alright, sounds good to me," Ralph said as he got out of the car and opened her door. "Should I go in with you since it's late to explain about the tire?"

"No, she's already in bed," Jeanie replied as they walked to the door. Ralph looked at her for a few seconds, smiling, and then said, "You know I had a great time and really enjoyed your company."

Jeanie smiled up at him shyly, responding in a small voice, "Me, too."

Knowing she was only fourteen and this was their first date, Ralph didn't think he should kiss her goodnight, so he said, "Well, what do we do now?"

Standing slightly on her toes, Jeanie leaned forward and pressed her lips gently into his, then pulled back and looked up into his eyes and said, "Thank you for a beautiful night." With that she turned, opened the door, and disappeared into the house.

Ralph was so taken by surprise by her kiss that he inadvertently stepped backward to the point of almost falling off the porch, recovering himself and regaining his footing just in time. It was about a six-mile drive to home, and even though this was just the first date, he was thinking, *This is the girl I want to marry. This sounds silly,* Ralph chided himself in his thoughts; *as a matter of fact, it's downright stupid.* But he thought it anyway and if felt good. They called each other on the phone and dated twice a month to school functions and really started to get to know each other. One thing they hadn't considered, though, was that there are no school functions during the summer months.

* * * * *

The waiting was over; Gid and Betty learned that they were going to New York to be based out of JFK airport. It was late in June of 1965. They had to be in New York for Gid to report to work for TWA by August 1. The damaged VW had been repaired, so they once again loaded up a trailer with all their possessions, the crib, the hope chest and the sewing machine, and they headed east. The plan was to spend a month at Betty's mother's house while they found a place to rent on Long Island. So with the trailer hooked to the '56 Mercury and Karla safe and secure in the VW with her mother, they left for Pennsylvania. This time they had one other precious piece of cargo with them; Betty was pregnant with their second child.

After arriving in Pennsylvania and settling in, the next task would be to secure housing in New York. With Karla safely placed in the hands of her grandmother, Gid and Betty left for a two-day trip to New York. It didn't take them long after arriving to find a place to rent. They had found a two-family house with the first floor furnished in Merrick, Long Island. It was just what they needed. It was an easy commute to work for Gid, and everything they needed was close by.

The month went by so quickly. Karla had just gotten to know her grandmother when it was time to leave already. With good-byes said and vehicles loaded once more, off they headed for their next big adventure.

They had no sooner settled in their home in Merrick when the phone rang. A lady on the other end introduced herself as Shirley Grace, and she was calling to welcome them to Long Island. She also invited them to the church that she and her husband, Carl Grace, attended, which was the House of Friendship Mennonite Church in the Bronx. Gid and Betty learned that people from Lancaster had notified people in the church here of their arrival. Carl Grace worked for American Airlines as a mechanic. They had a young daughter named Sharon who was only seven months older than Karla. Gid and Betty accepted their invitation and went to church with the Graces the following Sunday. At House of Friendship they met Grace Kautz, John and Marie Kauffman, Cecil and Dory Grove, Dave and Lois Bomberger, Jay and Ella Mae Lehman, and later on would come to know Ora and Rhoda Mast. This group would develop a friendship that would last for years to come.

Gid would now be starting work at JFK airport as a flight engineer on the Convair 880 and as a reserve pilot, which meant he was called in as needed. He was to expect one flight a month. This was new to Gid who had always worked a full weeks' work, so he needed to find something to do with all his free time. Since he was skilled at mechanics, he thought he could start a used car sales business, buying cars that he could easily fix up and resell. So that's exactly what he did during his first year at TWA.

Their friendships with their new found friends were very special and with the families growing, there were lots of children growing up together as well. They would take turns once a month and have carry-in meals at one another's homes. They really enjoyed each others company and they never had a dull moment.

* * * * *

In the summer of 1965, the Vietnam War was pretty much the topic everywhere you went. Ralph had already registered with the selective service and knew that he would probably get a draft notice before long. His father and all of his uncles had been to war; in fact, one of his uncles died at Iwo Jima. RH Walls didn't want to see any of his sons go to war, so he had, without Ralph knowing it, put Ralph's name on the National Guard waiting list thinking this would keep him safe from being called up to active duty.

Ralph and Jeanie had become close friends in the five months they had been seeing one another, but now school was out. Ralph wrestled constantly with thoughts of how they would get to see each other now. Jeanie wasn't allowed to go to the movies with a guy yet, so they hung out at her house a couple times a month, and he was allowed to take her to the miniature golf course just down the road. They were also allowed to go to the ice cream stand. Jeanie had lots of girlfriends and spent a lot of time with them, also. Plus she had a couple of paying jobs—babysitting and taking care of a lady down the road who'd had a bad fall from a horse and had broken her back. The summer went by fast that year. By fall school was back in session for Jeanie. She was a sophomore and fifteen now. School activities had started and she was allowed to go to the football games on Saturday.

On one fateful day as Ralph came into the house after getting home from work, the first thing he noticed was his mother just standing there with a terrible look of shock on her face. "There's a couple of letters on the counter for you," she said. Ralph picked up both envelopes and could see it wasn't going to be good news. One envelope had Selective Service written on the outside. The contents of the notice were short and to the point: *Report for active duty on December 25, 1965*. "Christmas Day, no less," was all he said aloud as flung it back down onto the counter.

"Oh my, oh my!" his mother said. "Well let's see what the next one says." After opening the second envelope he looked surprised. "What's it say?" his mother demanded, wringing her hands urgently.

"It must be a mistake," Ralph replied. "I'm supposed to report to the National Guard Amory for duty on November 12, 1965. How can that be? I didn't put my name on the list."

"You know what, Ralph, I think your dad did it for you a while ago," his mother replied. "We'll ask him first thing when he gets home from work." RH came in the house a little later and when they showed him the National Guard notice, he confessed he had indeed put Ralph's name on the list quite sometime ago. After the shock wore off Ralph thought about calling Jeanie to tell her the news, but soon decided he'd wait and tell her in person. On Saturday after the football game at North Hunterdon, Ralph told Jeanie about the letters he'd received. They both agreed that the National Guard was the best choice. By joining the Guard he would only have to report for duty one weekend a month and two weeks every summer for the next six years. He would also have to report for basic training, which lasted for six weeks. Being a member of the National Guard also meant that Ralph could still work for his father and continue to earn an income.

On November 12, 1965, Ralph reported to the Flemington Armory. At that time they were the Company "C", 6th Battalion, 50th Armor division. He was supplied with uniforms, shoes, and all the necessary equipment, and began attending some training sessions. There were a number of other young men who had come in that same day or within the month previous. They were told that their basic training would be on hold for a while since there were so many in training at this time due to the war. That sounded OK to Ralph because it would be winter soon, and he didn't relish the idea of training and doing field exercises in the cold.

Dating had now changed also. Since Jeanie could only go out with Ralph twice a month, they had decided that she should go with some of her friends once a week to school functions and they could just meet there. It wasn't like a real date; she was going anyway, and he just happened to be there. So in reality they were dating once a week. There were many times when Ralph attended school sporting events with his friends and not with Jeanie, especially if there was more than one wrestling match or basketball game during a particular week.

Ralph mainly hung out with his neighbor, Gary Wurst, who was still in school, and with his brother, Glenn. The three of them were avid wrestling fans. Gary was hired by Ralph's dad to work on weekends and during the summer months, and he and Ralph had become good friends and worked well together. Even though Ralph had always been fun loving and enjoyed a good prank, by contrast he had been a quiet kind of guy while in school. He had never caused any trouble to speak of and always tried to be a decent person while with a girl. He had plenty of opportunities with some of the girls he had gone out with, but he knew when to stop if things were going too far. This soon caused his peers to poke fun and tease about his timidity with girls, which was not the case at all. Ralph knew right from wrong, and he also knew that having sex should be between a husband and wife, not between teenagers in the heat of raging hormones.

But Ralph wasn't perfect by any means. He had discovered that drinking beer was a lot of fun and he was acquiring a taste for it. Even though he was only nineteen and couldn't legally purchase beer or alcohol in the state of New Jersey, there were other ways to obtain it. Sometimes on Saturday nights he and his brother and some other friends would take the springs out of the back seat of his '56 Chevy and drive into New York City where you could buy beer at the age of eighteen. They would stack the cases of beer under the back seat, put the cushions back on top of them, and then drive back to New Jersey. Ralph knew this wasn't the right thing to do, but he did it anyway. One thing he never did was drink while on a date with Jeanie. Their dating had become a little more intense, though, and time spent parking or saying good-night was starting to take a lot longer. Ralph kept reminding himself that she was only fifteen and a sophomore in high school.

Ralph did, on many occasions, get to see Jeanie's mother. They never said much to each other, just the usual greetings and small talk. Ralph could, however, tell that she wasn't happy about him dating her daughter. By December they had been seeing each other just three months shy of two years, and Ralph was totally convinced this was the girl he wanted to spend the rest of his life with.

Ralph had heard from his friends in school that there were always guys hitting on Jeanie and that some of them kept asking her out. This wasn't sitting very well with Ralph. This was his girl and no one else was going to take her out. The next time they were out, he asked her about all the other guys, and she said, not to worry because they were just good friends. All Ralph could think was, *Good friends, my foot! They only have one thing on their minds.*

It was almost Christmas, so Ralph decided he would shower her with gifts - a dozen gifts, to be exact. When he went to her house on Christmas day with all the gifts plus one for everyone else, Jeanie was in shock. He found out later that her mother was upset over his extravagance and said it was just foolishness. Ralph continued to shower her with gifts, and he even traded in his '56 Chevy for a beautiful '61 T-Bird. What Ralph was doing was showing Jeanie that no schoolboys could compete with him.

* * * * *

On December 12, 1965, Betty gave birth to their second child, Michael Scott. With Karla now twenty-seven months old, Betty had plenty to keep herself busy. They always looked forward to those evenings when their small group, which was growing rapidly with the addition of children, would get together to visit and play games, especially Rook. There was also lots of storytelling, and Gid would usually have a "doozie" of a story. One particular story that he told went something like this:

This morning when I got up I noticed that we needed milk for cereal, so I thought I would run over to Bohack's grocery store to pick some up. When I was ready to pay I noticed there was only one cashier to check out with, so I was forced to get behind a lady checking out a large order. I was getting change out of my pocket to pay for my milk when I dropped a quarter on the floor. The lady in front of me put her foot on it to claim it as her own. I said, "Hey, lady, that's my quarter!" She picked it up off the floor, looked at it and said, "It doesn't have your name on it," and put it in her pocket. While she was putting all her bags in the grocery cart, I quickly paid for the milk with the exact change, picked up one of her bags of groceries and started for the door. The lady hollered, "Hey, that's my bag of groceries!" I looked at the bag in my arm and said, "It doesn't have your name on it," and walked out of the store. By this time most people would ask, "No, you didn't, did you?" Then Gid would reply, "Yes I did, and do you want to know what was in the bag?" Usually someone would say, "Yes." And Gid would answer, "Baloney, just what I'm feeding you!" That was Gid; he always had a story to tell. If there was someone new to the group, the rest would be forced to hear the same story over and over again. The funny part was that you laughed just as hard each time he would tell it. These precious Christian friends were like family; in fact, as the years went by the children all thought of them as aunts, uncles, and cousins. It really is true–friends are friends forever.

6

THREE-STATE ALARM

In January of 1965 Ralph's father was called for jury duty, so he decided to send Ralph and Charlie to a new job located in Pottsville. They were both familiar with the roads because they had done numerous jobs in the area over the years. The night before there had been a sleet storm, but by morning the roads looked pretty decent, so he decided to send them out with his brand new truck. The roads were just a little slushy so they took their time. When they got to Pottsville they needed to make a right turn off the main road onto a side road that wasn't paved. Apparently the local road crew hadn't taken care of their roads as well as the county did because they were covered with ice. The directions said to go one mile and then the driveway would be on the left. Ralph and Charlie were sure they could handle this icy dirt road with no problem, but there was the challenge that every bit of it was uphill. After a lot of spinning the wheels and wearing the tires down to the rims, they made it to the driveway only to discover it was worse then the road. It was a solid sheet of ice, and to make matters worse once you turned into the driveway you had to turn to the right and go up an even steeper lane to the house. Once they had committed to turning into the driveway they instantly knew they were in trouble. The left side of the driveway had been built up with a rock wall to make it level; in other words, it was the downhill side of the driveway. From the rock wall the land sloped down into a huge field all the way to Pottsville. The scene was a beautiful picture of white snow and ice with bits of hay and weeds sticking up here and there through the snow. The truck slid to the left and came to rest on top of the rock wall. When Ralph looked out the driver's window he couldn't see the ground below unless he rolled down the window and stuck his head out. That's how high the truck was sitting in the air. They sat in silence for a moment, trying to come up with a solution to their dilemma, when suddenly Charlie said, "Wait here! I'll go find a big piece of wood and then come around to your side and try to pry you back onto the driveway." Before Ralph had a chance to respond Charlie already had the truck door open and was stepping out. Apparently he forgot that the driveway was covered with ice, because the second his feet hit the ground he disappeared from Ralph's view. Thinking Charlie was seriously hurt, Ralph figured he better try to help him, but to slide across the seat might make the truck move too much and cause it to slide over the edge. So his next thought was to carefully open the driver's side door and then slowly work his way around the ice-covered rocks to the other side, holding onto the truck for balance. Everything was going fine when suddenly Charlie's two feet appeared from under the truck startling Ralph and causing him to lose his grip and fall from the top of the rock wall.

The first thing that must be said here is that Ralph had always been a very good athlete; he ran cross-country and had tremendous balancing abilities. When he landed on the ground below, the force of momentum carried him forward down the hill toward Pottsville at a break-neck speed. With every step he could hear the crunch of ice beneath his feet as they pounded the ground below; he could also hear his knees hitting his jaw with every stride. He knew that after about a hundred yards of this propelled running he would either be knocked out by his knees slamming into his head or his heart would probably explode. There was only one solution, and that was to just dive ahead and hope the fall didn't cut him to shreds when he hit the ice. His biggest concern, though, was Charlie's condition and whether or not the truck was coming down the hill right behind him about to run over him. He had no way of knowing because he couldn't turn to look. Ralph knew he had to stop this dangerous, high-speed run, and eventually he willed himself to fall, which was hard to do at that rate of propulsion. The fall turned into the most beautiful snow and ice-plow slide that you could have imagined — that is, a beaten up human body had just plowed about sixteen feet of snow and ice. What seemed like an eternity had only taken a matter of seconds. Finally he slid to a stop and just lay there for a minute, looking up at the sky, stunned at what had just happened. After getting his bearings, he got to his feet that were connected to a pair of wobbly legs and looked up to see that Charlie and the truck were still sitting where he'd left them. Getting back to the top was another challenge, but he soon realized that the only way was to grab the pieces of grass sticking through the snow and pull himself up one slow step at a time. Halfway up the field he heard someone yelling and he stopped to see who it was. There was the builder hanging out one of the windows of the house yelling, "What are you doing down there? The job is up here." At that point Ralph just wanted to be standing next to him by that window so he could pick him up and throw him down the hill! When he finally reached the top he found that Charlie was OK, and the builder came down to help. They all decided to leave the truck right where it was and to just carry all their equipment uphill by hand. They figured that by the end of the day the ice would be completely melted and they could just back out and head home, and lucky for them, that's exactly what they were able to do. When Ralph got home that night, his father, mother, and aunt who was visiting wanted to know how his day went. Ralph told them this story with lots of humor and extra drama sprinkled in, of course, and the two women practically wet their pants they were laughing so hard!

Spring of 1966 found Ralph being sent to Fort Dix for a six-week stint in Basic Training. This didn't sit well with him – the thought of leaving Jeanie behind as easy prey for all those high school Romeos. They wrote letters constantly and he would call whenever he could get time off to use a phone. This was Ralph's first time away from home for an extended period of time, except for the times at Boy Scout camp when he was younger. Basic Training really wasn't bad at all. He had always been in good physical shape and enjoyed physical competition. His top Sergeant called him "a trooper" because he said he always gave 110 percent. There was an incident during a training ceremony one day, though, which caused quite a ruckus. The morning was chilly and everyone's fingers were a little frostbitten. They were in a dress right formation. The drill sergeant came running over and stood right in front of Ralph, hollering at him over and over, but Ralph didn't know what he was saying or that it was directed at him. The next thing he knew, he felt something on his hand. Then the drill sergeant left. They were all dismissed and everyone came running over to Ralph hollering, "Are you alright?"

Ralph had no idea what they were talking about until he looked down and saw blood running down and puddling on the ground. "What happened?" Ralph asked.

One of his friends said, "Your thumb was sticking up, and he said if you didn't put it down, he was going to cut it off."

"You're kidding!" Ralph said grabbing his thumb.

"No, I'm not, so the sergeant reached in his pocket and pulled out a pen knife and he started to cut your thumb off."

"I couldn't feel a thing," Ralph said, "my fingers were numb and I didn't know he was talking to me."

By then one of the platoon leaders came over and said, "We better take you to the Infirmary." They hopped in a jeep and drove to the Infirmary. When they got there the attending medic asked, "How did you do this?" Before Ralph could speak, the platoon leader said, "He cut it on his bayonet." When they got back to the barracks, the rest of the company was all complaining.

Ralph asked, "What's going on?"

One of the men said, "They've locked us down."

"What do you mean?" Ralph asked.

"We can't leave our barracks area all weekend or make any phone calls."

"Why did they do that?" questioned Ralph.

"Because they don't want the word to get out about what the sergeant did to you." They spent the rest of the weekend with no privileges and Monday everything went back to normal.

A couple of weeks later, the last week to be exact, the men had to make T-shirts to wear to run an obstacle course. Ralph thought this would be a great place to show that he hadn't forgotten the incident with his thumb. So he drew a big thumb on his T-shirt with blood dripping off it and wrote, "PVT Numb Thumb" across the top. The word must have spread to the sergeant, because as Ralph came across the twenty-five foot monkey bars, he could see the sergeant standing directly at the end staring straight at him and not leaving any room for him to jump down. Ralph managed to jump down, however, and then he stood chest-to-chest and eye-to-eye for a moment before going on to finish the course.

The six weeks had come to a close and Ralph was ready to go home, but just when he thought he was leaving they came to him with paperwork saying he was being sent to Seagirt, New Jersey, for two weeks of leadership training. He had been voted as one who would make a good leader, so this extended his time by an additional two weeks. Once the leadership training was completed, Ralph was able to return back home where he thought everything would be back to normal, like how his life had been before.

Ralph's attitude had been changing quite a bit in the last year or so, and he had become very self-centered. Whatever he wanted he was going to get. It didn't matter what it cost. He started spending his money on cars, booze, and just having good times in general, or at least what he thought were good times. At work he had become very competitive. Ralph always wanted to be the fastest and the best. He strived for perfection. Ralph and his father didn't see eye to eye on everything. RH would try to save pennies by skipping steps in the work process that would eventually be covered up anyway, like behind cabinets, vanities or paneling. Ralph always taped them anyway because he said when the wind blew, women would complain about the draft blowing from behind the cabinets. Ralph always argued it took longer to cut pieces than to just put one whole piece up. That was just a couple of many small disagreements that he and his dad were starting to have.

Then to top it off he found out that Jeanie had been getting rides home from school with other guys. This made him furious. *How could she do that to me*, Ralph thought. He didn't want her anywhere near another guy, especially in a car. When he confronted her about it, she said, "They just drove me home from school, that's all." Well, it mattered to Ralph and it bothered him, so he started looking around for other dates.

On three different occasions he went to the local dance hall, struck up a conversation with a girl, and made a date, but each time he was disappointed. He could only think about that girl named Jeanie. They dated on and off through the remainder of the summer, and in the fall Jeanie started her junior year of high school. During the summer Ralph's dad hired Jeanie's brother Herb on his son's recommendation. Herb was a fast learner, and Ralph liked having him on the job because he could get updates about Jeanie from him.

Ralph and Jeanie's dating had now gotten back on track and had become more consistent. Now that she was older, they were no longer confined to dating only twice a month. Now they went out every weekend and to the movies. Ralph always made sure they went to the early show so there would be time for "parking" later. They did push the limits, but neither one wanted to make a mistake. They had talked about the future and even about marriage when she was out of school. For now, though, they just had to control themselves and be patient.

1967 started out great. Everything was going fine until the spring. Jeanie had been asked to go to the prom by a class member. Ralph had no desire to go, having been out of high school for so long, and so she decided to go with her classmate. Ralph was off the wall with anger and jealousy! So in retaliation, he figured he should find someone to go out and have some fun with. It just so happened that a girl named Susan had caught his eye; her parents owned the farm where Jeanie's family also lived. He had met her on a previous occasion and she'd asked him if he would like to go to the prom with her. Ralph reasoned to himself, *well, since Jeanie is now going with someone else, why not?* So he agreed to take her, but he thought he should get to know her a little better. The night they agreed on for Ralph to take her out happened to be a night when Susan's parents were out and her grandmother was staying over. She didn't want her grandmother to know she was going out, so she climbed out the bedroom window and met Ralph out on the road, jumped in his car, and they drove down into the field behind her house. The only problem was that when Susan had left the room, she'd also left the window wide open with the curtains hanging out the window. She had also taken her pajamas off and put on regular clothes, but she had left her pajamas lying on the floor in front of the window.

Ralph and Susan had not been down in the field for very long when he noticed how bright it was up by her house. The house was hidden behind a hill, but they could see that the sky was lit up where the house was situated. He mentioned it, but in the usual nonchalance of youth they brushed it aside thinking it was just the moon or something. Ralph and Susan were still sitting in the car engrossed in a great conversation when about an hour later they saw a car coming through the field towards them. As the car got closer, Ralph could see that it was a police car, and in it was the local police officer that Ralph knew well. He pulled up along the driver's side of Ralph's car, rolled down his window and said, "Follow me, Ralph, you're in big trouble!" As Ralph looked past the officer across the front seat of the police car, he could see Herb sitting on the passenger side.

What had happened was that Susan's grandmother opened the door to check on her granddaughter, saw everything hanging out the window and the pajamas on the floor and thought she had been kidnapped, so she called the police to report a kidnapping. When the local town cop got there and started searching for Susan, the first place he went was across the street to see if she was there or if the neighbors there had possibly heard anything. When he knocked on the door, Herb had answered. When the cop told him what had happened, Herb told him she hadn't been kidnapped and that he knew right where she was and who she was with.

As Ralph followed the police car through the field and up the hill, it became quickly evident why the sky was so bright up by the house. Ralph counted 33 police cars lining the road and people with flashlights searching everywhere. *Now I'm going straight to prison*, Ralph thought somberly as he drove past all those police cars and was directed to park in the driveway. As he pulled in the driveway, there were Susan's parents standing on the porch with some detectives who looked like they were restraining her father.

When Ralph and Susan got out of his car, two detectives quickly came over to the car and began to search it. Meanwhile her mother was yelling, "What were you thinking?" to her daughter, and her father, who was slightly intoxicated, was yelling other things at Ralph. They continued to hold the father back and had Ralph stand at the foot of the stairs. The one detective asked Susan's parents, "Do you want to press charges?" There seemed to be a difference of opinion between them, but the officers listened to Susan's mother. Then the mother looked at Ralph and told him she wanted to see him tomorrow to talk to him. The father didn't want to wait; he wanted to talk to Ralph right now.

A detective turned to Ralph and told him to get in his car and go home. As Ralph turned and walked back to his car, the local cop walked with him and said, "You are one lucky guy. They had a three-state alarm out tonight. Just get in your car and go home."

Ralph turned to him and said, "Do my parents know about this?"

"Yeah, I called them."

As Ralph got into his car with a heavy sigh, all he could think was that it was going to be a long night. When his house came into view, he could see that one end of it was brightly lit, as if his parents had turned on every light while waiting for him to come home. It was after midnight by now, when normally they would have been in bed, but as he got closer, he could see his mother's face looking out the window. When he opened the kitchen door, he could see that it was a look of weary frustration.

Ralph looked at her and said, "Does Pop know?"

"Yes," she said.

"What did he say?" Ralph asked.

"Nothing, he just went to bed," she replied.

When Ralph went into the bedroom, he could see the covers on Glenn's bed shaking from Glenn's laughter. This almost caused Ralph to start laughing, too, but they both knew better. The wall between their room and their parents' room was paper thin, and there had been many a time when they were younger, that they thought their father's fist would come through the wall when they got a fit of laughing late at night. There had been a few occasions when he did come in and start beating them while they hid under the covers. Glenn would always get it first because his bed was closest to the door. Ralph had planned it that way so that his father was worn out by the time he got to him. The funny part was that after one of those beatings, when his father left the room, Ralph would start laughing under the covers again because he hadn't gotten it as bad as Glenn had. Of course this would always make Glenn whisper nervously, "Stop it! He'll be back!" Ralph knew that, but he knew Glenn would be first again.

The next morning Ralph made sure he heard his father leave the house before he got up. When he went out to the kitchen, he asked his mother, "What did Pop say?"

"Nothing," she replied. "He just grabbed his lunch pail and went out to the shop."

Now Ralph was usually out the door the same time as his father, but today he thought he'd wait till he saw Charlie pull in the driveway. *There's safety in numbers*, he thought. So when he saw Charlie's truck pull in he walked out of the house. By the time he got to the shop, Charlie was walking to Ralph's truck and getting in on the passenger side. Ralph looked over at his father and said, "Where am I going today?"

"Go second coat the Fisher job. When you're done there, come over to the Bush job. That's where I'll be."

"OK." Ralph got in and backed out the driveway and headed down the road. He looked over at Charlie, who had a smirk on his face. "What's so funny?" Ralph asked.

"Your father said there was a little excitement in the township last night," Charlie said with a laugh.

"Yeah, I guess you could say that, but nothing happened."

"Yeah, right!"

"No, really, nothing happened. Believe me, I'm not a total fool."

"If you say so."

"So what did he tell you?"

"Not much, he was laughing too hard and said, 'serves him right, that'll teach him.'" Then Charlie said to Ralph, "You need to find something else to do with your time; why don't you do what I'm doing and take flying lessons?"

"You've got to be kidding, you're flying?"

"Yeah, I took my first lesson this weekend."

"Really? Is it expensive?"

"Heck no, the first time up is only a penny a pound."

"Where are you doing this?"

"Over at Sky Manor Airport."

"When are you going again?"

"I'll probably go after work tomorrow night. Why don't you check it out?"

"Sounds good, I will."

The rest of the day Ralph had only one thing on his mind - meeting with Susan's parents this afternoon after work. He was supposed to be taking this girl to the prom. She had already bought her gown and he'd ordered his tux already. He ran every possible scenario through his head of what their meeting might be like, and then he came up with a plan. When he finished work, he ran home to wash up first, and then he changed and drove over to Susan's house. No sooner had he knocked on the door than Susan's mother was opening it. "Come in, Ralph," she said tersely. Then she walked to the kitchen table where her daughter was already sitting, but there was no sign of the father. They all sat down, and after a long lecture consisting of, "What were you two thinking?" she turned to Ralph and said, "So what do you think I should do about this situation?"

Ralph hadn't had any time to talk to Susan about this, and at this point he was only thinking of saving his own skin, so he blurted out, "I think we shouldn't be allowed to go to the prom."

"What?" Susan screamed, shooting him an angry look.

"And second," Ralph continued undaunted, "I think that we should not be allowed to see each other for two weeks." (Actually, he had no intentions of ever coming back.)

Susan jumped up out of her chair, screaming, "But I have a gown already!"

Her mother said, "I've been thinking along the same lines of what Ralph just suggested."

"But, Mom, nothing bad happened. Why should I be punished?"

"You don't think you did anything wrong? What do you think, Ralph?"

"I think we messed up big time, and I'm really sorry for any stress that I might have caused your family."

"I'm glad to hear you say that."

"But, Mom!"

"Be thankful, young lady, that I'm handling this and not your father." That was one word Ralph didn't want to hear, 'Father.' "By the way, Ralph, he wanted to have you put in jail, but I talked him out of it. I sent him away today so we could talk." Now Ralph wasn't a praying man, but under his breath he said, "Thank you, God." "I think its best if you two don't see each other again."

Inwardly relieved but not wanting to look too obvious about it, Ralph mumbled, "OK" with just the right amount of repentance in his voice.

Susan turned to Ralph and said, "Thanks a lot!"

Bringing the conversation to a close, despite her daughter's still seething anger, Susan's mom announced, "I think we're done here now, and I hope you both learned a good lesson."

"Yes, ma'am," Ralph said humbly and politely as he pushed his chair away from the table. But he was thinking, *I hope she doesn't ask me what the lesson is.* As he pulled out of Susan's driveway, he could see Jeanie's house across the street and figured she most likely knew about this whole fiasco. He figured he better just stay away awhile till things cooled down. He was hoping that Herb would come to work this Saturday so that he could thank him for sending the local cop down to the field instead of letting them send a cop who didn't know Ralph personally. He couldn't imagine what would've happened to him if that had been the scenario. Probably he would've been handcuffed and roughed up a bit for good measure. But the main reason Ralph hoped Herb worked on Saturday was so he could get Jeanie's take on the whole episode. One thing he knew for sure was that he could never come past this house in his white T-bird again, so it was time to get a different car. But there was an even more important reason in Ralph's mind for getting another car: he knew that even if Jeanie would go out with him again, she probably wouldn't get in the T-bird because he had taken someone else out in it!

* * * * *

Word had spread quickly in school that day. Herb hadn't told Jeanie anything about the night before. He figured she should find out from someone else. When a friend came up to her and asked her, "Aren't you still dating Ralph?" she said, "Yes, we are still going out. Why do you ask?"

"Didn't you hear about last night?"

"No, what happened?" Her girlfriend then told her everything she had heard.

Jeanie was in disbelief. "I can't believe that!"

"It's what I heard," her friend retorted with a shrug and a wry smile. Throughout the day more people would tell her slightly different versions of the story, but all agreed on one point - that Ralph had indeed been out with the other girl. One girl even told her that her brother was involved. Now she was going to find out the truth.

In the cafeteria during lunch hour, Jeanie found her brother, and before she could say anything, Herb said, "Well I guess you've heard."

"I've heard quite a few things, but what role did you play in all of this?"

Now Herb, who was enjoying this immensely and had a big grin on his face, began to tell his dramatic version. "Well, you were going to the prom with what's-his-name and I knew that what's-her-name didn't have a date yet, so I kind of told them about each other."

"You did what? How could you?"

"Well, that was only part of it."

"Go on, tell me more."

"That night she called me and said she needed to sneak out of the window so her grandmother wouldn't see her, but she couldn't get the screen off so she asked me if I could help. "You have *got* to be kidding me!" Jeanie fumed.

"No, I'm not, so I went over and removed the screen and left it lying against the house."

"Do her parents know about you doing this?"

"No, and if they did, I'd be in big trouble now wouldn't I, so be quiet about it."

"Well, go on, so then what happened?" Jeanie demanded impatiently, wanting to know all the details.

"I went back home, and later that night when I looked out my window and saw Officer Bill Brown pulling up, I went outside to meet him because I figured he was there to scold me about racing again or something, and I didn't want Mom to know."

"Where was I when all this was going on?"

"I think you were in your room talking on the phone or something. So anyway, when he said that Susan was missing, I told him she wasn't and that I knew right where she was."

"Wait till Mom hears about this," interrupted Jeanie, shaking her head disdainfully.

"I'll worry about that later; anyway, I jumped in the patrol car and took him down to where they were."

"Do they know you turned them in?"

"Oh, they saw me in the car, I couldn't very well hide."

"So what happened then?"

"I don't really know. Once we got back up to the house there were cops everywhere and Bill told me to go home, so I did."

"So what happened to Ralph?"

"I haven't a clue."

* * * * *

On Saturday Ralph got to talk to Herb when he came to work. Ralph thanked him for, as he put it, "saving my butt." Then he wanted to know what Jeanie had to say about the whole thing. Herb said she really hadn't said anything. Ralph then wanted to know how her prom date went. "Alright, I guess. She really hasn't said much about that either." Then Herb added with a sly grin, "But I bet when I get home from work today she'll want to know everything we've talked about."

"Well, tell her I was asking about her, will you?"

"Yeah, I will. Why don't you just call her, Ralph?"

"I think I'll wait awhile and then maybe just stop in some night, but don't tell her that."

"OK."

In the two weeks that had passed since the incident with Susan, Ralph had taken two flying lessons and had traded his T-bird in for a 1965 Malibu convertible. The flying lessons were a lot of fun, and he had already scheduled another. Before taking these lessons he had never been up in a plane, and he loved it, especially the plane they were flying. The instructor said it was a Cessna 150 and that it was a real easy plane for learning to fly. Ralph had grown up in Hunterdon County and knew his way around the roads. Since 1960 when his father had taken him to work that first night, he had traveled almost every road in the county doing drywall jobs. From the air it was fantastic seeing all the roads with their twists and turns and all the fields with different crops planted or just tilled. He would often have the thought, *I could really get used to this.*

One Wednesday evening Ralph got up his nerve to face Jeanie, so he pulled into her driveway. As he pulled in, he could see her walking down the lane. He figured she probably didn't know who it was since he was driving his new '65 Malibu. He pulled up alongside of her and said, "Hi, stranger. Want to go get some ice cream or something?"

She stood there for a second staring at him, then responded, "I really shouldn't," but reached for the door handle anyway, opened the door and jumped in. "Nice car."

"Thanks."

"Did you just get it?"

"About a week ago."

"Wow, it's a convertible."

"Hey, I'm sorry about everything that happened."

"Yeah, me too," said Jeanie, looking at Ralph with a shy smile

"So what do we do now?" asked Ralph.

"I don't know. What do you think we should do?"

"First, do you still want to go out with me now?"

"Do you still want to go out with me?"

"Of course I do!"

"Are you sure?" Jeanie asked.

"Yes, I'm sure. I don't want to go out with anyone else ever again."

With that reassurance, Jeanie slid across the seat, leaned against Ralph and said, "Do we have to go for ice cream?"

7

DECEPTION

Things were going great that summer. Ralph and Jeanie were seeing a lot of each other. They went to movies, stockcar races, and to the drag strip on the weekends at Island Drag way. In the fall Jeanie started her senior year of high school. All throughout high school she had been taking college prep courses and had always made excellent grades. Some of her teachers noticed how well she was doing in her schoolwork and asked if she had considered going to college. Jeanie had thought about the possibility of college now and then, but she'd never given it any serious consideration. Also, she didn't know how Ralph might react if she told him she was thinking about college, so she just avoided the subject.

At home it was a different story. Jeanie's mother had been against her relationship with Ralph from the beginning and had told her many times it wasn't right. "It's not biblically correct for you to be going with him, because he's not a Christian." Her mother would repeat this statement many times throughout their dating years. She had even suggested college to Jeanie hoping that would separate them. Jeanie would've loved to further her schooling, but she also loved

Ralph and was afraid to even suggest it to him, so for now she decided to just put it on hold. She told herself that when the time was right she could test the waters by dropping little hints to Ralph.

Ralph was still taking flying lessons whenever he could find the time after work. In a two-week period Ralph had experienced some close calls while flying. One evening while Ralph was flying with an instructor, practicing touch-downs, a flock of pheasants took off from an adjacent corn-field and flew directly in front of the plane. The instructor grabbed the stick, pulled up, and narrowly missed the birds. The following week Ralph was approaching the field to land and had clearance to do so, when a plane took off without clearance and headed right for him. Again the instructor took the stick, hollered some words, and got on the radio to call the tower. The tower said they hadn't given clearance to take off to anyone, so with that the instructor turned the plane around, chased down the other pilot and got wing tip to wing tip with him and began yelling at him on the radio. They later found out that the other pilot had been drunk at the time.

That was probably when Ralph first started having blood pressure problems. When Ralph had gotten home from each one of these harrowing experiences, he had told his parents all about them. Little did he know that they had called his insurance agent to tell him Ralph was flying airplanes, and upon hearing this, the agent immediately called Ralph to set up an appointment to see him. When the agent asked Ralph if he was going to continue flying, Ralph said, "I guess so."

Then the agent said to Ralph, "Well, we will have to attach a rider to your life insurance policy."

"What does that mean?" Ralph asked.

"If you're hurt or killed while flying, there won't be any coverage. Plus your premiums will be going up."

Ralph began weighing all his options. *Let's see, two close calls, higher premiums, and no coverage.* "I think I've changed my mind about flying," Ralph said.

"I think that's probably a good idea," replied the agent laughingly.

That year at Christmas, Ralph invited Jeanie over to his house for dinner. His parents had been teasing him for some time about dating such a young girl, but they hadn't mentioned much about it recently. So Ralph figured they better start getting used to her being around. He had brought her over to the house here and there over the last few years, but now he wanted them to really get to know her. Ralph's father always acted a little silly when she was around. Jeanie could make him blush just by sitting next to him on the couch. Another reason Ralph had her over at Christmas was so he could give her a lot of presents without her mom seeing them.

* * * * *

January started off with a trip to Florida in a Twin Beech. Gid and Betty invited their friends, Fred and Mim Martin, to go along on this quick little vacation. They spent four days hopping from West Palm, Opa-Locka, Ft. Lauderdale, Immokalee, and Sarasota. When they arrived back in Pennsylvania, there was snow on the ground and the roads were icy. While driving Mim and Fred to their house, they had to maneuver a ninety degree turn just before they reached their farm, but with the roads so icy the car just kept going straight. Gid just gave it some gas, made a nice big circle in the field, came back onto the road and drove the rest of the way to the farm as if nothing had ever happened. He did mention with his usual humor that he thought they might enjoy the scenic route through the field first! Gid timed the trip back to Long Island right to the wire and made it back in time to take a flight out of JFK on the 7th. Flying had now become an everyday occurrence. Betty didn't even have to ask if he was flying that day, as she could tell by the smile on his face. With Gid's friendly smile and quick wit he soon became a very popular guy around the airport. Everyone knew Gid and loved to hear his stories. He just had a way of cheering up everyone he came in contact with.

Betty kept very busy taking care of the children and the house and keeping track of Gid, as well as she made all of her clothing and the children's. She was involved in church activities and a community women's Bible study, which met once a month. Her friend Shirley Grace was the chairman, and Betty thoroughly enjoyed her company and loved being with her. She also took an Adult Education class on Conversational German hoping it would help her understand Pennsylvania Dutch. Time just seemed to be flying by, and their friends and their families were all growing and becoming inseparable from one another.

* * * * *

The New Year started off well. Everything seemed to be going great until the end of April. Jeanie had waited long enough. She had to break the news to Ralph that she really wanted to go to college. One Friday night while they were on their way back to her house, she told him a teacher had suggested that she continue on in her schooling and that she thought that might be a good idea. Ralph's first impulse was to blow up, but he didn't. He tried to stay calm, but Jeanie could tell he was very upset. He asked, "But what about our plans to get married?"

She said, "What are a couple more years? We can still get married."

Ralph knew that if she went away, he'd probably never see her again. How would he be able to keep track of her? She would be an easy mark. He just couldn't let that happen.

He said, "Well, let's talk about this tomorrow. Let's sleep on it tonight."

"Alright," Jeanie replied. They kissed goodnight and parted. As Jeanie walked to the house she thought, *That didn't go too bad. I thought he would be really upset.*

What Jeanie didn't realize was that Ralph was in a rage; he'd just hidden it from her, that's all. His thoughts went round and round in a continuous loop of, *how could she even think that? I've got almost four years in this relationship and I'm not going to lose her.* He tossed and turned all night trying to think of a way to change her mind. Finally he thought of a way that would keep her from going. At work the next day he told Herb, "When you go home tonight ask Jeanie if she knows where I've been. When she asks, "What do you mean?" just say, "Well, his dad says he didn't come home last night and he wasn't at work today."

"Is there any reason why you want me to do this?" Herb asked.

"I just want to scare her a little, that's all," Ralph mumbled his reply, finding it hard to meet Herb's questioning stare.

"OK..." Herb responded with a sigh, feeling a little puzzled over this strange request but deciding to be loyal to his best buddy.

Ralph's parents were going to be away that weekend, so if the phone rang he planned not to answer it. He figured that once Jeanie heard what Herb said she would call. But he wouldn't answer. He would wait a couple of hours, and then later he would just show up at her house acting all depressed. Everything went just as he planned, and when she saw his car pulling in the driveway, she came running out with concern written all over her pretty face. "Where have you been? Is everything OK?"

"Yeah, I'm OK, I've just been doing a lot of thinking."

"About what?" she asked as she got in the car.

"About us. Let's just go for a ride tonight and talk."

"OK."

They drove and talked, then parked the car and started to make out. Up until now they had been very careful and had never gone all the way. That was until now. He assured her of how much he loved her and was afraid he would lose her if she went away to school. "Please don't go, I love you too much," he told her. They were both crying and it just happened. They both knew they had done wrong. They both knew the consequences of their actions. But only one knew it hadn't been an accident, and that it had all gone as planned.

A little over a month later, Jeanie approached Ralph and told him she thought she might be pregnant. The next day they made an appointment in Lebanon with the local doctor, whom they both knew. The doctor was very pleasant and kind and confirmed Jeanie's beliefs. He then asked her if her mother knew she was at the doctor's office, to which Jeanie replied, "No." Jeanie was only seventeen-and-a-half at that time, and Ralph had just turned twenty-two. The doctor asked them both what their intentions were, and they reassured him that they planned to get married and have the baby.

They both knew that the next thing they had to do was tell their parents. Ralph asked Jeanie if she wanted him to be with her when she broke the news to her mother. "My gosh, no!" was her response.

Jeanie's mother had told her from the beginning that she shouldn't be dating so soon and especially not with a non-believer, and that no good would come out of it and that he would lead her astray. So now Jeanie knew this would lead to a bunch of "I told you so's," plus her mother would be totally embarrassed in front of the church family for not controlling her daughter and for allowing her to date so young, especially with a non-believer. She had even quoted the relevant Scripture to her from 2 Corinthians 6:14: "Do not be bound together with unbelievers; for what partnership have righteousness and lawlessness, or what fellowship has light with darkness?" Jeanie knew she was in for it, so why put it off? So she broke the news the first chance she had alone with her mother. It was just as she had expected. Her mother kept saying, "Oh, the humiliation! Oh, the humiliation." Ralph, on the other hand, waited to see what happened with Jeanie. When she asked him if he had told his parents yet, he said, no, that he was waiting to see if she was still going to be alive first, because if her mother had killed her, then he wouldn't have had to tell his parents. Jeanie punched him in the arm and said, "You better tell them or I'm going right over there and tell them myself." Ralph assured her he would tell them that night.

When he got home, he told his mother she was going to be a grandmother. "Oh, my goodness, what did you do? Does Jeanie's mother know?"

"Yes, she knows."

"How did she take it?"

"Not too well."

"Ralph, she's still in school."

"I know."

"What are you going to do?"

"I'm going to marry her."

"When?"

"When she's out of school, I suppose."

"Oh, my, that poor girl."

"Mom, relax, it's not the end of the world, I will take good care of her. Oh, and when you get a chance, you can tell Pop he's going to be a grandfather."

Jeanie had gotten a part-time job working after school. She had her driver's license but didn't have a car, so someone would have to take her to work. Ralph would go down and pick her up when she was done. On different days it was Ralph's mother's turn to pick her up at school and make the drive to Flemington. One rainy day after dropping Jeanie off at her job, she turned and headed home. As she approached the light at Bartel's Corner, it turned green, so she continued ahead. Suddenly a car that had tried to stop struck her; they found out later that its brakes had failed. About two hours later, Ralph and his father were sitting at home wondering what had happened to her. Usually dinner was on the table by now. As they stood by the window, Ralph saw a State Police car coming down the road. He knew instantly something had happened. He thought the worst - they both had been killed in a car accident. As the car pulled in the driveway, he could see his mother in the car. The car stopped and she got out and came in the house. Now that he saw his mother was OK, his only concern was whether the accident happened coming from or going to Flemington. His mother started talking right away. "We had a terrible accident." Ralph interrupted, "We?"

"The other car and I."

"Is Jeanie OK?"

"Oh, she wasn't with me." She continued to tell about the crash and said that the car was totaled. Ralph's dad didn't care about the car; only that no one was hurt. Later that night Ralph went to pick Jeanie up from work and told her what happened. Jeanie started blaming herself because she had to be taken to work. Ralph told her not to be silly; it was just something that happened. He reassured her that it could have happened to anyone and that it wasn't her fault.

The night of the school prom was their last chance to go to a prom together. Ralph had agreed to take her. That night before the prom Ralph officially asked Jeanie to marry him and gave her an engagement ring.

While at work one day Ralph had been discussing the need to find a place to live once he got married. This particular day a carpenter was on the same job and overheard Ralph's discussion. He approached Ralph and asked, "Would you be interested in buying a small house?"

Ralph answered, "Sure, but I guess it depends on where and how much it is."

"Well," the carpenter said, "it's near Bloomsburg, and I'm asking $12,500.00." Ralph asked if he could look at it after work, which was fine with the carpenter, so directly after work he went straight to the house. When he pulled up he thought, *this can't be the place; it's way too nice*. But then he saw his friend, the carpenter, walking out back, so he got out of his truck and went over to him. He asked him why he was selling it. "It was my mother's, and I'm moving her into my house to watch over her more closely." He then began to show Ralph the property and the house.

The house sat on one and a half acres of land, half woods and half landscaped lawn. The property was located in the country next to a small farm. The house was a tiny, old-fashioned, two-story that was picture perfect. The whole house only measured twenty-four by twenty-four. There were two bedrooms and a bath upstairs, and a kitchen, living room, and dining room downstairs. It had a full basement and nice-sized porch just off the living room. Ralph told him he wanted it, but there was one problem. Ralph had just recently made some big purchases: he had purchased a Corvette and then Jeanie's engagement ring. He used to have a lot of money in the bank, but now he was running low on funds.

As he left the property and headed back home, Ralph thought, *how am I going to come up with the money to buy that house?* Then he remembered how his father had gotten the funds he needed to build the ranch house when he'd left the farm. He had asked Russell Haver, the owner of the farm he worked on for a loan, and he held the mortgage. So Ralph thought he would do the same. After cleaning up that evening, he drove straight over to Mr. Haver's new home on Mountain Road, walked up to the door and knocked. Mr. Haver had just finished his meal and asked him in. "Mr.

Haver, I don't know if you remember me," Ralph began, "But I'm Ralph Walls's son, Ralph."

"Well, I'll be. You sure have grown. How old were you when you left the valley?"

"I think I was twelve then and I'm twenty-two now, sir."

"So do you work for your father?"

"Yes, sir, every day.

"I hear he is quite busy."

"Yes, sir, we are always busy."

"Well, what brings you down to my neck of the woods?"

"Well, sir, I'm getting married in a few months..."

"Well, congratulations!"

"Thank you, sir ... I want to buy a house, and I remembered how you helped out my parents when they built their home. So I was wondering if you might be interested in helping me out with a loan so that I can buy my house."

"I'm getting up there in years now and really don't try to get involved in mortgages anymore, but how much would you need?"

"Well, sir, they are asking $12,500 for the house, and I would need the whole amount."

"Zow wee, you need it all?"

"Ahhh, yes, sir."

"When would you need it?"

"We haven't drawn up any papers yet, sir, but I would imagine in about a month."

"I'll tell you what, you seem like a hard-working young man and you come from a good family, so I'll take a chance on you. Get me all the information about the property and I'll have my lawyer draw up the paperwork."

"Thank you very much, sir, thank you!" And with that they shook hands and said goodnight. When Ralph left he had to go past Jeanie's house on the way home, so he stopped to tell her the good news. She was excited, to say the least, and wondered when she could see it. Ralph made arrangements to show her the house on the weekend.

When they pulled in the driveway, she couldn't believe this was going to be their home. The paperwork was completed very quickly and in a matter of weeks, Ralph had title to the house. Ralph and Jeanie would spend every spare moment they had now cleaning and painting and getting the house ready to live in.

In July Ralph's brother, Glenn, informed the family that he had volunteered for the draft. His basic training was to start immediately at Fort Dix. His parents were speechless and couldn't believe he had done that. Glenn said this way it would be over in two years and he could get on with his life. He joked with Ralph telling him he would be out before Ralph was done with his National Guard service. The war in Viet Nam had suddenly become very personal to their family. Ralph's parents were glued to the TV during the nightly news accounts. Glenn had been dating a girl named Carolyn Burns now for two years, and it was a very emotional goodbye.

The weeks prior to the wedding were trying times for Jeanie. Her mother was a wreck about the whole thing. The one thing she insisted on was that Jeanie couldn't wear a white dress. So Jeanie made her own dress in a lovely shade of pink. No extended family members were invited and it would be very simple and plain.

On August 31, 1968 they were married in the Lambertville Mennonite church by Pastor Warren Wenger. Those present were Ralph's parents and best man, Gary Wurst, Jeanie's mother and her brothers and sisters and her maid of honor, Debbie Luster. Ralph's brother, Glenn had finished his basic training at Fort Dix and had already been sent to Fort Polk to receive his advanced training.

After the wedding, they went to Ralph's parent's house where they had a very small reception. They hadn't even thought about a honeymoon, so they just went to their new home in Bloomsbury where they began their new life together.

By Monday morning Ralph was back to work and Jeanie began setting up housekeeping. A few weeks before the wedding Ralph had traded in his Corvette for a '68 Malibu because, in his words, they were going to need a family car soon. Now he was driving one of his father's trucks to work, so this made it possible for Jeanie to have a vehicle at home. From the start, Jeanie had a passion for cooking, decorating, and gardening. She loved creating things and she was very good at it. In school she had received the Betty Crocker award, and if she had been able to go to college she would have liked to become a decorator. She was also very skilled at drawing and sewing clothes. Even though she was very young, Ralph had married a girl who was very skilled at taking care of a house. She was never afraid to try something new and would often create or rearrange things at home before Ralph would come home, hoping for his approval. This often led to heated arguments and sometimes fits of rage. Jeanie was a very intelligent girl and Ralph was probably a little jealous of her creativity and suggestions. Right from the beginning their marriage was on shaky ground.

* * * * *

It seemed just like yesterday when Karla was born, but here it was September and Karla was starting kindergarten. It was hard to think of her starting school, but her parents knew she was ready for a bigger challenge. As Betty walked with Karla to the school, she couldn't help but notice that Karla seemed quite proud of her new dirndl dress that her mom had made for her. It was yellow with blue flowers.

Within that same week Gid met a man named Will Haines. Will, like Gid, had an interest in small planes and had been a pilot of small planes for many years. Will told Gid about a plane he would like to own. It was a Meyers/ Aero Commander 200. Gid, being the entrepreneur that he was, said he would keep his eye open, and if he found one, he would let Will know. By November he found a Meyers 200 in Connecticut. When he first saw it, he fell in love with it right away. The Meyers first came into production late in 1958. It had a great reputation for quality and performance. Being a man of his word, Gid felt obligated to call Will and tell him he found the plane that he wanted. But before he did he needed to test it out. So on the 26th of November, Gid took the Aero Commander 200D -N2988T up for a trial flight. Gid was hooked; this was the plane he had always dreamed of, but a promise is a promise, so he called Will. Will, who lived in California, flew to JFK, purchased the plane, but decided to keep it on Long Island. From that point on, Gid knew what plane he wanted to specialize in. Will went back to California, but he left instructions for Gid to use the plane and keep it ready for him when he came east for business, and of course Gid was happy to oblige. Gid became Will's flight instructor whenever he came to New York.

8

IT'S GOT A LANDING STRIP

In November of 1968, Glenn had finished his training at Fort Polk and was home on leave before he was to be sent to Vietnam. Glenn and Carolyn were inseparable during his leave, and on November 24 they were married. Their time together quickly came to a close when Glenn had to pack and leave. He was sent right into the thick of it. On his first day in the field he had just arrived and set his duffle bag down when a fire destroyed everything he owned including clothes, personal items, and all his pictures of Carolyn.

Back home the families were either glued to the television set or running to the mailbox to see if there was any word from Glenn. It was not a good time for those who had loved ones fighting in the war, especially when the evening news kept flashing the number of combat deaths on the screen every night.

* * * * *

On Sunday, January 19, 1969, Jeanie woke up knowing something was happening.

"Ralph, wake up! I think my water has broken."

Ralph not quite awake yet, said.

"Wha...wha...what?"

"I think my water broke."

"Oh, OK," he said sleepily, but then snapping fully awake, he jumped to his feet and ran down the stairs leaving Jeanie and her packed suitcase upstairs. After she cleared her throat a couple of times at the top of the stairs, Ralph finally noticed and ran back up to grab the bag. Then he ran to the car throwing the bag in and wondering where she was. Finally with the car running and Ralph sitting in it, she came out of the kitchen door making sure it was locked. Ralph meanwhile was sitting in the car yelling, "Hurry up, we're going to be late!"

"How can we be late? I'm the one having the baby and they can't have it without me!" She got herself into the car and Ralph took off before her door was totally shut.

"Will you relax, you're going to get us both killed," Jeanie said as she was trying to put her seat belt on. The drive to the hospital would, under normal conditions, take about forty minutes, but they pulled up to the emergency room entrance in about twenty-five minutes. As they pulled up a nurse was coming out, and she grabbed a wheelchair when she saw Jeanie. Ralph parked the car and then ran back into the hospital. The people inside directed him to where they had taken his wife. Once he found his way and went through a set of double doors, there was a nurse waiting there.

"Mr. Walls?"

"Yes, that's me."

"Your wife said that you would be going in with her."

"She said what?"

"She wanted you in the room during the delivery."

"We never talked about that," he said.

"Mr. Walls, in that room over there you'll find some gowns, just put one on and I'll come get you."

"You mean I've got to get undressed?"

"Oh no, it just goes over your clothes."

So Ralph proceeded to find the room where the gowns were and then tried to figure out how they went on. Well, he finally decided which way he thought was right and put it on. When he had finished, a doctor came into the room to change. He took one look at Ralph and said, "You've got that on backwards."

"Thanks," Ralph replied as he took it off.

"Is this your first one?"

"What?"

"Is this you first baby?"

"Oh, yeah."

Just then the nurse stuck her head in the door and said,

"Mr. Walls, are you ready?"

"I guess so," he answered as he walked toward her. This was something he hadn't planned on. He thought he'd just sit in a lounge and read a magazine and then they would bring the baby out to show him, but now he was expected to watch this whole thing go down. The only other births he had seen were in the cow barn when he was younger.

As they walked down a long corridor, a set of double doors opened and there was a lady lying there with the bottom half of her body exposed. Now, from the position she was in, it was hard to tell who it was. The nurse attending to her said,

"Oh, Mrs. Godown, here's your husband now."

As the lady struggled to look up, she yelled,

"That's not my husband!" Then the nurse quickly grabbed the curtain and pulled it shut around the bed.

The next thing Ralph heard was,

"Ralph, over here, I'm over here, honey." As he turned and looked to where the voice was coming from, he could see Jeanie motioning for him to come. When he reached her bedside, he said through clinched teeth,

"Why am I here?"

And Jeanie answered with a big smile on her face,

"Why, honey, don't you want to see what you have done?"

"I guess so."

It wasn't long at all before someone yelled, "She's ready, let's go."

They pushed her into another room and told Ralph to stand at the head of the bed by his wife's side. Jeanie reached out and grabbed Ralph's hand. Ralph thought, *oh how sweet.* He had no idea that he was about to lose all feelings in that hand for some time to come! Jeanie told him to look in the mirror and watch the baby being born. Every time they said, "push," Ralph almost went to his knees from the squeezing of his fingers that Jeanie was applying. Then before he knew it, someone yelled, "You have a beautiful baby daughter." They had already decided on names depending on what they had, so the baby girl was named Stephanie Lyn. Ralph was excited beyond belief. Now he wanted to tell the world. He called both of their mothers and promptly told them they were grandmothers.

With the new addition to the family, things were different around the house. Ralph had been used to being the center of attention, but that suddenly changed. Stephanie now became number one. When Ralph came home from work, he expected dinner to be on the table and things in order, but now with the baby's demands, things didn't always happen when they were supposed to.

Then throw into the mix his relationship with his father at work. Ralph's father never liked to turn anyone down, especially customers, which caused quite a lot of stress. With too much work, someone would have to wait, and what usually would happen was that they would start a job, then go and start three more jobs and so on, then go around trying to get them all completed in a timely manner. Before long there were three jobs half done, six jobs started and some who had been waiting for weeks. Many times Ralph would be sent to start a job where the builder had been promised three to four weeks ago that they would show up. So when Ralph showed up on the job to begin work, the builder would be in an uproar, and Ralph would usually take the brunt of the abuse. When he would get back to the shop and ask his father, "Why didn't you tell them you couldn't start for three weeks?" his father would just smile and say, "I knew they would wait."

Quite often Ralph went home from work already in a bad mood. Another thing that didn't help was that Ralph would stop on the way home from work and buy a six-pack of beer for the evening. In fact, if there was no beer in the house, he wouldn't eat dinner till there was. The slightest thing would upset him and cause him to fly off the handle. He made it clear that the feeding, changing, and washing of the baby were none of his concern. In his loudly stated opinion, he went to work all day, so it was Jeanie's job to take care of the baby.

Needless to say, Jeanie was starting to wonder what she had gotten herself into. They were only five months into the marriage and she was starting to dread the thought of Ralph coming home every night. Living in fear of his erratic temper and what would happen next was terrifying. She had a baby now to think about. This was a time in her life that she wanted to cherish with her child and husband, but Ralph was not bringing joy into this marriage. She needed to talk to someone, but she was afraid to make a call and admit to her mother that she had been right. She finally did call her mother, knowing what she would say. Her mother said, "Don't say I didn't warn you. You need to stay there now and pray that he will change." She also told Jeanie that she had been praying for him from the beginning and would continue to do so. Jeanie had suggested to Ralph that they start going to church. Well, of course Ralph thought that was silly. He went to church when he was little and told her he didn't need it now, and besides, he told her his grandmother was a good Christian woman and she didn't go to church anymore but she still read her Bible everyday. His standard answer was, "They're just a bunch of hypocrites there anyway." And that always ended the discussion.

For a couple of weeks Ralph had been thinking about putting an addition on their house. Since he was in construction, it would be nice to have a garage for equipment and supplies. He had been doing small jobs at night on his own and making a little extra cash, plus he thought it would add value to the house. So they talked it over and decided to go ahead with the plan. Ralph heard that a second story is less expensive to build because you don't have the cost of a foundation or another roof, so they decided to make it a two-story addition. Ralph's father had just contracted a large domed church ceiling to do and needed to buy lots of lumber to plank and scaffold the job out. When they completed the job, Ralph's father had to get rid of all the lumber, so Ralph offered to buy it from him. His father gave him a good discount and Ralph hauled it home for his future addition. Over the next couple months, they completed the addition. The original house measured only 24 x 24 and they added 32 x 24 to it. This was Ralph's first experience with the actual construction of a house from the ground up, and he loved it! At work he used to say to his father, "We should build houses, because we've covered up everybody else's mistakes for years and made them look good. If they can do it, I know we can." His father would just laugh. One day he made that statement and a builder was standing there and heard him. His name was Bob Ronquist. Bob turned to Ralph and said, "Look, I've got a lot of building lots here and I would like to slow down a little. If you want to build some houses on them, you can."

Ralph said, "Yeah, right!"

"No, I'm serious," Bob said.

"Well, that's nice of you Bob, but I don't have the money to buy a lot."

"You don't have to pay me for the lot till the house sells," Bob replied.

"Wow! You'd do that?"

"Sure."

"Well, let me think about that." Ralph thought, *how could I ever afford to build a house*? When he got home that night he told Jeanie what Bob had told him, but both decided it probably wasn't going to happen. They just couldn't afford to do it. *But an offer like that doesn't come along too often*, he thought.

At work the tension was mounting with each day. Ralph and his father didn't agree on how jobs should be done and whose job should be done first. Ralph thought they should take care of their regular builders first. "Don't make them wait; they're our bread and butter." But RH figured they'd wait out of loyalty, so he always tried to squeeze a couple of homeowner jobs in first. But Ralph knew that, once again, he would be the one sent to the builder's job to make peace after the builder had waited three weeks already. One day a builder came into the house where Ralph was working in a real huff and started throwing things around, screaming, yelling, and cursing. Ralph never yelled back; he just kept working quietly. But he carried his anger home with him and took it out on his innocent family. One night while sitting at the dinner table talking about the problems of the day, he became so enraged that he raised his fist and brought it down hard on a half-gallon container of milk, smashing it flat. There sat his baby daughter, Stephanie, dripping wet from the exploding carton. The entire room was covered with milk. Jeanie jumped to her feet, comforting her baby, and Ralph stormed out of the house.

This was enough for Jeanie. She waited till the next day for Ralph to leave for work, and then she packed a bag, put Stephanie in the car, and went to Ralph's mother's house. Ralph came home that night and found a note on the counter telling him where she was and that she was afraid he would hurt them. Ralph soon picked up the phone and called his parent's house. His mother answered the phone and Ralph asked if Jeanie was there.

"Yes, she is." He could hear the stiff tone in his mother's voice.

"May I talk to her?"

"I'll see if she wants to talk to you, Ralph."

The next voice he heard on the phone was Jeanie's.

"Hello."

"What are you doing down there?" he demanded in his usual angry tone.

"Waiting for you to calm down and control yourself."

"I'm calm, so come on home."

"You don't sound calm," Jeanie replied hesitantly.

"Well, I'm calm, just come home."

"How do I know it won't happen again?"

"Nothing's going to happen, I'm sorry, I wasn't thinking. I'll try to be better."

"You'll *try*?" Jeanie responded with a touch of sarcasm in her voice. By this time she had begun to lose faith in Ralph's ability to control himself or to keep his promises.

"I will be better — is Mom listening?"

"No, she's playing with Stephanie in the living room."

"When will you be home?"

"In about an hour."

"Be careful."

"I will … bye."

About an hour later, Jeanie and Stephanie arrived home. Ralph had been working in the upstairs addition nailing flooring down. Jeanie yelled upstairs, "I'm home."

Ralph answered back, "OK" and kept working. Neither one of them brought up the incident again, and before long, everything was back to being just as it had been before. Ralph was doing small jobs in the evenings and working forty-eight hours a week for his father. Jeanie loved to work outside in her flowerbeds and vegetable garden. Once in a while they would get Ralph's mother to watch Stephanie and they would go to a movie. When winter came everything would change. Winter meant high school wrestling season, and Ralph didn't miss those matches. So on those nights Ralph went out and Jeanie and Stephanie stayed home. Jeanie kind of liked the peace and quiet at home when Ralph was gone.

* * * * *

While deadheading on a flight back to JFK, Gid met a pilot named Bud Malone. In the course of their conversation, Bud told Gid he had a place in Frenchtown, New Jersey, and that he had his own airstrip. Gid expressed his excitement by saying,

"That's what I would like to have someday."

Bud quickly responded,

"Well, there is a plot of land for sale right next to mine that connects to my strip." After getting all the information and directions, Gid was anxious to tell Betty. When he did tell her about this property for sale, he made sure he reiterated to her, "It has a landing strip."

It didn't take long before Gid had Betty, Karla and Mike loaded into the Aero Commander and heading for Frenchtown, New Jersey. As they approached the property, Gid made sure everyone noticed, "It has a landing strip." The Aero Commander touched down and they proceeded to check out the piece of land that Bud had told Gid about. It was a seven-acre lot with woods behind it. Mike really liked that and thought of all the fun he could have playing in the woods. In the front was a dirt road called Tinsman Road. Gid noticed that there was plenty of room to build a house and a barn big enough to hold airplanes. He and Betty were sold on the property and could really envision starting the next chapter of their life there. After returning home, Gid soon had to leave again for Kansas City to begin simulator training on the Boeing 727. He was in training from October through the 15th, and then he returned back to Long Island. He and Betty had definitely made up their minds to purchase the piece of property in New Jersey, so in November they flew to Frenchtown and signed a contract to purchase it.

* * * * *

By spring of 1970 things at work had reached a boiling point for Ralph. One day while working with the whole crew, Ralph had had enough and just walked off the job. He knew there were two builders who had been waiting for them to start their houses. And, as usual, they were holding them up. When Ralph left his father's job, he went straight to the two builders and told them he could start their jobs immediately if they wanted him to. They both were elated and Ralph started that same day.

That night he told Jeanie he no longer worked for his father and that he already had two jobs to do. Jeanie was a little skeptical. It was always nice having a regular paycheck coming in and she wondered how often he would be getting paid. He assured her not to worry, as he also had three or four small jobs that he had promised people he could do nights, so now he would just move them up to daytime.

The next day on his way home from work, he stopped at Bob Ronquist's house and asked him if he was still serious about letting him build on a lot. Bob said, "Anytime you're ready."

Ralph said, "OK, I think I might try it."

After telling Jeanie the news and his plans to build a house, Jeanie asked him how he planned on financing this idea. “Remember,” he said, “I don’t have to pay for the lot until it’s done. And also, Bob has equipment, so we can do our own septic systems and he also has a full-time painter. He said we could pay for all those services when the house sold. And don’t forget I’m going to keep the drywall business going also. One more thing — I figured we could sell our house and use that money.”

“Sell the house, where do you plan on us living, then?’

“I haven’t got that far yet, but someplace closer to Bob’s development. Maybe we could just rent a place near there.”

“When will all this happen?” Jeanie asked doubtfully.

“Well, it’s going to take a little time. We have to decide on a house plan and get all the permits and then sell this house.”

“Let’s just think about this for a little while,” Jeanie said.

“Fine, OK,” Ralph responded.

“Also, this probably isn’t the best timing since I’m expecting in June.”

“You’re probably right.” Ralph didn’t want to start his first house in the winter months, so by waiting meant this wouldn’t happen till next year. A couple days later Ralph stopped at Bob’s house and told him of their plans. While there, Bob gave Ralph a stack of books with house plans to take with him. Meanwhile, Ralph’s business was doing really well. New jobs kept coming in, plus Ralph’s father asked him if he would do some sub work for him. This worked out great for both of them and their relationship was greatly improved by their new business arrangement.

On June 6, 1970, Jeanie woke up during the early morning hours knowing she needed to go to the hospital. Ralph called his mother to let her know that they were heading to the hospital and would drop Stephanie off on the way. Everything seemed to be going fine until they realized the baby needed to be turned 180 degrees. Ralph was barely holding his own and as usual, Jeanie was the strong one. Ralph was holding his own, that is, until they brought out a needle to stick in Jeanie that looked like it was about a foot long. That made his knees buckle and he had to grab onto the bed. Jeanie had noticed he was turning white and said,

"I think someone should check on my husband."

A nurse said,

"Mr. Walls, are you alright?"

"I think so," Ralph said, as he wobbled around.

"Here's a chair, why don't you sit down a minute." Jeanie's labor and delivery lasted for hours. Finally the baby had been turned and their second child had come into the world. "It's a boy!" the doctor yelled. Someone asked,

"Do you have a name yet?"

"Yes," Ralph said proudly, "His name is Rodney Bryant." After leaning over and kissing Jeanie, Ralph exited the delivery room, running for the phone to call his parents and Jeanie's mom.

The rest of that year was a really busy time for their family. Jeanie now had two children and a husband to take care of. Ralph was still in the National Guard and gone one weekend a month, which usually meant he might come home in a bad mood. In the summer the family would get a two-week vacation from him while he was in Watertown, New York, fulfilling his service obligation.

In July, Ralph's brother Glenn returned safely home from active duty, and for the first time he held his baby daughter, Nancy, who had been born in November. She was his pride and joy. In a matter of days Glenn began working for his father and quickly settled into life as a private citizen. Everyone in the family noticed, though, that Glenn had become quiet; he kept to himself and didn't really like to talk about the war and the things that had happened while he was there. He had been awarded the bronze star for heroism in action while engaged in military operations against a hostile force in Vietnam. But now he just wanted to get on with his life and leave the war behind him.

Ralph didn't socialize well with other people; he just thought it was a waste of time. So the only people Jeanie ever got to see were their parents and Glenn and Carolyn, whom they had over quite often.

* * * * *

In December, Gid flew the family out to their new piece of property in New Jersey. They landed on Bud's strip, which they now referred to as Malone Field. They got out of the Aztec and walked their property, visualizing where the house would be built and dreaming about the future. The conditions didn't permit for a long stay, so they soon were back in the Aztec and headed for Smoketown where they landed at Mel Glick's.

This was a good time of year to see the family during the holidays. Keep in mind that Gid had seven sisters, and by now some of them were married and had children. Being a large, extended-family Amish gathering, there were also lots of aunts, uncles, and cousins there too. It was not unusual to have fifty or more people visiting at a home, especially when they knew that their pilot relative and his family would be there. Gid loved these special times. He didn't like being the center of attention, but everyone loved getting him to tell his stories, and he had many good ones to tell. It didn't matter if there were fifty people in a room, when Gid began to tell a story, you could hear a pin drop and shortly afterward you could almost guarantee a roar of laughter.

But first things first; Gid knew he needed to say Hi to his good friend Mel and let him see his family. They were the one thing Gid was ever guilty of showing off. Gid's precious family was always first in his life.

Betty's mother lived about fifteen miles away and this is where they usually spent the night when visiting for the holidays. The children loved seeing Grandma Herr and visiting their cousins Ken, Sandy, and Brian and Aunt Ruth and Uncle Don, who lived on a farm.

* * * * *

By March of 1971 Ralph had all the necessary permits to start his construction business, and the sub-contractors were lined up and ready to go. Ralph's idea was to work with them or just watch so he could learn how to do most of the work himself in the future. He met with the excavator and staked out the house. The man who worked for the excavator that was to do the actual digging turned out to be a friend who had been a year ahead of Ralph in school. They had been on the track team together. This was one person who Ralph really liked. The man's name was Rodney Sutton. That's why Ralph named his son Rodney. Rodney Sutton had taught Ralph how to high jump and had made him a set of standards that he could take home and practice with. Rodney was still a good teacher. He taught Ralph everything he could about excavating, and Ralph soaked it up. At home Jeanie had always heard Ralph speak highly about this Rodney guy, but she had not met him yet. But she was always glad to know when he was going to be on the job because it seemed like those were the times when Ralph came home in a better mood.

The first week they had the hole dug out, Ralph kept having the nagging thought that he and Jeanie had better get their house sold so they could have some money to invest in the business. So after a discussion on "where are we going to live if we sell?" Ralph answered by saying, "I don't know; let's wait and figure that out after it sells." Ralph made a quick sign that said "House for Sale" printed in big block letters with their phone number underneath. He marched out into the front yard and started to hammer it in the ground. As he was hammering the sign a passing car stopped, backed up, and pulled into the driveway. The passenger rolled down the window and said,

"Are you selling your house?"

"Ahhh, yes," Ralph answered.

"May we see it now?"

"Right now?"

"If that's OK."

"Let me check with my wife," Ralph said as he ran to the kitchen door.

"Jeanie, is the place decent, some people want to look at the house!"

"Now?! I thought you were just putting the sign up."

"I was."

"Just give me a minute to grab the kids."

"OK." The young couple was already out of the car, walking arm in arm around the property.

"My wife just needs a minute to catch the kids."

"That's OK," they said laughing.

Then Ralph realized he made it sound like his kids were animals running loose. The couple stayed about an hour, said they loved the house, but they were leaving to go to Europe for two weeks but that they would be back when they returned home from their trip.

After they left, Ralph said to Jeanie,

"Yeah, right, we'll never see them again." For two weeks not one person called to look at the house. On Sunday afternoon Ralph was out mowing the yard when the couple pulled in the driveway again. They asked him if the house was still for sale and he answered, "It sure is."

They got out of the car, handed him a check as a binder and a piece of paper with all their information on it and said,

"How soon can we close?"

Ralph said, "I don't know; can I call you back tomorrow night?"

"Sure, that would be great." He gave them a receipt for the check and they left.

After they left Ralph and Jeanie just stared at one another, and then Jeanie said,

"Where are we going to live?"

Ralph replied,

"That's the least of my worries; what do I do next?"

Neither one of them had ever sold a house before.

"I guess you better call a lawyer tomorrow."

Ralph added, "Who? I'll call Pop and ask him."

Ralph called his father and got the name of a real estate attorney, and before he hung up his father said he had been talking to a friend named Rin who had his house for rent in Lebanon. Ralph knew the man, so he called him and inquired about the house. After getting all the information, they loaded the kids in the car and went to look at it. It was huge and beautiful. They made the deal and now Jeanie was happy, because she knew they would have a home and this one bigger than their first, which was even better now that they had two children.

Ralph had met a man named Willie Stasyshyn on one of the job sites who wanted to break away from his current employer and start his own business. Willie knew block work and framing and every other aspect of the building trade, so Ralph had asked him if he would be interested in his project, but Ralph wanted to work along with him as time permitted since he still had obligations to his drywall customers. Willie agreed, and he was the next man to help Ralph on the house.

Willie could build a house from the ground up, and he turned out to be one of the most important people Ralph ever had a chance to work with. He always said that what he learned from Willie was priceless. Willie always exhibited a lot of patience and took the time to explain things in detail. Ralph learned how to do his own footings, how to layout a house, how to do framing, siding, roofing and many other details involved in general contracting. Everything was going great until Ralph realized he needed to pay the man at the end of the week. The problem was that he hadn't closed on the sale of his home yet, so he needed funds and needed them quickly. After thinking about it for a while he went back to Bob to ask him what he should do. Bob said, "Just go to the bank."

"But I don't own the land; it's still in your name."

"Just mention the deal we have and I'm sure they will help you out," Bob said. It just so happened that the man he had to talk to at the bank went to the same church that Ralph had attended so many years ago as a child, and he knew Ralph's parents well. On Friday around noon Ralph, dressed in his work clothes, walked into the bank and asked if Mr. Young was in. The lady at the front desk asked, "Do you have an appointment?"

"No," Ralph replied.

"Who should I say is here?" asked the receptionist.

"Ralph Walls," Ralph replied.

"Have a seat, Mr. Walls," she said. As she made the call, Ralph figured Mr. Young would probably think it was Ralph, Senior there to see him.

Mr. Young came to the door of his office and said, "Ralph, come on in. I haven't seen you in years. What can I do for you?"

Ralph began to tell him the whole story, including the sale of his own house and the closing being only days away.

"So how much are you thinking you're going to need?"

"Well, sir, I figure the whole house is going to cost around $35,000 to build, but I'm going to need about $10,000 to start."

"When are you going to start?"

"Oh, it's already started."

"It is?"

"Yes, sir, as a matter of fact the house will be totally framed this afternoon."

"You have a house already framed?"

"Yes, sir."

"When were you thinking you needed the money?"

Ralph looked at his watch and then said, "In about three hours — that's when the framers will be done."

Mr. Young just sat there looking at Ralph for a long moment. "Your family has quite a good reputation, so I'll take a chance on you. If you can wait around about twenty minutes, I'll have a check cut for you."

"Thank you, thank you very much, Mr. Young."

"No, thank you for coming to our bank. We like to see young, hard-working people starting businesses. I hope you will continue to give us your business in the future."

"Yes, sir, I will, thank you." They shook hands and Ralph went out to the lobby where a secretary greeted him and began the paperwork. At the end of the day Ralph showed up on the job site and handed Willie his paycheck.

The house continued to move right along. Then one day late in July, Ralph was standing out in front of the house talking with Bob when a car pulled up and asked if the house was for sale. Ralph answered,

"Not yet..."

Bob immediately said to Ralph,

"Let them see it."

"But you can look at it," Ralph hollered back to the driver. As they were getting out of their car, Ralph turned to

Bob and said, "I didn't think it's a good idea to let someone see it unfinished."

Bob responded,

"Don't ever pass up an opportunity to show your product, because some people can see past the dirt and clutter." Ralph ran over to meet the people and take them through the house. The house was a small ranch house with three bedrooms. Ralph had eliminated the walls surrounding the cellar stairs and put railings exposing the basement, which was unfinished, giving the house a modern, open look. The couple only had one son and introduced themselves as the Andersons. They loved the house and asked what he was asking. Ralph stood there dumbfounded and had to say,

"I haven't even figured up a price yet. I had planned on finishing it first and then advertising it."

"Let's go out to our car and talk things over."

Ralph didn't have his figures with him, so he said, "I'm not really prepared to talk price right now."

Mr. Anderson laughed.

"Let's pick a place and time when we can sit down and talk it over, OK?"

"OK, that sounds good to me!" Ralph replied heartily. When they met the next time both parties agreed on a price and the house was sold. They wanted to be in the house in time for their son, Tommy, to start school in the fall.

* * * * *

In Massapequa, Betty and Shirley were thinking of sending their daughters to summer camp. Ella Mae had found a Christian camp in the Pocono Mountains where they were going to send their daughter, Glenda. They all thought it would be nice if all the girls could go together. The camp was called Spruce Lake Retreat Center, and it had a wilderness camp for the children and also a center for the adults. They all agreed, so Karla, Sharon, and Glenda went to the wilderness camp, and the adults decided to spend the following weekend at the retreat center when they went to pick up the girls. This would turn out to be a tradition that eight couples continue doing to this day. At first they called themselves the Gid Miller Gang, because Betty usually made the arrangements. Later, as everyone started making their own arrangements, they became known as the Spruce Lake Group.

In September Betty was preparing Michael for kindergarten, and he was so ready for a new challenge after spending a year in pre-school. Karla was now in the third grade and loved school.

Gid and Betty decided that it would be better if they lived closer to where their house was being built in New Jersey, so they listed their bi-level house on Rhode Island Avenue for sale. They rented an old farmhouse in Spring Mills, New Jersey, and moved there in March of 1972. They had to leave the TV behind because it was built-in, but the children didn't miss it. They never had trouble finding things to do. Living in the country and having a dog was a new experience for the children, and they loved it. One day Mike was fed up with something and decided to run away. He started walking down the lane, but it was pretty long, and before he made it to the end he had changed his mind and returned home, deciding it wasn't so bad there after all.

9

I REFUSE TO BELIEVE

In Lebanon, New Jersey, Ralph and Jeanie were well into their stay in the rental house and loving it. Ralph had his own office in the basement with counter space that stretched around two sides of the basement, but the counter was almost never visible because of plans and building books spread all over it. Ralph had already picked out a plan for the second house. One thing he always did was to make sure it was one they wouldn't mind living in also, just in case it didn't sell. This one had a nice ten-on-twelve pitched roof which Ralph thought added special charm to the house. The idea was to get this house closed in before winter, so he would have inside work when it got cold outside and just in case he didn't have enough dry wall jobs.

By late fall he had the house closed in, and one day a neighbor from across the street came over and wanted to talk. Ralph never liked to be interrupted while he was working, but he paused briefly to chat with the man. Turned out the man said he and his wife would come over nights after Ralph left and checkout the work progress on both houses. They were thinking they wanted to upgrade and buy a new home. Suddenly, Ralph was all ears, hearing that word "buy." They talked throughout the next week and worked out details and price, and the house was sold before it was even finished.

The one detail Ralph didn't realize was that the man was a longshoreman who was on strike, and he ended up being there all the time watching over Ralph's shoulder, checking every little detail, sometimes even with his carpenter's level and square. This made for a lot of tension in Ralph, which of course he took home with him. He got up every morning knowing there would probably be a list of changes waiting for him at the job site. As it turned out, the longshoremen were on strike for something like fifty-five days that year.

The one thing that helped was looking forward to playing with his children at night. They were getting to the age where Ralph enjoyed having fun with them. They had a very large yard that was adjacent to a gas station, which was closed on Sundays. Ralph would spend lots of time pushing Stephanie and Rodney around the gas pumps and down the driveway in their wagon. Jeanie loved it when Ralph took the children out to play. This would free up some time for her to run to the store to do some shopping alone. She always knew she had to get out of the house quick because if there was an accident while she was still there, Ralph wouldn't know what to do and he'd come running to her for help! For example, he had never changed a diaper until this one particular day. Stephanie didn't usually have many accidents, but with all the excitement and laughing, one happened. She said,

"Daddy, I need to have my diaper changed."

"Oh, your mother will be back soon, you can wait."

"I don't want to wear it."

"Just wait."

"Daddy!"

"OK, let's go in the house."

After making sure Rodney was safe and secure, he said, "OK, where does she keep the stuff?" Stephanie walked to a closet and showed him where it was. Ralph lifted her up to the table hoping Jeanie would walk in right at that moment. *No such luck,* he thought dismally. After removing the diaper and cleaning her up he got a new one out and put it on her.

Stephanie never said a word. Just then he heard,

"Hello, I'm home!" as Jeanie called out from the kitchen. Ralph had just put Stephanie down on the floor when off she took, crying all the way to her mother.

"What's wrong, honey?"

"Daddy changed my diaper and it's all wrong."

"I'll fix it, honey."

That was the only attempt Ralph ever made at diaper changing. Jeanie always wondered if he did a bad job of it as a handy excuse to get out of diaper-changing duty from then on!

By November Ralph had completed his military obligation and now was free from the National Guard. Christmas was a lot of fun that year. The children were so excited coming downstairs and seeing all the gifts under the tree. Jeanie had made everyone a stocking that hung on the mantel in front of the large fireplace. Since the house was so big, Jeanie had both families over for Christmas dinner. One of the things Jeanie loved to do was cook, and her meals were always excellent, but Ralph would always challenge her by asking, "Are you sure we have enough?" which then always resulted in their having too much food. Jeanie had a fine eye for decorating also, and she would always know just where to put the right accent or special touch.

The thing that she especially missed, though, was going to church. She knew better than to bring it up. Ralph would say, "Oh, we just went last Easter, didn't we?" Then there was the time Ralph's mother asked if he was going to get the children baptized. Since they lived in Lebanon and close to his parent's church where he had been baptized, Ralph thought that might be a good idea. Jeanie, however, knew that infant baptism for salvation wasn't what she believed, but went along with his idea because it was at least church. She had tried to explain about baptism to Ralph, but she could see he wasn't even interested in what she had to say.

By spring the construction of the second house was a memory, and Ralph was busy with his regular builders doing drywall and had already begun construction on the third house.

* * * * *

About twenty-five miles away in Frenchtown, New Jersey, another construction job was underway: Gid and Betty were excitedly having a new house built. Gid wanted to use as many of his Amish and Mennonite friends as possible in the construction of their house. They lived in Lancaster County, Pennsylvania, so Gid moved a trailer onto the property for the workmen to live in for a few days at a time. He hired Mahlon Newswenger as the general contractor. On the masonry crew was one of his childhood friends, Emanuel Fisher. One day while on the job site, Gid had flown in to check on the progress of the house. Gid and Emanuel were standing by the plane talking, and Gid asked Emanuel if he would like to go for a ride. Now Emanuel had never been in an airplane before and Gid assured him it would be OK. They took off from Malone Field in Frenchtown and headed out towards the Delaware River, which separates New Jersey and Pennsylvania. As Gid started to fly over the river, Emanuel was awestruck and just kept looking down saying how beautiful it was, when all of a sudden the plane made a sudden jerk and it felt like they'd hit a bump. Emanuel's hands just grabbed on to whatever he could grasp and he looked at Gid to see what was happening. Gid sat there with that big grin on his face that he was noted for, and he said,

"Oh, that must be the state line." (The author of this book must admit that he got me also with this stunt, some sixteen years later! If you're reading this book and you're lucky enough to be one of Gid's friends, be honest, did he get you, too?)

* * * * *

The third house was on Windy Hill, the same street as the previous two; there were other homes on it that Bob had built, and Ralph knew all the people on the street. So whenever he drove down the street, Ralph would always see someone he knew. On several occasions one or more of the neighbors would want to have some work done in their homes. This was adding more work to his already busy schedule. He always told anyone who wanted him to do work for them that he would start their job, but if one of his regular builders would call, then that would become his first priority and he would have to leave the work unfinished to meet the builder's needs. If the neighbor agreed to that, then he would do their work. Surprisingly, they always agreed (his good reputation and quality workmanship spoke for itself). Ralph's workload was getting big, and he knew that he was going to need to hire some help. The house he decided to build was a two–story, and he didn't waste any time. The house went up quickly and he had been advertising it from the beginning, but there were no takers. Ralph and Jeanie weren't taking any chances, so they decided to stop paying rent and just move into the two-story, so in August they moved their family in. Ralph decided that since they were living in this one, why not start another one, so that same month he started construction on a large "L"-shaped ranch, hoping once again to have it under roof by winter.

Ralph found out that his cousin, Nolan Walls, was in the work-study program at the high school, so he asked Nolan if he would be interested in working for him. He was very interested, and he started right away. So every day at noon he would show up to help Ralph. Nolan was a quick and very conscientious worker. He also was a comedian and loved to tell a story or two. Those two traits he had inherited from his father, James Walls, who was known as the family storyteller. Ralph was very close to his Uncle James and his Uncle Leon, both of whom would do anything for you. If Ralph had a car problem, they could always solve the problem. When Ralph had worked for his father, Leon also came in on weekends to help, and he and Ralph would usually get teamed up together to hang drywall, which Ralph liked because Leon was a hustler. Ralph used to kid with him saying, "You're pretty fast for an old guy!" They even went to a lot of high school wrestling matches along with Glenn and Gary. It wasn't uncommon to see the four of them sitting together in the stands cheering on the home team.

Jeanie enjoyed this time when Ralph was away two nights a week watching the wrestling matches, because it gave her some peace and quiet at home with the children. She would always pray that their team would win, because she knew if they didn't, Ralph would more than likely come home in a bad mood. Ralph was louder than most people when he talked, but when he was angry his voice picked up a couple of notches, which usually ended up waking the children. Jeanie always hoped the referees didn't make any "bad calls" that night, because then Ralph's mood would be even worse.

Living in a neighborhood was good for Jeanie because it gave her the chance to interact with other wives and mothers. Jeanie had lots of friends while in high school, but since being married to Ralph, her social life had become much more limited. Ralph figured she didn't need to sit around drinking tea all day with other women, talking about their husbands. "No good could ever come of that," he would always tell her. Now all she had to do was just walk up the street and it was very likely that she would just accidentally run into someone who wanted to visit awhile.

Jeanie was the type of person who made friends quickly and easily, and in no time at all she was friends with everyone in the neighborhood. She enjoyed having friendships and now felt alive again. Even though she had only been married four years, the stress and pressure of living with an explosive husband was taking its toll. She lived in fear almost every day, wondering what sort of mood he was going to come home in that night. When things were going well, he was the sweetest man in the world to be around, but if one thing went wrong at work, then everyone at home paid the price. Now at least Jeanie had a way of escaping the stress of everyday life with Ralph for a couple hours when she would visit with her girlfriends. She had to be careful though, because if she went home all excited about the great day she'd had talking to one of her friends, Ralph would become upset even over that! He would stomp around and yell, accusing her of neglecting the house and kids while she sat around gossiping. Jeanie always secretly thought in her heart that he was just jealous because he didn't have any friends, but she never said that to him.

With Ralph being in construction, Jeanie was able to discover and put to use some of her natural talents. She loved to design and decorate the new homes that Ralph built. When it came to the final touches like cabinets, countertops, tile, paint and carpet, she was the one who knew what a woman wanted, because the house is a woman's domain. This gave her a chance to use her creativity. She had done a little wall-papering in her mother's house and in some small bathrooms before, but now she had the opportunity to coordinate an entire house of paint and wallpaper.

Ralph was a little skeptical at first, but soon he realized she was very good at it. She often thought how some day she would like to be a decorator, but she knew that would have to wait at least until the children were in school.

* * * * *

The work on the Miller's house in Frenchtown was in the final stages. They had hired their dear friend John Kauffman to do the electrical work. Gid had made a lot of changes in the house design along the way, and every time he asked John how much longer it would take to accomplish the new work, John would always reply, "That will only take about five minutes."

That saying became the standard line everyone used on the job when Gid would ask how long something would take. John was also a teacher at Christopher Dock High School, and he'd offered his services during his summer off that year.

Betty kept herself pretty busy that year also. When they had moved into the house in Holland Township they wanted to find a Mennonite church to attend, but the closest one was Doylestown Mennonite, which was a considerable drive. After driving there two times she realized that if the children got involved in church activities, she would be making a lot of trips back and forth, which wouldn't be very economical. One Sunday while Gid was away on a flight she remembered the Baptist Church they passed every time they drove out to the house, so she loaded the children into the car and decided to give it a try. When she walked into the building, a man named Herb Kemme greeted her. Herb and his wife, Doris, were members of the church, and they had a four-year-old daughter named Gail. Herb took Betty to the church office and found out where Karla and Mike needed to go for Sunday school. Then he showed Betty to the adult class where he introduced her to everyone and invited her to join them. Betty and the children found the church very much to their liking, and she decided that if Gid agreed when he got home and she was able to tell him about it, then they would worship and fellowship there.

There was a lot of work for Betty to do in the finishing process of the house. The whole house was to have all the wood trim stained, and that was Betty's job, as well as she also helped paint most of the rooms. There was one little incident just prior to finishing the house that made for some special memories. Little Mike saw all the tools lying on the kitchen counter and decided he would be a little helper. He thought he would help them staple the Formica countertop down. By the time they got to him he had put four little holes in the new counter top. (About twenty-five years later, when Mike was building his solar house in Colorado and Betty was helping him finish his kitchen cabinets, Mike asked his mother if she wanted to put some staple holes in his countertop!)

Gid, Betty, Karla, and Mike spent Christmas Day, 1972, in their new house even though it wasn't finished. A good memory they have is of the beautiful gingerbread house that Gid had brought back from Germany. A few days later they were moving in, regardless of a few unfinished items. One important item was the kitchen sink, which wasn't hooked up yet. So being the good sport that she was, Betty carried all the dishes into the laundry room every day for a week and washed them in the laundry tub. Things soon got completed and they established a normal routine. The children were now attending Alexandria Township Grammar School, with Karla in the forth grade and Mike in the first.

Spring was there before you knew it and that meant it was time for planting a lawn and garden. The soil there was very rocky and needed a lot of work to prepare it for planting. It seemed like Gid's flights were always perfectly timed for when Betty needed help in the garden, but not to worry, they had children who could help. So for the next few weeks Karla and Mike became expert rock picker-uppers, but if you asked them they wanted to know about child labor laws! Betty had become quite skilled at running the tractor with the front-end loader on it; she had run equipment back on the family farm, but now with Gid frequently away on flights, she had to do most of those things involving a tractor by herself. She always said it seemed like when Gid would leave for a flight during the winter, that would somehow make it snow, so there she would be, up on the tractor, clearing the driveway, which was a rather long one; it ran all the way from the barn to the road. While working on her lawn and garden project she would drive the tractor over, drop the bucket down, and then she and the children would fill it with rocks. Once it was full she would drive it back to the edge of the woods and dump it. Betty was also an expert at running the rototiller at a time when most women didn't even know what a rototiller was (and probably still don't know!). She was so gutsy with the rototiller, in fact, that she would get some planks and drive the tiller right up into the back of the station wagon to haul somewhere else. What a woman! Back to the rocks, I wonder if Mike ever thought he was being forced to pick up rocks as punishment for his stunt with the kitchen counter? But then the question begs to be asked, why did Karla have to pick up rocks, too? Maybe she was supposed to be watching her little brother when he had stapled the countertop down! Betty was a smart woman, and she knew that the best way to keep both kids out of mischief was to keep them busy with good, hard work.

* * * * *

The spring of 1973 was a little tense for Ralph. He was about three weeks from completing the ranch house, and that meant he would have two mortgage payments to make if he didn't get it sold quick. Needless to say, things at home were very stressful. Jeanie knew that there was no way they could hold onto both these houses much longer. Money issues always seemed to cause the most tension. Ralph would start meddling with her household budget, trying to find ways to cut back. It usually meant checking out everything Jeanie was buying to make sure they really needed it. Ralph would start by saying things such as, well the kids don't need those snacks, or their shoes still look good, or why do you need those lotions? So cutting back on groceries, clothes, and extra trips in the car, and always turning off lights in empty rooms of the house, were always the first cutbacks they made, but they always seemed to be able to afford his beer and cigars. Jeanie always had to make sure there was a six-pack of beer in the house. Jeanie didn't drink, but now she was old enough to purchase it, so one of her duties was to keep the refrigerator stocked. If Ralph came home from work and there wasn't beer in the fridge, no one could eat dinner till he went back out and got some.

The children had learned at an early age when their father was upset just by the look on his face, but Ralph never hit his children. He was afraid he might hurt them with his uncontrollable temper. All he had to do was stare at them and they would run away in fear, crying.

While Ralph was at work one April day in 1973, Jeanie received a call from a realtor who wanted to show the two-story house they were living in. Jeanie said that would be fine, and so the realtor brought the people right over. That afternoon when Ralph came home from work, Jeanie told him that some people had looked at the house today and really liked it.

"How do you know?" asked Ralph.

"Well, the first way I could tell was how they were already saying where they would put furniture, and secondly, the realtor just called and wanted to know when you would be home so she could bring an offer over."

"It's probably going to be too low of an offer, so don't get your hopes up," Ralph replied dryly. No sooner had the words come out of his mouth than doorbell rang. "They must be in a hurry," Ralph said as he walked to the door.

"Hello, Mr. Walls," the realtor introduced herself, and they went in and sat at the dining room table.

Ralph said, "Sorry I look so messy, but I just got home from work." He was covered with dust from sanding all day. The realtor presented the offer to them. Now Ralph and Jeanie had played the "what if" game a long time ago about what prices would work and what wouldn't, so they had a good idea of the price they needed on the sale of their home. The offer wasn't what they really wanted, but it was in the doable range. They both were afraid that if they turned it down, the couple might not make another offer. Ralph knew there were a lot of two-story houses on the market at that time, so he said to the realtor out of earshot of the couple, "How soon are they thinking about? The reason I ask is because if they will do a quick closing, then I will agree to the price, but if they are thinking of dragging this out, then I say no."

"What do you call quick?"

"Thirty days would be nice."

"That's funny, because that's what they told me to say to you," she responded.

"Well, I guess we have a deal, then, so where do we sign?"

Jeanie had been quiet the whole time. When the transaction was complete, she walked them to the door, said goodbye, then promptly turned to Ralph and demanded, "OK, now where are we going – and in less than thirty days?""To the ranch house," answered Ralph. "But that could sell right away, too."

"That's OK; I guess we just won't unpack a lot of boxes." They hadn't unpacked a lot of boxes this time either.

Thirty days went by quickly. The move was done over a couple of nights and one weekend. The lot that the ranch house was situated on had a nice slope to the rear of the property, so Ralph had made sure the basement was partially exposed on the sides and in the rear so that he could put a basement entrance in at ground level. Now the house was already a decent size, but with this big open basement with windows, Ralph figured he would finish it off. So on nights and weekends, being the consummate workaholic that he was, Ralph worked on it nonstop, adding about 1400 square feet of living area to the house.

Within six weeks they had a contract on the ranch house. When Jeanie heard this news it put her straight into panic mode, exclaiming, "Where are we going now?"

"Just relax," Ralph would say, "We've got lots of time." The closing wouldn't be for ninety days, so that gave Ralph lots of time to decide where he would move his family. Every night after dinner they would load the children in the car and travel the roads searching for a house that needed some work. Ralph figured if he could find a fixer-upper, he could move them into it while he worked on it. Plus, that way it would be cheap. Within days they were driving down a road in Pittstown when they passed an old house with a "For Sale" sign in the yard. Ralph proclaimed, "Now *this* is what I'm looking for," as he backed the car up and then pulled into the driveway.

"You have *got* to be kidding!" Jeanie exclaimed. Their children had only known nice houses. They had never seen anything like this.

"Is this our house, Mommy?" asked Stephanie as she stood up in the back of the car trying to get a better look with little Rodney pushing her out of the way, demanding, "Let me see!" The house had obviously been abandoned. The weeds were two to three feet high right up to the sides of the structure. There was a large barn in the rear of the property that looked fairly new, and there was a lane that led to the large opening in the front. They were sitting in a circular driveway that connected to the lane. Four huge maple trees, a chicken house, and what looked like the remnants of another barn that had been burned down all surrounded the circular drive. The "For Sale" sign was barely visible through the weeds. As Ralph hurried out of the car he said, "It's a miracle I even saw that sign."

"A miracle for who?" Jeanie asked dryly.

By now everyone was out of the car. Rodney quickly grabbed his mother's hand and asked, "Who lives here, Mommy?"

"I don't think anyone does, honey," she said as they walked toward the house. Ralph told everyone to stay in the driveway while he went up and looked in the windows. "What does it look like?"

"It's pretty bad; it looks like a bunch of hippies were living here." Jeanie could tell Ralph was interested. He was running down the lane toward the barn to have a look inside when Jeanie yelled, "Do you think you should do that?"

"Don't worry, I'm just looking; I'll be right back." Jeanie started to get the children back in the car. In the next moment Ralph was already back at the car and ready to go.

"Do you have the number written down?" Ralph asked impatiently, sure she would've already done this.

"No. I thought I'd wait and see what you said when you came back from the barn," Jeanie replied, still feeling a little incredulous that he seemed serious about this house.

"Well, write it down," Ralph barked in his usual commanding style.

"OK, Ralph, just a sec, let me find a pen." Jeanie dug in her purse for a pen and a scrap of paper and jotted the number on it. They couldn't get home quick enough for Ralph. He wanted to make the call tonight and get all the details.

"Give me the paper," Ralph said as the car rolled to a stop in their driveway. By the time Jeanie and the children got into the house, Ralph had already made his phone call and was slamming the phone down. "The office hours are 9 to 5," he exclaimed. "You need to call them first thing tomorrow."

Jeanie just shook her head and sighed, knowing it was pointless to argue; she had become very accustomed to this routine.

Ralph was anxious to get home the next day. He was barely in the door when he was yelling, "How'd it go today? What did you find out?"

Jeanie came out of the kitchen with a smile on her face said, "Well, I got all the information you wanted and …"

"Yeah, so what do they want?" Ralph interrupted.

"If you let me finish, I'll tell you."

"Why are you smiling?" Ralph interrupted again.

"I think I could like it."

"What do you mean, you think you could like it?"

"If you would give me a chance to talk, Ralph, I'll tell you."

"OK, OK, go ahead," he demanded, as he folded his arms impatiently on his chest.

"Not only did I get all the information, but he asked me if I wanted to see it."

"What, you mean you've already looked at it without me?"

"I saw the whole house and everything. And I think you could make that place look great."

Now who's the one trying to make a sales pitch, Ralph thought. "So when can I see it?"

"I told him you would probably want to see it tonight." Jeanie replied confidently.

"You did?" Ralph seemed a bit stunned that she had managed all this without his intervention.

"Yes, and he said it was no problem."

"Well, let's go; get the kids in the car."

"Ralph, we haven't eaten yet, the kids need to eat."

"We'll stop at the pizza place afterwards." The kids jumped up and down screaming "Yay!" when they heard the news of this fun diversion.

"Come on, kids, let's get in the car before Daddy has a fit!" Jeanie said with a smile as she got the kids ready to go.

"Yeah, and you can tell me all the details on the way there."

"Just give me one second, Ralph, because I told him I'd call his house first before we came over; he only lives a few miles down the road."

Ralph knew he would want the house no matter what, but he didn't want to appear too anxious. He also knew there wasn't anything that he couldn't renovate. The thing that he was really excited about was the land itself and the barn.

As it turned out, the realtor was also the owner of the property. After they'd all had a chance to look the place over, he asked, "So what do you think?"

Now Ralph already thought the price was cheap considering the house sat on five acres, but with the property looking the way it did and with the sign being partially covered with weeds, he figured it had been sitting quite some time with no takers. "I'll tell you what, I'll give you $30,000 if you can close in thirty days." Ralph wanted a quick sale here, but he also wanted enough time to make a couple of rooms livable before he had to move his family out of the ranch house. The realtor then said, "Well, let me go home and crunch the numbers and give you a call." Ralph then said, "Oh, I forgot to tell you — this is a cash sale, so we don't need to take time with setting up a bank loan; just a title search and the proper paperwork is all we'll need to do."

"OK, Mr. Walls, I'll get back to you."

"Will that be tonight or when should I expect your call?"

"When do you go to bed?" asked the realtor.

"Not till 11:00 pm," Ralph answered. "But I have to stop and feed these little ones on the way home first."

"OK, I'll give you a call later tonight."

"OK, let's get in the car, guys, and get some pizza." As they were pulling out of the driveway, Jeanie asked, "So what do you think?"

"This is what I've always wanted. We could have a big garden, keep some chickens, and I could fence in a section and we could have some steers. What do you think?"

"It's going to take a lot of work, and I don't know how you're going to make this livable before we have to move in, but I love it. It has great possibilities. Another good thing is that the grammar school is just down the road around the corner. I know because I went that way today on my way back home."

"Mommy, are we going to live in that house?" Stephanie asked inquisitively.

"Maybe, honey."

"It's not very nice."

"I know, but Daddy can fix it up, you'll see."

"Are we getting pizza now?" interrupted Rodney.

"It won't be long."

Later on in the evening when they'd gotten back home and put the children to bed, the phone rang at about 9:30 and Ralph answered it on the first ring with an exuberant, "Hello!"

"Hi, Mr. Walls?"

"Yes, that's me."

"This is John Smith."

"Oh, hi."

"I've got those numbers for you."

"OK, let me have it."

"I will need another $5,000.00 to make this deal work."

"I'll tell you what. I'll give you $33,000.00, but we have to close in thirty days or less." There was silence on the other end. "Hello, Mr. Smith?"

"Yes, I'm here."

"Actually, if you want to sell that house tonight, I'm ready," Ralph replied.

"OK, it's a deal; when can you sign the papers?"

"I can come right over."

"No, no, I don't have them ready, they're in the office. How about tomorrow at 12:00 noon?"

"Fine with me as long as you don't care what I look like. I'll be coming straight from the job site."

"That's fine."

"OK, I'll see you at noon."

"OK, goodnight."

"Goodnight."

Ralph was cheering so loud that he woke up the children who thought Mommy and Daddy were having a fight. They both knew this was going to be a rough road ahead. Ralph was busier than ever with the drywall business and really had no time to spare at all. His plan was to work twelve-hour days from now till the closing, then go back to eight-hour days and work nights and Sundays at the house till they had to move.

By the middle of June the house in Pittstown was theirs. Everyone was anxious to see the house Ralph and Jeanie had bought. Ralph's Aunt Eleanor, his mother's sister, did Ralph's bookkeeping and was always impressed with the beautiful homes he built and moved into. So one Sunday afternoon her son, Bruce, and her mother, Ralph's Grandmother VanOrden, got in their car and drove out to Pittstown. When they got to the property they slowed down to get a better look. Ralph's grandmother couldn't believe it; in fact, she said, "Keep driving, I refuse to believe he would buy that and move his family in there." She wasn't the only one. No one in the family could believe it.

That didn't bother Ralph. He said, "I'd like to find two of these a year for the rest of my life. Most people can't see past the tall grass and ugly siding, but I can see a beautiful piece of land here with a fenced-in pasture and someday a beautiful house on it."

Ralph started work on the property right away. The plan was to get two rooms ready for the kids to sleep in and also to make sure the family had a functioning bathroom and kitchen. Someone had previously closed in the front porch with windows and doors. Eventually that would become Ralph's office, but for now that would be fixed up as a temporary bedroom for the kids. That was the easy part. The kitchen and bath were going to take a little more work. The whole upstairs would be left till after they moved in.

By August Ralph was spending nights at the Pittstown house putting the finishing touches on the downstairs. He knew you should always start the upstairs first, but he had bigger plans for that and decided it could wait till another time. The barn was fairly new, and its entire second floor was constructed of sturdy plywood. Now that the house was livable he could start hauling stuff over and storing it in the upstairs of the barn. The kids loved all that space in the barn to ride their bikes and hot wheels in. They had been doing that on the weekends while their father worked on the property. Ralph had bought a big riding mower to handle cutting all the grass and had finally gotten the five acres looking half decent.

Jeanie was anxious to get moved in, not that the place was anything to brag about yet, but just to get settled and stop living out of boxes. In five years' time she had lived in five houses counting this one, and in the last twelve months alone they had moved three times. She said she was starting to feel like a gypsy, but she always kept a good sense of humor about it. Nevertheless, she reminded Ralph that they needed to put down roots, because the children would be starting school in a year and needed to get settled into a stable environment.

On the last day of August they received a call from Glenn announcing the birth of their second child, a boy named David. When they grabbed a chance to go see the new baby, they could tell that Glenn sure was one proud father, beaming from ear to ear.

By the first of September they were completely moved in, and the children slept in the two rooms that would eventually become the office and the sewing room, and Ralph and Jeanie slept in the living room with a mattress on the floor. They basically were camping out, but in a couple of weeks Ralph would have two rooms upstairs done for the children. Fall and winter were pretty cold living in that old house with the old windows that rattled every time the wind blew.

* * * * *

The school reunion was a very special time for Gid, and he couldn't wait to see his old friends, especially the Fisher brothers. As his plane touched down at Mel's he turned to Betty and said,

"Did you see that big hay field over there?"

"Yes I did, honey, and I know, you could have landed there."

"Why, have I told you that before?"

"Only every time we see a big field." Gid had a big grin on his face, knowing full well he did it all the time. Once out of the plane Gid had to find Mel and say hi, then they went down to his family's house, which was only a little ways from the schoolhouse. There was something special about being with his family, and he wouldn't miss it for anything. The Amish have very close family ties, and that's one thing that Gid valued dearly. This time, however, he wouldn't be spending a lot of time visiting family because this was a school reunion, not just a class reunion.

Since this was a one-room schoolhouse, that meant everyone who'd attended the school would be there, including his sisters. This was always a great time of renewing friendships, and for Gid this was important. When he left home he had determined that he would distance himself from his friends so he wouldn't be a bad influence on them, since Amish young men don't usually leave the community. Now they were all grown up and just couldn't wait to hear all about the things he had done. Gid never bragged and always made things that he had done seem insignificant. He always wanted to know all about their lives and especially their families.

10

THE GREAT IGNAGUA

During the month of January, Gid and Betty and Jay and Ella Mae took a vacation to Africa. The Lehmans were familiar with travel in Africa because years earlier they had lived there and started Menno Travel Service. So they made the perfect tour guides for Gid and Betty. After landing in Nairobi, Jay took them to meet their good friends Kerm and Sharon Yoder who had worked with them when they were in Africa. For the next two weeks the six of them were on safari together. From the beginning they were captivated by the immenseness of the country and the variety of animals that were just roaming everywhere. They would drive for miles on end through what seemed like barren land, and then almost like magic, a luxurious resort would just appear right in front of them. One particular resort that they loved was made to look like a Massai village, with mud huts scattered about. Another amazing thing was that from the resort you could see elephants wandering on the plain close by. The food was indescribably delicious and the service was extraordinary. Their nights were spent sleeping under mosquito nets, which did a good job of keeping the pests away. Early in the mornings after breakfast, it was back into the safari vehicles and off to explore new things. The roads were very unpredictable, and they suffered three flat tires on the way. Along the way they made a stop on the plain of the Serengeti to visit their missionary friends Chris and Lavern Pfiefer, who were working there. A moment that made a lasting impression on Gid and Betty was when Chris and Lavern took them to a leprosy colony. They left there feeling sad and at the same time encouraged with the progress that was being made in the efforts to help those afflicted with leprosy.

The safari continued on to Ambeselli, where they saw the gerenuk, and Ngorongoro Crater, where they saw many hippos. They traveled to many more locations and saw a vast array of wild animals, and by the time they had to go home, they left there with a tremendous sense of awe. It seemed that the giraffe was photographed the most, and there is even an old home movie of Gid chasing some giraffes. They were so excited about their trip that they all agreed they would soon return with their children.

* * * * *

By spring Ralph and Jeanie were eager to get outside and start work on their property. The first thing they wanted to do was get a big garden underway. Someone had introduced them to a couple named Richie and Betty Atkinson, who had a small gentleman's farm. They lived a few miles from their home and had a tractor and plow. Ralph asked Richie if he would come over and plow up his garden. Ralph knew that the first year's plowing usually didn't produce a terrific garden, but when he saw the color of the soil he had high hopes. With the garden underway Ralph turned his efforts to fencing in a large part of the property so they could raise two steers and some sheep. He also turned an outbuilding into a chicken house and began raising chickens. His construction business was booming and Ralph was having a hard time keeping up with the calls from his regular builders, so before it got out of control he hired two subcontractors to do all his drywall hanging. Richie and Betty became great friends and introduced them to some of their other friends as well. One particular lady became one of Jeanie's closest friends, and her name was Michelle Allen. Michelle was filled with life and had a quick wit that Jeanie loved.

By summer Ralph was ready for his next big project on the house. He hadn't totally finished the upstairs yet because he had bigger plans, but he wasn't going to tell Jeanie and the kids his whole idea yet. He wanted to surprise them all. The one section of the house that contained the kitchen, bathroom, and laundry was a single story that butted up to the two-story main house. Ralph's plan was to rip off the roof and put bigger floor joists in and build a second floor addition on top. By the Fourth of July he had all the materials shipped and laying in the backyard. That day his parents were having Ralph and Glenn and their wives and children over for a picnic. Ralph had called his brother earlier in the week and asked him to help that day with a small project. Glenn loved it when Ralph said that, because he always knew that when Ralph said small it meant just the opposite, and he never knew what to expect, but that was part of the fun.

Ralph had told Jeanie and the kids to get their breakfast early and not to use the back door. He told them to just stay out of the kitchen area totally. Jeanie now knew what he was about to do. Glenn arrived early and Ralph was ready; Ralph knew he wanted to have this whole thing back under cover by evening, in case of rain, so there was no time to strip shingles off the old roof. With the whole family watching, Ralph climbed the ladder with a chain saw in hand and began to slice the roof into pieces; sparks were flying everywhere, and Jeanie thought for sure he was going to burn the house down. In less than an hour there were big sections of roof laying in the yard, and the children's eyes were as big as saucers as they watched their daddy work. By 10:30 they had the new floor joists put in and the plywood decking down.

Jeanie and the children left to go to the picnic as Ralph and Glenn stood the last walls up. Ralph had prefigured almost everything well in advance, which made the whole project go much faster. While Ralph was cutting rafters Glenn was putting all the ceiling joists in. By 4:00 that day the new addition was all papered in and water tight, and they still got to the picnic in time to have a burger, potato salad, and baked beans. When the children got home that night they couldn't believe their eyes, and they wondered how they were going to get in to that new part of the house. Jeanie explained to them that Daddy was going to cut a hole in the wall upstairs and make a new doorway. Then she added in a much louder voice, "After he puts all the new windows in." Ralph figured she didn't know he already had the windows and a sliding glass door sitting in the barn. The only real dirty part of the whole project came when he broke through the wall, as it was quite an old house and the walls were filled with mud and straw.

* * * * *

The big yellow bus pulled up in front of the house. Getting Stephanie used to the prospect of riding the bus to school had been a work in progress for a couple of weeks. Stephanie wasn't too keen on the idea of going somewhere without her mother and with strangers at that. But after a final push she was on the bus heading down the road two miles to the Alexandria Township School. That was the easy part. Getting off the bus every afternoon was the nightmare. She would happily get off the bus after having a great day at school, but as soon as the bus pulled away, the tears would flow in a show of dramatic anguish, worked up just in time for her mom to see when she walked in the house. This happened almost every day through kindergarten. Stephanie had always been with her mother, helping her around the house and with her little brother, but now her best buddy and mom put her on that big yellow bus and sent her away every day. *How could she do that to me,* she thought. Now her way of getting even was to make her mother feel sorry she did that.

So crying became a daily ritual. She didn't want her mother to think she had a good time while she was away, so every day there was a different reason for crying: someone looked at me funny, someone said something, my hair was all wrong, my dress wasn't right, and so on. But as soon as her father came home she would stop crying, making it look like Jeanie was exaggerating when she would tell Ralph all about it. This would eventually lead to tension between Ralph and Jeanie, who had different views of discipline. Jeanie would tell Stephanie to wait until her father got home, and that he would deal with her, and then when Ralph got home he felt it wasn't up to him to deal with the problem. He felt that if one of the children did something wrong they should be disciplined at the moment the wrong was done, not threatening them with discipline from the other parent. So while Mom and Dad were arguing, Stephanie would be hiding around the corner taking it all in. Ralph had noticed this early on, and he had always suggested they discuss these things somewhere out of the reach of the children's ears. But both had a hard time obeying their own rule. As a result, little ears usually heard their disagreements.

The summer gave them an abundant amount of produce from the garden and Jeanie canned and froze everything she could. Ralph had made her some shelving in the basement and said with all the jars of canned goods on it, it looked like a picture in *Better Homes and Gardens* or *Good Housekeeping* magazine.

Halloween was one of Ralph's favorite times of year. Year in and year out he would do the same thing; he would wait till Jeanie handed the candy out to some children, then run out the back door with a big trench coat on screaming and yelling with his arms flailing, chasing the terrified little kids down the driveway. This year everything was about to change though. He succeeded with the first two groups of kids, but on his third attempt he exited the house and went a little too far into the yard before turning toward the driveway. Running at full speed he suddenly felt something strike his neck and wound up on his back in the yard. He had run into the clothesline and almost broke his neck. He lived to tell about it, but he never chased trick-or-treaters again.

Another one of Ralph's favorite times was when they would have Glenn and Carolyn and their children over for an evening of playing games and eating pizza. He would always try to have a big finish for them when they left for home, something to keep them laughing. Sometimes he would just climb out on the porch roof and yell to them as they rode by, or he would be standing up the road hitchhiking as they drove by. One of his antics that Glenn and Carolyn laughed about all the way home was the night he was able to get about a hundred yards up the road and was standing there dressed like one of Clint Eastwood's characters. He had a trench coat on with a big cowboy hat and a lit cigar in his mouth and was holding a shotgun. They drove right passed him, and about a quarter of a mile up the road, one of the children asked, "Wasn't that Uncle Ralph standing along the road back there?"

The more they thought about it, the harder they laughed. He'd gotten them again. When they got home that night, they had to know for sure, so they called. When the phone rang, Ralph knew it was Glenn calling.

"Hey, was that you standing along the road tonight?" Glenn asked. Ralph could hear Carolyn laughing in the background.

"Yeah, I was out looking for cattle rustlers."

* * * * *

Gid had leased a Meyers 200 to a man in Florida. The man would send a lease payment to Gid every month, but suddenly one day the payments stopped, and Gid couldn't get in touch with him.

After about four months, Gid received a phone call and was informed that his plane was in Great Ignagua, the southernmost island of the Bahamas, and that Sheldon, the lessee, was in the hospital in London. Steve, who worked for Gid, went to Sheldon's house in Florida only to find that he wasn't in, but that a pet lion was guarding the house! Soon after that, Gid had to fly to London for TWA, and while he was there he went to the hospital to look for Sheldon, but to no avail. What he eventually found out was that Sheldon was in Nassau in prison. Apparently he had made an emergency landing in the middle of the night and some drugs were found in his girlfriend's handbag.

Gid was in close communication with the Bahamian government to have the plane returned to him, but they said he could claim the Meyers 200 only if he could prove that he owned the plane. Gid proved it easily by sending them a copy of his ownership papers, but the government still was not cooperating.

Gid and Steve, who both liked challenges, especially concerning aviation, decided maybe they should go down and try to find the plane, but thought it might look a little strange for two men to be touring the island together. So, Steve's wife Amelia suggested that she and Betty go along so they would appear to be regular tourists. They left Friday, the day after Thanksgiving, 1974, at 2:00 am from Pennsylvania in a Cessna 310 - twin engine. Karla and Mike stayed with Grandma Herr, Betty's mother.

The heater in the plane was "touchy" and decided it wasn't working on this particular day, and they were freezing, as it was a really cold day, so they stopped in Virginia to fix the heater. Gid and Steve had to crawl under the plane and reset the circuit breaker.

After landing in Florida and making a short visit with a relative, they returned to the airport and made another call to Nassau about picking up the plane. Gid was told, "Mr. Miller, you don't seem to understand. That plane belongs to the Bahamian government." Well, Gid flatly disagreed, and soon they were headed for Great Ignagua Island. It was about a three-hour flight, but they landed on Little Ignagua first to refuel and clear through customs.

They landed on Great Ignagua on a huge runway that had been built during the war, and the first thing they saw was Gid's Meyers 200, tied down with electrical wire, with flat tires, a loose panel on the belly where they apparently had been looking for drugs, and a dead battery.

Soon a pickup truck came down the road towards the airport, and their interest in the Meyers had to be suspended for the time being. The man driving the truck was Mr. Cartwright, who worked for Morton Salt; since there were very few motels or restaurants on the island, the Morton Salt Company owned a guesthouse there, which was staffed with a lady who would cook. He wondered if they were interested in staying there and they said yes. Since there were no car rentals at the time, they borrowed Mr. Cartwright's pickup truck, which had a large toolbox in the back, and drove to the guesthouse.

After they got settled in at the guesthouse and had dinner, they went for a drive and, of course, ended up at the airport. Now that it was nighttime they could check out the Meyers a little more closely under the cover of darkness. Gid brought a box of airplane keys along in hopes that one of them would fit the Meyers. Sure enough, the first one they tried fit in the lock, and when he turned it, the door opened up with no problem! Then they realized the battery was dead, but of course they weren't surprised. But they did wonder how they were going to charge it up, and then Gid and Steve looked at each other in unison and said, "Mr. Cartwright's truck!" So they put the Meyers battery in the truck and connected the two batteries with a piece of wire that Steve had found on the ground and then had stripped it down to the copper, so he could use the wire as a jumper cable to charge the abandoned plane battery.

Betty and Amelia sat in the truck, and Betty held her foot on the accelerator to charge the battery while they both kept their eyes on the road for headlights in case a car was approaching. This was a little more stress than they needed and they weren't sure that they made good accomplices!

Meanwhile, Gid and Steve were digging through the contents of the toolbox on the back of Mr. Cartwright's truck and found a garden hose, a five-gallon gas can, and a tire pump. Just what they needed! They knew God was looking out for them! Immediately they started siphoning gas from the Cessna 310 to put into the Meyers. Steve did a little coughing and spitting after getting some fuel in his mouth to start the siphon. They inflated the tires with the tire pump, but then they pushed a little sand against the tires so that no one would notice they had been inflated and get suspicious.

Finally they decided that enough had been done that evening. They went back to the guesthouse and went to bed. Gid didn't sleep well that night, lying wide awake wondering what time it got light in the morning here in the Bahamas; he knew that he wanted to leave at daybreak on Sunday morning. Gid had only caught a few hours' sleep when the roosters began crowing, and if that wasn't bad enough, a band came down the street very early, making lots of noise. But at least he was awake at daybreak!

While the four of them were eating a delicious breakfast the cook had made for them, Mr. Cartwright came in and asked if they were having a problem with the truck. He had opened the hood to check the oil and noticed an extra battery in it. Of course, it had "Aviation" written across it in big letters. Gid and Steve told him they were having trouble with the battery in the plane and hoped he didn't mind that they were charging it with his truck. Mr. Cartwright had no problem with that at all. Gid then paid him for a couple days rental of his truck.

After breakfast they drove around the island to do some sightseeing and also to give the battery for the Meyers a better charge. They saw the big piles of salt at the Morton Salt Company's mines, and then they spent some time on the beach where they found some coral and large conch shells.

Then it was back to the airport to put the battery back into the Meyers to see if it would start. Fortunately, no one was at the airport while they were there, and while Gid and Steve were working on the plane, Betty and Amelia were up by the road watching for any cars that might come along. While watching for cars, they found some long sticks and were drawing the American flag in the sand. When the two young women stood back to admire their artwork, they burst out laughing over how much this accomplice job was really stressing them out, reducing them to drawing in the sand to relieve the tension!

Back at the airfield, after sputtering and choking for a while, the plane finally started and they were all ecstatic. Now they could enjoy the rest of the day and leave early the next morning - or so they thought. After lunch, Gid and Steve made arrangements to have gas put in the 310, since they had siphoned it empty to fill the Meyers. Betty and Amelia stayed at the guesthouse for a relaxing afternoon. While the men were at the airport, another plane came in, and suddenly the customs people were all over the place, asking Gid and Steve questions. Then a priest came along, and noticing that the 310 had six seats, asked if he could have a ride to Nassau. They finally convinced him that they had too much weight as it was, and that it would be illegal to take him along. Of course, they had no intentions of stopping in Nassau!

Gid and Steve didn't have a good feeling about the way things had transpired at the airfield, and so when they got back to the guesthouse, they told Betty and Amelia to pack. They decided they should leave that very afternoon. They paid the cook for a couple days' work at the guesthouse and told her that they were going to do some island hopping, and that if they weren't home by supper, not to cook for them. They also instructed the cook to tell Mr. Cartwright that his truck would be at the airport with the keys under the floor mat.

When they got to the airport, thankfully no one else was there, so they quickly put their suitcases in the 310 and took the one emergency raft from the 310 and put it into the Meyers. They all got into the Cessna 310 and started the engines. After taxiing beside the Meyers 200, Steve jumped out, ran over, and jumped into the Meyers. He was taxiing almost before he had the engine started! The tires were a little rough from sitting so long, but they soon rounded out. Both airplanes headed for the runway and took off. No one knew for sure if the Meyers would fly, but it was the chance they took and it was not without a lot of prayer. They climbed to a couple thousand feet immediately and communicated by radio.

Everything was going well and both planes traveled at about the same speed, so they kept in sight of each other all the way to the U.S. Not sure if they could be picked up on radar from Nassau, they flew about 50 to 100 feet off the water as they flew by Nassau, then climbed up again before landing in Florida. When nearing Ft. Lauderdale Gid was asked about a flight plan and he said, "Oh, we need a flight plan?" Of course, he knew that they were supposed to have one, but under the circumstances, it was not a good idea. As they were in the traffic pattern, Steve radioed to Gid to ask him to check if his landing gear was down, because the hydraulic line had ruptured on takeoff and sprayed the interior of the plane with oil. The gear was down and both planes landed safely. Betty and Amelia were so glad to be back home safely that they wanted to kiss the ground, but didn't want to do anything that looked too suspicious!

Gid and Steve had already discussed how they would keep this a secret, like possibly changing the N number. So you can imagine their surprise when they got out of the planes and a voice came over the loud speaker saying, "Congratulations, you did it!" They were wondering who found out about this already, and then they remembered that the people at the airport knew what they were planning to do. They needed to fill out some papers upon reentering the U.S., and one question asked how long they had been gone. To them it seemed like a week, but it had only been a little more than 24 hours!

* * * * *

In the spring of 1975 Ralph and Jeanie decided to try their hand at raising a couple of Hereford steers. The pasture area had been completely fenced in, and Ralph had built stalls into one end of the barn. They purchased two young steers and decided to name them. Ralph thought that they should name them something they liked to eat, so when it came time to eat them, the children wouldn't get too upset because they would have been calling them food names all along. After a little thought he decided on Pot roast and T-bone, which to his surprise everyone liked. They also bought two sheep and two geese. The geese were a little strange; they must have had a birth defect or something, because their wings were always facing the wrong way when outstretched, but when they were tucked in they looked fine.

Another funny thing was that the ram liked to play basketball. That's right, basketball. One day, quite by accident, while Ralph was shooting hoops out at the barn, one of his shots went over the fence and landed in the pasture, and before he could get to the ball, the ram had it in his line of sight. The ram charged the ball and began to push it with his head around the entire pasture until he finally collapsed from exhaustion. When the ram was finally done with the ball, Ralph retrieved it and got the whole family to come out and watch their crazy ram. The children were hysterical with laughter and wondered why he was doing that. Being the wonderful dad that he was, Ralph told them the truth: "He used to play for the Harlem Globetrotters and wanted to see if he could still handle the ball." Even though the children were young at the time, I don't think they believed him. Besides, their mother told them that the ram probably thought of the ball as an enemy and he was defending his wife. Ralph thought his story was better.

The steers became a little problem in the spring when the clocks were moved ahead. Ralph had been giving them a small amount of grain in the morning before he left for work, and he usually left at 6:00 am, but the steers didn't know anything about the time change. So, on Sunday morning at 5:00 am, when everyone was sound asleep, the steers began mooing loudly for their feed. This wasn't just a little cute sort of mooing; it was downright bellowing so loud that it made the house vibrate. To make matters worse, the geese thought something was wrong so they added to the cacophony and started to honk, really loud, demanding honking.

You guessed it; the sheep didn't want to be left out, so of course they joined in with their bleating, which now made it a sextet ensemble.

Ralph couldn't get his pants on quick enough; as a matter of fact, there was a small hole in the one pants leg that his big toe caught in, and he ripped the entire pants leg off in his hurry to put them on. Jeanie watched as Ralph hopped around, trying to get into his pants, and when his pant leg ripped off, that's when she lost it. Now with the pillow over her head trying to keep from laughing so loud, it was obvious to Ralph she was laughing, especially since the entire bed was shaking. Hopping on one leg because his foot was still stuck in the pant leg hole, he lost his balance and fell onto the bed, knocking the lamp over in the process. By now the children had been awakened and were knocking at the bedroom door, wondering what was going on. The children had never seen Ralph in his underwear, so he was hollering to Jeanie to get the door. Jeanie ran to the door laughing so hard it hurt, and she gathered the children and took them into one of their bedrooms to try to explain to them what was happening. But she was laughing so hard they couldn't understand what she was saying.

Ralph could hear her laughing and then he began to laugh too, and finally he found another pair of pants to slip on. By the time he got outside to feed the animals, half the lights in the neighborhood were on and there was one neighbor standing on his porch as Ralph ran across the backyard. The animals all quieted down instantly and it wasn't because Ralph shot them; there's nothing like eating a good meal to keep animals quiet! When Ralph got back in the house he found that Jeanie was in bed, and as soon as she saw him, she burst out laughing again. He got back in bed and they laughed till their sides hurt.

On Mother's Day Ralph went out to the barn to do the usual morning routine but when he got to the last stall there was quite a bit of activity going on in there. It seems as though the ewe was giving birth to a set of twins. That was something he desperately wanted to get a picture of. You see, Ralph had put his Irish setter in the pasture with all the animals because that's where she wanted to be. The truly amazing part was that she was helping with the delivery. The ram was standing there watching while the setter was cleaning off the lambs. Ralph hurried to the house to get everyone else so they all could see this. Everyone thought it remarkable that the lambs had been born on Mother's Day.

The geese weren't about to be out done; they had a nest of eggs that they were guarding closely. Sometime later the eggs hatched, and suddenly there were an additional six goslings running around, and they all copied the parents, running with their wings turned the wrong way.

* * * * *

In the summer Gid's plane business, along with his TWA schedule, was keeping him very busy and he needed to make some time for Betty and him to be together. When his schedule permitted it, he would take Betty along on a flight. If a particular flight were going to be a layover for a couple of days, Betty would accompany him to that location. One of the first flights she accompanied him on was a flight to Lisbon, Portugal. This turned out to be one of the best ways for them to spend time together and to see the world. Most of these layovers were only for a couple of days, but still it was exciting to experience the flavor of another country. Betty took lots of photos and kept a detailed account of all the countries they visited. When they arrived back home, the new school year was starting at Alexandria Township School where Karla was beginning the seventh grade and Mike the fourth. It was back to work as usual, but the brief pause to spend time together was very important to both of them.

Also in September, Gid's airplane sales business had really taken off. With his close proximity to Sky Manner Airport in Alexandria Township, he was able to bring prospective clients right to the planes. He had named his business **Gid Miller's Aero Sales, Inc**. Gid had become pretty well-known for a particular little plane, and to do justice to Gid and the plane, I will share with you some quotes of the six-page article that was written about Gid and his favorite plane in the September 1975 issue of *Air Progress* magazine (with text and photography by Budd Davisson):

> Gid Miller toed the ground in his aw-shucks manner, listening quietly to my accusation that he was a flaming fanatic. Then as my spiel ended, he smiled a slow country-boy smile and said, "Well, we've got the best, fastest, strongest, easiest, most reliable and finest-looking airplane ever built in the U.S. It's not that we're fanatics, we just know a good airplane when we see one.
>
> And that sums up a unique little one-man show called Gid Miller's Aero Sales Inc. Miller sells and leases airplanes (between hops as an airline pilot), but not just any old airplane. Oh sure, once in a while he'll let an occasional Aztec or Mooney trickle through his hands. But 99 percent of the time, when he uses the word "airplane" he's talking about one particular little bird, the Meyers/Aero Commander 200, a pugnacious little iron and aluminum ingot for which Miller makes many claims, most of which, it should be noted, are absolutely true.
>
> My initial contact with Miller was more out of curiosity than anything else. I'd been seeing his frantic ads in Trade-A-Plane for some time and I got tired of passing them off as typographical errors. At times he had as many as four OTW's, as well as

mini-herds of 200s listed. I shouldn't have called. It was all true.

Cornering Gid Miller was no easy process. In the two weeks I worked with him, he bought and sold two 200s, picking one up in Colorado and another in California which he ferried to Long Island in 13 ½ hours. Business appeared to be booming, and when I finally ran him down, he was walking through one of his stockpiles of airplanes at Sky Manner Airport in central New Jersey, one of several places where little heaps of Miller-Meyers are to be found in the Frenchtown, New Jersey area he calls home.

Gid had the entire six-page article reprinted, with pictures and all, to be used for advertising handouts in airports. The title of the article is **"Best Airplane Ever Built?"** The rest of the article described the Meyers in complete detail. The full-size picture in the center of the article was of Gid sitting in the right seat of his favorite plane, the Meyers 200. The man flying the plane was stunt pilot Ed Mahler, who was later tragically killed while flying at Suffolk Air Force Base.

11

THIS IS THE DAY

Five miles to the north it was back to school for Stephanie, but this time she wasn't going alone, because her little brother, Rodney was now ready for school as well . With both children in school, this freed up some time for Jeanie to do things that she wanted to do. One of those things was to spend more time with her friend, Michelle. One day Jeanie stopped at Michelle's just to visit, and when she knocked on the door she could hear Michelle yell out, "Come on in, I'm in the back."

When Jeanie located her, she started to laugh, "Michelle, what are you doing?"

"What does it look like I'm doing?"

"It looks like you're trying to paint."

"Duh, how'd you guess?" Michelle rolled her eyes jokingly and smiled.

"Well, it's obvious that you are painting. But my question is why are you using that tiny brush?" Michelle was painting the entire room with what looked like a one-inch brush.

"What should I use? This is the biggest brush I have and it's what Paul gave me to paint the room with." Paul was Michelle's husband and he liked to have fun too, so he must have thought this would keep her busy for a week if her arm could hold up that long.

"Michelle, you are too funny! I can't believe you fell for that. We're gonna have to get back at Paul somehow. But meanwhile, you need a pan and roller, and then you could finish this room in a couple of hours."

"Wait till I get a hold of Paul tonight, I've got just the place for this brush." Needless to say Jeanie and Michelle went out and bought a pan and a paint roller that same day and tackled the job having lots of laugh while doing so, making the work quick and easy.

Since Rodney only went to school for half a day, Jeanie always had to make sure she was home by noon. But having her mornings free was still enough time to get herself into mischief. In the evenings she always wanted to tell Ralph about the fun she was having with Michelle, but Ralph would just comment, "No good can come from it. All you women want to do is sit around drinking tea and talking about your husbands." Ralph had started to notice a change in Jeanie lately, and it worried him. She used to just let whatever he said go by, but now she was giving some smart aleck remarks back at him.

"We might drink some tea, but we have better things to do than to waste our time talking about our husbands; that would be too boring," she commented.

Autumn was always a special time of year, bringing with it cooler temperatures which made it enjoyable to work outside. With the final harvesting done in the garden, it was time to turn the garden over in preparation for next year's planting. They would rake the leaves into piles and haul them off to the composting pile, that is unless the children ran through them first, and then they had to be raked all over again. Ralph didn't mind that double work; in fact, he loved playing with the children, but most often Jeanie would yell at him for being a little too rough with them. And eventually someone would get hurt or get something in their eye and go running to Mommy for help. It always seemed to Ralph that Mommy was the only one who could fix things. Even if he offered his assistance, they didn't think he could help. Most often the times of fun would end on a sour note, and Ralph would wind up going back to his work knowing he was the bad guy once again. Sometimes the smallest incident would get Ralph into fits of rage, especially if he thought he was being accused or blamed for something. He would let it fester in his mind, and before long he would just blow up. He was noted for putting his fist through walls or doors if his temper flared up. One time, after attempting to start the push mower a dozen times and having it fail to start a dozen times, he picked up the mower by the handle and swung it like a hammer throw in the Olympics, sending it sailing and crashing into the side of the barn. Everyone knew about his violent outbursts and knew enough to stay away when he was in one of those moods. That probably explains why the children would run to their mommy when they were hurt. If Daddy couldn't fix it he would probably get upset as a result, so they ran to the one whom they felt safest with.

The New Year didn't bring many changes, except for the fact that Jeanie was enjoying her newfound freedom of being able to get out and go places during the day with her friends. And of course this inevitably caused trouble with Ralph. He would come home from work and ask what she had done that day. If the answer weren't what he wanted to hear, an argument would ensue. It was ok if she was going to help someone do something, but if she was just visiting and spending her time talking, then she might as well stay home, in his opinion. Like he had said before, no good could come of that. Ralph's solution was that he should do less around the house so that she had more things to do to fill up her time.

So he came up with a plan: Jeanie would continue to do the housework, but now she would also take care of all the animals, the garden, and the lawns. Ralph thought this would keep her home and off the roads. Not too much changed, though, because Jeanie came up with her own plan: she took care of the animals in the morning and let everything else go until she had to be home for Rodney at noon. This didn't sit too well with Ralph, especially if he came home and the grass was only half cut out front where everyone could see it. In his firmly expressed opinion, there wasn't any reason not to get the front lawn cut in one session. When he cut the grass, the front yard would take no more than twenty-five minutes on a riding mower, so he knew she had to be running around and not leaving herself enough time to get home and complete the job.

The property had about an acre and a half of lawns and field to cut, and Ralph didn't expect her to mow it all at one time. He had divided it into three sections, and he thought that each section, once started, should be completed the same day. Jeanie loved to cut the grass, just like Ralph did, but she wanted to be with her friends, too. Her reasoning was that she had been cheated out of part of her life by having to get married at such an early age. She had been thrust into marriage and motherhood and missed all those special relationships that she would have had with her girlfriends. She had dated Ralph for four years in high school, starting at the very young age of 14, and they had now been married for almost eight years. That was twelve years of her life that she had given up, and now she wanted a little freedom to have some fun with her friends. This difference in opinion between them would always lead to heated discussions, and many times to explosive arguments. She reminded Ralph that in the last eight years of marriage, they'd never had a honeymoon or a single vacation.

Ralph's business was doing very well, so when he would say that they couldn't afford to go on vacation, she knew that it was a lie. She knew he meant he was afraid to leave his work for even a week, for fear that he would make a customer upset. He had always maintained a high standard of keeping his word with his clients. That was the one good thing Jeanie could say about him. Jeanie had become quite a strong-willed individual, and she didn't back down in their arguments. Ralph would usually just give up by throwing his arms in the air and muttering something about there being no sense in wasting his breath arguing with her. Then he would retreat to the barn or go weed the garden in an effort to try to calm down.

One day after one these sessions, Ralph came back in the house and told Jeanie to go ahead and plan a trip somewhere. First of all she couldn't believe she was hearing him right, but she wasn't about to challenge that for fear he'd change his mind too quickly! Second, she wanted to call Betty Atkinson right away, because they had just been talking about taking a trip somewhere also. Later that year the four of them flew to Bermuda and had a wonderful vacation. While on the island the most convenient way for them to get around was by moped, and they had some harrowing incidents while going from place to place. Driving on the opposite side of the road took a little getting used to. One time when Ralph had crossed a bridge and began to make a right turn he suddenly realized he was in the wrong lane, and an oncoming bus was heading straight for him. Another time they were racing down the road as fast as those bikes would go, and Jeanie was in the rear of the group trying to catch up. Suddenly a ninety degree turn appeared in front of them, and three of them made the turn, but Jeanie was going too fast to make the turn, so she decided to just leave the road and go straight ahead, and when it was too late to change her mind, she realized she'd wound up in a parking lot trying to maneuver between about a hundred cars. The others had anticipated her not making the turn and had stopped along the road and watched the whole thing happening. They had quite a laugh when Jeanie finally found her way out and rejoined them.

Roads weren't exciting enough for Richie, so he suggested they try jumping sand dunes on their mopeds. When looking through the vacation photo album, it wasn't long before the next picture you saw was that of Richie and Betty riding double on a tiny moped. The other bike had bit the dust – literally – buried in a sand dune. They spent a lot of time at the beach, and Ralph was amazed at the beaches and the clear water. One day an octopus swam directly beneath him, and it was truly an awesome sight. The trip was wonderful, a welcome break from kids and work,
and for the time being everyone was happy.

* * * * *

In December of 1976 the much-awaited second trip to Africa was underway, except this time the two couples, the Millers and the Lehmans, took all their children with them. On Christmas Eve the four Millers landed in Paris, France, with their final touchdown in Nairobi on Christmas Day, where they met up with the Lehmans. After spending a couple of days sightseeing in Nairobi, they started out on the safari that the children were anxious to begin. The children's excitement was written on their faces as each new spotting of animals was announced. One morning as they were getting ready for an early animal run everything began to shake. Glenda had laid her glasses down on the back of the toilet tank and they slid off and broke. They had all just experienced their first earthquake.

While on the animal run, they saw a huge herd of elephants. Gid said, "That wasn't an earthquake that we experienced, that was all these elephants getting out of bed at once!" One of the things that stuck in Gid and Betty's mind was how almost everyday while riding in the tour van, Kevin, who would have been around eight years old at the time, would start to sing, "This is the day, this is the day, that the Lord has made, that the Lord has made." Before long the entire group was riding across the African plain singing "This is the Day."

When I first heard that story, I wondered how many of the tour guides or natives had heard about the Lord for the first time because of an eight-year-old boy's exuberant praises. Think about the possibilities; it's a very catchy tune and there could have been people all over Africa singing about the Lord and not even knowing what they were singing about. We have so many opportunities to share God's Word; a very simple song from an eight-year-old boy could have planted many seeds on that African safari. If I ever made a movie, I would definitely include the scene of an open-top VW bus driving across the African plain with six children in it singing that song at the top of their lungs.

Another memorable moment was when they were eating breakfast on the patio of a restaurant, and a baboon ran up and stole a piece of bread right out of Mike's hand.

After the safari, the Millers flew to Rhodesia (now Zimbabwe) to see their friends, the Hueberts. They spent a few days visiting and sightseeing, and then they flew to Victoria Falls on the border between Rhodesia and Zambia. The falls are so tall and wide that they create their own rain forest, and you have to wear a waterproof coat or else you'll get soaking wet. The trip was a wonderful time for the family to spend together, and it left an especially lasting impression on the children.

* * * * *

Not long after Ralph and Jeanie returned home from their wonderful vacation, things fell back into the same old routine between them, and everything returned to the way it had always been before. However, Ralph was drinking a lot more now and was complaining about everything. Jeanie was determined not to be a stay-at-home housewife and wanted to be able to spend time with her friends without Ralph going into a rage about it. She had also told Ralph she would like to get a job. Ralph insisted that she didn't have to work because he was making enough for them to live on. Jeanie didn't want to hear it and would insist that she should be allowed to seek employment. This argument was fought on a regular basis, always ending with the same result, with Ralph saying, "End of discussion, you're not working." With the pressures of work that Ralph was putting on himself, it left very little time for family interaction. The children knew just from their father's facial expression when he came home whether they should stay away from him or not. If it looked like he was in a bad mood they simply disappeared into their rooms and waited for the explosion. Nine times out of ten it didn't take much to start him going on a rampage. In fact, most of the problems started before he even got home.

From the very beginning of running his own business, Ralph had vowed not to hold customers up like his father had done. To keep his promises he was putting in twelve to fourteen hour days, and Jeanie would never know when he was going to arrive home for dinner. But she also knew that when he walked in the door he expected his meal to be ready and it had better be hot ... and this was in the days before you could just quickly reheat food in a microwave. Many a night he was in a bad mood before he even walked in the door.

* * * * *

During the year Gid and Betty managed to sneak another trip together into their busy schedules. Gid was going to make a trip to London with a long layover, so he asked Betty if she would like to come along. While in London they took a tour to Stonehenge and Winchester Cathedral and enjoyed some of the more popular sights around the city. When they were in London they found a place called Wolfe's, close to Buckingham Palace, which was noted for its hamburgers. This would turn out to be one of their favorite stops during their many return trips to London. It turned out to be a nice short break away from home for the two of them.

* * * * *

By the fall of 1977 Ralph was getting the itch to move again, so they put a sign in the yard and their home sold instantly. In fact, they weren't prepared for such a quick sale. They decided to rent a house for the winter so they could take their time looking for just the right home to own. They located a ranch house to rent in West Portal and began the usual moving process, a little at a time, on nights and weekends. With all the moves they had made, they were getting pretty skilled at it. In about a month's time the day of the closing came, and as usual everything went well. The people who bought the property were really excited and couldn't wait to move in. They hadn't sold their home yet, but they were anxious to go to their new house and spend the day. Ralph and Jeanie had already moved out completely and were settled in their rental house. That night Ralph got a call from one of their former neighbors across the street from the house they had just sold. They said the house was on fire and it looked like it would be a complete loss. Ralph and Jeanie were devastated. Even though they no longer lived there, it still felt like home to them, and they had many good memories from that home. They wondered what could have happened? They found out the next day that the new owner had started a fire in the fireplace and had left it burning unattended. The real sad part was that his nine-year-old daughter asked him if he was going to put out the fire before leaving. Sources said that he responded by saying it would be OK to leave the fire burning in the fireplace. The building officials condemned the house, so eventually it was taken down and a new house was built farther back onto the property, where Ralph and Jeanie had their garden.

It was a cold winter that year, and the rental house was situated on a wide, open area with no trees around to give any buffer to the strong winds that blew across the property. The grade on the property was such that water would pool in the driveway and not drain out properly. One particular morning Ralph went out to jump in his truck and go to work, only to find that all four tires were frozen in three inches of ice. Ralph was not a happy camper that day; it took him four hours to hand chip all the tires loose, and he had to keep running back into the house every so often to get warm.

Ralph and Jeanie didn't have time that winter to look for another house because of the amount of work he had to do, so he had a realtor looking for him. He had given the realtor explicit instructions on what to look for, and he made sure Jeanie had the same copy.

Some of the items on the list were:

1. It must be a two-story
2. It must have a garage or barn
3. Nice piece of property, well drained
4. Don't even consider anything on the south side of Route 12

Jeanie and the realtor looked and looked, and every time they thought they had found the perfect house, Ralph would say no, that it was not quite what he had in mind. After a couple of months the realtor told Jeanie to bring Ralph into the office and let him look through the listing books himself. One Saturday they all sat down in her office, waiting for Ralph to find the perfect house. Within minutes Ralph exclaimed, "Here it is, this is the one I want to see."

Everyone was in disbelief. The house in the book was a ranch house with no barn that was located on the south side of Route 12.

"That's nothing like what you had us looking for all this time!" Jeanie said.

"I know, but something is telling me to check out this house."

The realtor just sat there, not saying a word. She'd heard enough about Ralph to know it was best to let Jeanie handle him.

"*Something* is telling you to check out this house?"

"Yeah, it's a gut feeling I have."

Jeanie looked over at the realtor, who was sitting there with a droll expression on her face, and Jeanie said, "Well, OK then, let's go look at this gut feeling he has."

Jeanie was a little upset because both of them had been looking for two months for the complete opposite thing based on Ralph's 'Explicit Instructions.' Into the vehicles they piled and made the drive to Delaware Township, situated on the south side of Route 12. As they approached the house, they could see a stone wall around the front of the property. The house, a ranch style, had a stone veneer with a wood shake roof. In the front yard there was a large mimosa tree, and on the east side there was a long row of weeping willow trees, which usually indicates a wet area. They got out and began walking around the property, and right off the bat the ground was so saturated that everyone's shoes were getting wet. The house was empty but it had a lock box on the door, so the realtor opened it and they all went in. Up until this point Ralph hadn't said a word. He made one quick tour through and said, "I'll take it, let's make them an offer." Needless to say, Jeanie and the realtor were both speechless.

"I know you all think I'm nuts, but I just feel I'm supposed to buy this house. I can't explain it, but when I saw the picture in the book I saw our name on it."

Jeanie could sense the sincerity in Ralph's explanation, but she still felt a bit frustrated that she never would've looked at this one based on Ralph's guidelines. "I like the house too, Ralph, but if I'd have known, I wouldn't have looked at a lot of those other houses."

Ralph had that look on his face that Jeanie knew so well by now, the look that told her the wheels were turning in his mind.

He said to the realtor, "As we drove in I noticed that the house next door was for sale also. Can you find out for me what they are asking for it?"

"Give me a minute to check the listing and I'll be right back." The realtor went out to her car to look in the MLS book that she'd brought along with her.

"Why do you want to know about the other house?" Jeanie asked.

"Just curious, that's all; if it's cheap enough we could buy it and put a second story on it and then sell it, or just rent it out the way it is."

"Why on earth would you want to rent it?"

"That way we could control who our neighbors are," Ralph said quietly, and just then the realtor came back into the house to give them the details on the property next door. The realtor told them that some missionaries had lived there, but they had gone back to the mission field, which was why it was up for sale. After hearing all the details, Ralph said he'd think about it. In two days' time the sellers accepted their offer, and forty-five days later they owned the house in Delaware Township. This time they were in no hurry to move in, at least that was what Ralph said. He wanted to respackle and repaint some of the rooms and Jeanie wanted to do some wallpapering in the bedrooms.

But that didn't mean he wouldn't be moving things to the new house, so every time he made a trip over to work, he had to have the truck full of items to be moved. This way by the time he was done working on the house, they were half moved in.

By late spring they were moved in and Ralph had a garden all ready to plant. The children began attending Delaware Township School and Jeanie had again expressed her interest in finding employment. After seeing an ad for a dental assistant position in the paper, Jeanie called the number. The lady answering the phone told her what they were looking for and set up an interview for her. Jeanie had no experience as a dental assistant, but she was told it didn't matter and that they would train her if they accepted her. The interview was with Dr. Drew Vigilanti, DDS, and his wife Mary Ellen. Jeanie was accepted and started work immediately. From the first day Jeanie was excited about her new job and her new friends. Drew was a very good dentist and a good teacher, a man with great patience and a pleasant attitude. Mary Ellen looked like a model and was a lot of fun to work with, and soon she became a dear friend to Jeanie. Ralph had to admit it — he could see a difference in Jeanie's demeanor immediately. She had a new sense of value and self-worth about her, and Ralph had to begrudgingly admit, even if to himself, that he loved her all the more for it.

Another interesting thing happened in 1978; Rodney had developed an interest in music. Jeanie thought that maybe he should start piano lessons, so she stopped in at the music store on her way home from work one day and asked if they could recommend anyone to teach her son. They recommended a young man by the name of Chris.

In October the house next door had been sold and a young couple moved in. Ralph had noticed them outside one day, but he had no intentions of walking over and introducing himself. He figured they would probably want to talk, and that would just take time away from what he wanted to get done. One evening about a month later, Ralph came home from work to find that Jeanie had gone next door and had met the young woman who lived there. Jeanie said her name was Bonnie and her husband's name was Mike. She also said that their last name was Hudock. They didn't have any children yet but wanted to have a family eventually. Jeanie said that she seemed very nice and that Bonnie had asked all about their family. Jeanie had suggested that the four of them get together sometime. Ralph told her that was nice, but he didn't have time to sit around and chitchat with the neighbors. *How is the work going to get done around here if I sit around visiting?* As usual this was going to wind up in an argument about having friends. The argument ended this time with Jeanie saying to Ralph, "You know, you haven't got a friend in the world."

That phrase that Jeanie said to Ralph would have a lasting effect on the rest of Ralph's life. He just walked away as usual, but this time this man who never took anything from anyone, who always had a reply to everything, had been hurt to the core. But he never let on. He kept running the names of all the people he knew through his head, the ones he had always considered friends. Were those people true friends, or did they just stay friendly to him because they needed something from him? What is a true friend? He had a wife, and your wife is supposed to be your friend, but she just stated that he didn't have a friend in the world. That meant that she wasn't his friend either. Ralph started to think, are people just tolerating me, do they all hate me, am I really that bad of a person? No matter what he did the rest of that night, that phrase repeated over and over in his mind — "You know, you haven't got a friend in the world." The next few days at work it continued to eat at him, and he would purposely go out of his way to pause if someone was working near him and he would strike up a conversation with them. He would ask questions about their families and try to act concerned. He really wanted to know about this friendship thing. Finally one night he decided to break down and ask Jeanie about the neighbors.

"So have you been talking to the neighbor anymore?" Jeanie immediately felt as though she had to be on the defensive. Coming from Ralph, a question like that could be a lead-in to an argument. Jeanie's mind was racing trying to think, *was there something I was supposed to do today that I didn't get done and he thinks I was out visiting?*

"No, I haven't seen her in awhile. Why do you ask?" Jeanie made an effort to keep her tone calm and detached so as not to stir up trouble.

"No reason; just thought you wanted to get together with them." Ralph spoke with the same calm tone of detachment, which baffled Jeanie considerably. *Is this a new technique he's using on me?* She had become very accustomed to second-guessing his moods.

"Well, I did want to get together with them at one time, but you said you were too busy and didn't have time for chit-chatting, remember?"

"Well, I've got most of my work caught up, so if you want, we could meet with them sometime. As long as it doesn't become a habit." Jeanie was not one to let an opportunity that falls into her lap pass by, even though she was filled with curiosity as to why the sudden interest in meeting the neighbors.

"What night do you want me to see if they are available?"

"Friday or Saturday is fine with me, whatever suits you guys, but just a visit, no meal."

"Ok, I'll ask Bonnie." Ralph turns and heads for the TV and sits down for the evening. Jeanie has no idea what's going on in his head, and knows enough not to ask questions. Ralph had been so engrossed in his TV program that he hadn't heard Jeanie talking to Bonnie on the phone. A little while later Jeanie came into the room and said, "I just got off the phone with Bonnie, and she said Saturday night would be better for them."

"Fine, they're coming over here, right?"

"Yes, at 7:00."

"OK, I'm watching something now." Ralph turned up the volume on the TV and Jeanie left the room, mad at Ralph but excited that she had company coming on Saturday. By Saturday Jeanie had the house all cleaned up and ready to entertain the new neighbors. Right at 7:00 there was a knock on the back door. Ralph and Jeanie both went to the door to greet them, and the girls introduced their husbands. They went to the living room to sit down, and Jeanie called for the children to come out of their rooms and to meet Mike and Bonnie Hudock. Mike and Bonnie were great with the children and talked with them for quite some time. Mike was really interested to learn that Rodney had just started piano lessons, and he wanted to know what he had learned so far; with a little coaxing from his mother, Rod (what he preferred to be called) sat down at the piano and played some of the beginning things he had learned. Mike and Bonnie both encouraged him by telling him they thought he had natural talent. The children went back to their rooms and the adults went back into the living room and talked. They spent this first visit just learning more about each other, talking about things like, where they grew up, where they went to school, their work, and hobbies. Mike was a very easy guy for Ralph to talk to and Jeanie could see that Ralph was enjoying himself talking with him. The only problem was that the guys started talking and the girls had a conversation going of their own, and Jeanie wanted to hear both. This was a good thing, but Jeanie wanted to know what they were talking about because if she had to ask Ralph after they left, he would probably say "nothing much" and just walk away.

Jeanie invited everyone into the dining room for snacks, and the kids heard the word 'snacks' and came running too. To Jeanie the night seemed to go well. But time would tell if Ralph had enjoyed himself.

After the neighbors had gone home, Jeanie started to clean up and Ralph headed for the TV. She was dying to know what his impressions were, but she knew if she asked him he would give some smart remark. *Besides,* she thought, *he just wants me to ask him so he can say something like, "well I'm glad that's over with." It looked like he was having a good time,* she thought, but she knew from past experience that Ralph was a great faker; he could put on a good face until everyone was gone, and then he would blow up saying how rotten a time he had. What happened next floored her. Ralph returned to the kitchen and went to the fridge to get a beer, and then he leaned against the counter and said, "That was fun; we'll have to get together with them again sometime."

Jeanie looked directly into his eyes when he said that to make sure he wasn't being sarcastic or something. But he looked totally sincere when he said it.

"I thought so to, and we probably will. I'm glad you had fun, Ralph."

Jeanie thought, *OK, now I've made myself vulnerable for his witty comeback, and it will be something like, "I was only kidding, I was bored out of my mind and we are never doing that again."* She busied herself around the kitchen, but he just got his beer and left the room. Jeanie let out a huge sigh of relief.

As the days went by the year was drawing to a close and the Hudocks had invited Ralph, Jeanie, and the children over to visit one evening. Jeanie was amazed because Ralph couldn't wait to go. This was a first, no kicking and screaming; he just said, "When?" The visit was great, and Mike had fun showing Rod his guitar, which he played really loud. He also showed Ralph what he intended to do to the house and asked for Ralph's advice. Once again the evening went really well. There was one time when Ralph asked Mike about a term he had mentioned that he didn't understand. Mike had said that he belonged to the Navigators. Ralph said, "What are the Navigators?" Mike was a pretty intellectual fellow; he was great at reading people and a master at knowing how much to say and when not to say something. So he just gave Ralph a very simple answer: that the Navigators are a ministry for spreading the Gospel.

At this point Jeanie was all ears, thinking with dread, *OK, this is the end of our friendship with these neighbors.* But then Ralph asked Mike, "So, are you a minister or something?"

"No, I'm just a regular guy."

At that point Bonnie asked, "Would anyone like some cookies and ice cream?" Jeanie followed her lead and said, "Let me help you!" as they both headed for the kitchen. There was never any mention from Ralph about Mike being a Navigator when they got home or in the days to follow. The winter found Ralph feeling a little bored with no barn or animals to run to and take care of, so he decided he needed a new project to keep himself busy. He really did miss not having a barn and a shop area. His plan was to build one, but not during the winter. He decided he needed to work on an indoor construction project during the winter, and since the house had a two-car garage attached to it, he decided he would turn the garage into a great room with an all-wood cathedral ceiling. Without any notice he started his project, and by spring there was a beautiful and very large room added to their home.

In the spring Ralph and Jeanie decided to put in a pool, so they found a local contractor who installed pools and hired him to do the job.

Ralph always scanned the paper looking for properties or homes to fix up. On this particular day he came across a mini farm for sale in Benton, Pennsylvania. He went into the house and got the map out to see where Benton was. After locating it on the map, he showed Jeanie the ad and said, "Do you feel like going for a ride?"

Her response was. "What, are you crazy?"

"No. I really would like to see this place. We've always talked about having a small farm when we retire, so let's go look at this one now."

"Ok" she said, knowing there was no other answer to give him when he got an idea in his mind. As she was breaking the news to the children, Ralph called the number to see if they could look at the property today. The man who owned the property said, "Sure, when will you be here?"

Ralph replied, "I'm not really sure how long it takes to get there. But we live in New Jersey and we'll be leaving shortly."

The man said, "That's fine, just come to where I live and then I'll take you to the farm." Then he proceeded to give Ralph the directions to his home.

The trip took two hours to make, and the directions were very good. The man came out as soon as he saw a car pull in with New Jersey plates on it. He introduced himself to Ralph and Jeanie, and then he told them it would be about a four-mile drive to the farm, and to just follow him. The area was absolutely gorgeous, and it reminded Ralph of the valley he had grown up in when he was a child. It wasn't long before they were turning right into a long dirt lane. What they saw was just what they were looking for. There were sloping fields on either side of the lane, and the right side was lined with trees and had an old barn at the bottom of the drive; the left side had a pond at the bottom with a two-story home sitting behind it. Farther down the property, behind the house and the barn, there were two very large fields divided by a tree line. As they came to a stop at the end of the drive next to the house, Ralph told them all not to act too excited. But as they piled out of the car Ralph shocked everyone and broke his own rule immediately. "Wow, this is great! Why on earth are you selling this property?" Jeanie was thinking the price of the property probably just went up by $10,000.00 because of Ralph's excitement.

"Well, I really didn't want to. You see, it actually belongs to my parents, but they can no longer take care of a place this size. We just moved them into a retirement home and need to sell the property. By the way, my name's John," he said, as he extended his hand to give Ralph a handshake.

"Nice to meet you, John. That's too bad they have to sell, because this is a nice place." Jeanie wanted to kick Ralph because she figured the price had just gone up again.

"Why don't you folks just look around? I'll open the house for you. I'm going to be in the barn with my horses. If you have any questions just holler and please take your time."

"Ok, thank you, that sounds great," Ralph still had a hard time keeping the excitement out of his voice.

As they walked around the house Jeanie said, "I thought you said not to act excited."

"What, was I acting excited?"

"Kids, was Dad acting excited?"

"Oh, I couldn't tell … but I'd say he was excited a little … too much!" Rod said, and they all had a good laugh over his perfect comedic timing.

"Well I can't help it, it's everything I've ever dreamed of," Ralph replied, surprising his family with the wistful tone in his voice. They spent over an hour looking around and exploring the place and were unanimous in their decision to buy the farm. They found John and asked him about all the particulars, and within a half hour they had settled on a price and date for the closing. They drove down to John's house, signed some papers, gave him a deposit, and started for home. The kids immediately started to sing, "Old Mac Walls Had a Farm," so Ralph thought they should celebrate by stopping at McDonald's to eat, which was followed by loud cheers.

* * * * *

That summer in Alexandria Township, Karla had felt lead by the Lord to go to the mission field with a group of teens. Her best friend Sharon also felt the call to the mission field, so the two of them joined a group of teens going to Honduras. Before they could go, however, they had to spend two weeks training in Merritt Island, Florida (the Lord's Boot Camp). There they learned to live in tents, bathe in ponds, lay block, and run an obstacle coarse, as well as many other things that would help them on the field in Honduras. The only time their parents were allowed to see them was at their commissioning service when their training was completed. There were thirty-two teens that completed the training and headed for the eight weeks of service in Central America.

Once they arrived in the field their first task was to set up their own shelter. During the next seven weeks they built a schoolhouse for pastors from the ground up. The work was hard but very rewarding. During their time there the girls were blessed in many ways; they had experienced answers to many prayers and saw the hand of God at work. They found it to be a time of real spiritual growth and it would impact the rest of their lives. After seven weeks of work they were given a week of relaxation in the capital city of Tgucalpa. Back at home four parents were anxiously waiting for the return of their daughters so they could hear all about their trip. Karla wasn't home more then two days when she had to start her junior year at Lancaster Mennonite High. Mike was starting eighth grade at Plumstead and always busy with something. The children seemed to be growing up so fast.

* * * * *

The pool was a much-needed addition to Ralph and Jeanie's property, and the kids put it to good use. Whenever they could chase the kids out, the adults got their turn and had just as much fun horsing around. Ralph was really enjoying Mike and Bonnie as neighbors and would often just stop and chat with Mike as they passed each other on their riding mowers. This was the same guy, who, not too long ago, had thought chitchatting was a waste of time. If Jeanie teased him about it, however, he would say, "It's different with Mike; we're not chit-chatting."

The one thing Ralph had noticed though was that every Sunday morning Mike and Bonnie left to go to church, and he didn't think they seemed like what he'd pictured church people to be like. Anyway, Ralph was occupied on almost every other weekend with the farmhouse. Now that they owned it they had been going up on Friday nights and coming home on Sunday afternoons. With the help of his brother, Glenn, they had been loading up their trucks on Friday evening with building supplies and driving up to Benton, where they started the remodeling process of the house. They usually got there in time to go to bed, and then they would work all day Saturday, play a little on Sunday, and then head home later in the afternoon. They had been keeping quite a hectic schedule all summer, so in August Ralph and Jeanie took the kids to Disney World, another first for Ralph, and they all had a great time.

When they got back home from vacation the new school year was about to begin. Jeanie had noticed that Ralph was not being as strict with her "running around" since she had started to work, so she thought she would test the waters a little bit by taking the kids to Sunday school. Her mother had been after her for some time to take the kids to church, but she always told her that Ralph would have a fit. This was the Sunday she was going to start. Ralph had plenty to do outside, so he was out the door early. While Ralph was on the riding mower out back he saw her and the children getting into the car and leaving, so he just waved, thinking they were probably going shopping or something. By the second week he had them figured out but he thought, *Who cares?*

November had brought an end to all the outside work around the house; all the lawn and garden equipment had been put away. Trips to the farm had changed to Friday nights and back home Saturday evening. Ralph had been putting in long days at work and was getting pretty tired, so having nothing to do on Sunday felt good for a change.

12

NEW LIFE

The friendship with Mike and Bonnie had really grown and they had been spending a lot of time together. One day when Ralph came home from work, Jeanie informed him that she had invited Mike and Bonnie to come over that evening after dinner. Ralph had no problem with that at all. He actually thought that would be fun. With dinner over and the dishes put away, the knock on the door meant that they had arrived. After exchanging greetings they headed into the living room and sat down. Right from the first time Ralph had met Mike and Bonnie he had felt very comfortable around them, so just sitting and talking wasn't threatening to him. Mike always had a way with words that could hold your interest, and Ralph enjoyed the back and forth dialogues he shared with him. They had arrived at about 8:00 that evening and everyone was just having fun talking about everything under the sun.

They had been there about an hour when Mike asked Jeanie about her faith. Mike already knew that she had been raised in a Mennonite family, and this change in subject was something that Ralph didn't really want to have. In his mind Ralph thought, *Heck, I went to church and Sunday school as a child and had all those perfect attendance bars that I wore so proudly on my jacket, so this shouldn't be too bad for a little while.* They talked about the Mennonite faith for about half an hour, and then they started to talk about the Bible and Scripture verses. Ralph felt confident that he could join in, because he knew the 23rd Psalm and the 100th Psalm by heart, but as he sat there looking for an opening to join in, it became apparent he didn't have a clue what they were talking about. They started to use words like Justification, Grace, Mercy, Saved, Born Again, and Rapture. Ralph sat there wondering what Bible they were talking about. He had never heard any of those terms before, so until 11:30 that night he just sat there listening. A couple of minutes later Bonnie looked at her watch said, "Mike, we've got to get going."

"Oh, you're right, I didn't realize how late it had gotten to be," he replied apologetically.

Goodbyes were said and their neighbors went home. Jeanie had sensed all night Ralph's quietness and figured this was going to be a bad night once they were alone. After locking the door and waiting for Mike and Bonnie to get closer to their own home, Ralph turned off the light and headed down the hall. He was totally embarrassed by what had just occurred in the last three hours, but he wasn't about to let Jeanie know. Jeanie was now getting ready for bed and expecting Ralph to have one of his rages at any moment. When Ralph finally came to bed and leaned over to kiss her goodnight, she was somewhat shocked. *This is not normal,* she thought. *What is going on with him? Is he up to something and is going to get even with me tomorrow?* Just then her thoughts were interrupted by Ralph's voice saying calmly, "That was fun; we need to do that again."

"Yes ... it was fun," Jeanie answered hesitantly, assuming that was his attempt at a sarcastic remark and the punch line would come next. But to her surprise, the next thing she knew he was rolling over on his side and sleeping. Actually,

Ralph was wide awake, wondering how he could learn what they'd been talking about that night so the next time he could participate in the conversation.

Jeanie had been taking Stephanie and Rodney to Sunday school in Clinton for about a month now without any objections from Ralph; he had been acting like he just didn't care. Ralph was usually pretty busy on Sundays with grass cutting and garden work, so Jeanie would just slip out of the house with the kids, trying not to draw too much attention to herself. What happened next was a complete shocker to her. He actually asked her if she was going to take the kids to church today or not. At first she didn't know what to say, wondering, *is this a trick question?*

She answered carefully, "Well … I was planning to."

"Oh, good" came Ralph's reply, which totally stunned her. Jeanie's thoughts went through the usual litany of questions as she tried to second-guess Ralph's motives. *Now what is he up to? Is he trying to get us out of the house because he's up to no good, or is he planning on starting another building project while we are out? I just bet that's what he is up to and when I come home there will a big mess to contend with.* But she didn't respond, figuring it was best not to push the issue.

Ralph went outside and made himself look busy, but the whole time he kept his eye on the back door waiting for Jeanie and the children to leave. It wasn't long and they came out the door and headed for the car. The car was barely out of sight when Ralph was heading for the house. He went straight to the living room and turned on the TV, then ran back to the window to make sure Jeanie hadn't forgotten anything and had turned back. After taking one more quick look outside, he settled in front of the TV. He had looked in the TV guide earlier when no one was around to find the times of the programs he wanted to watch. Perfect timing, he thought, they just finished the singing and the preacher is about to speak. He had decided that he was going to find out what all this stuff meant that Jeanie, Bonnie, and Mike were talking about the other night. He didn't like feeling left out of a conversation. Well, the TV church service just sounded like the same old stuff he had heard sitting in church with his parents when he was little, but he stuck it out and listened to the end. The program ended with some sales pitches so Ralph left the TV on and headed to the bathroom.

When he came back to the living room to turn off the TV, another Christian program was coming on. Knowing that Jeanie and the kids would be gone for about two and a half hours, he figured he could squeeze in another program. This time he found it a little more interesting and was really starting to enjoy it, but then it ended. Ralph looked at his watch and thought, *they have been gone about one hour and forty-five minutes, I could probably catch one more but it would be tight. The ride alone to the Baptist Church in Clinton would take at least thirty minutes. Plus she never goes out and wastes a trip without stopping to pick up some necessary food items.*

Again Ralph found another Christian program and watched right to the end, just in time to hear the car doors slamming and voices talking. He quickly turned the TV off and ran to the sink acting like he had just come in for a drink. Jeanie and the children came in carrying bags of groceries just like Ralph had thought.

"Sorry I'm late, Ralph. I'll have dinner ready real soon, OK?"

"Take your time, I'm in no hurry," Ralph responded pleasantly, as he headed out the back door. Jeanie and the children just stood there staring at one another, baffled because this wasn't the usual response he would give. Usually he would be saying something like, "Well, it's about time you got home; I'm starved! What have you been doing, out ramming the roads all day?"

Jeanie then said to the children, "Go check your rooms and the rest of the house and see if he made a mess or something."

Stephanie was always the first to see if she could spot something out of place, but she quickly returned and reported dutifully.

"Everything looks fine, Mommy"

"He wasn't in my room," came Rodney's reply.

Ralph kept this whole routine up for about two months; he even dug out his old King James Bible, but he found it to be too hard to follow. He kept hearing this word 'salvation.' *So what is this salvation they are talking about? They keep referring to this Bible verse, John 3:16: "For God so loved the world that he gave His only begotten Son, that whoever believes in Him should not perish but have everlasting life" (NKJV).*

A few things Ralph knew for certain. He had always believed there was a God and that He had a Son named Jesus; He had learned all that years ago in Sunday school. But the other part had him baffled: "whoever believes in Him should not perish but have everlasting life" *What's that all about?* Ralph wondered. *I believed that God's Son's name is Jesus, so does that mean I will live forever?* He thought. *That doesn't make sense.* But after listening to what they were saying, he discovered that God sent His Son to die on the cross for Ralph's sins, and there was more; not only did He die for his sins, but the sins of the whole world. Then the TV preacher explained that this was a gift from God and was only available to those who trust in Jesus Christ's sacrifice on the cross, and that doing so brings eternal life, as well as peace and joy while here on earth. Ralph needed to hear more about this. *How could one person pay the price for the sins of the whole world? Besides, what are they calling sin in the first place?*

Ralph remembered the Ten Commandments; he already knew how much he loved the movie, so then he thought, *maybe I should look them up.* He remembered they had all those "Thou shalt nots" at the beginning of them, so he figured maybe those were the sins they are talking about. Then one of the preachers said there is no level of severity concerning sin; basically, sin was sin. Murder and gossip are both sins, and it only takes one sin to separate you from God. Then they said you are sinning even if your thoughts are bad. *I'm in big trouble*, Ralph thought. *I must be sinning all day long, and how am I supposed to stop that? I can't stop thinking.* (Ralph knew there would be those who jokingly said he never seemed to be thinking in the first place!). Then they went on to say that when you ask Jesus into your life, His Spirit comes to live inside of you to teach you and convict you of any sin in your life But as it is written:

"Eye has not seen, nor ear heard, nor have entered into the heart of man the things which God has prepared for those who love Him" But God has revealed them to us through His spirit. For the Spirit searches all things, yes the deep things of God. For what man knows the things of a man except the Spirit of the man that is in him? Even so no one knows the things of God except the Spirit of God now we have received, not the spirit of the world, but the Spirit that is from God, that we might know the things that have been freely given to us by God. These things we also speak, not in words which mans wisdom teaches but which the Holy Spirit teaches, comparing spiritual things with spiritual. "But the natural man does not receive the things of the Spirit of God, for they are foolishness to him; nor can he know them, because they are spiritually discerned. But He who is spiritual judges all things, yet He Himself is judged by no one. For "who has known the mind of the Lord that he may instruct Him? But we have the mind of Christ" (1 Corinthians 2:9-16, NKJV)

Ralph thought this was all pretty heavy stuff. And then the preachers went on to say , "When you are ready, He will draw you close to Him. He is waiting for you with open arms. Just ask Him into your heart." Ralph had a lot to digest and he could sense that something definitely was happening in his heart, but he didn't understand what it was. His inability to understand caused him to really start getting bolder now in his search for the truth. Sunday evenings while the family was in the house, he would watch a gospel program. His whole attitude had begun to change, and he would ask if there was anything Jeanie needed help with. Jeanie thought from the beginning that he had done something terribly wrong and was probably worried about it, and that if he was nice now she wouldn't be so mad whenever he broke the news to her.

Christmas and New Year's had come and gone and it was Sunday, January 11th, the day before Ralph's birthday. This was no different than all the Sundays of the last two and a half months. Jeanie got the kids ready and headed for Sunday school in Clinton. As soon as she was gone Ralph turned the TV on and to watch his regular programs. The first program had a powerful message that day that really grabbed Ralph's attention, and at the end they gave an invitation to all the viewers to ask the Lord into their hearts. They explained what this meant and said they would pray a prayer with everyone in a moment. One pastor looked into the camera and said, "If you're ready, truly ready, pray this prayer with us." It seemed as though he was talking straight to Ralph and no one else. Ralph remembered how he had prayed his prayers before bed when he was little, so he got on his knees in front of the TV and prayed along with the pastor. When the pastor had finished praying, he said, "Friend, if you have prayed that pray from your heart, then, welcome! You are a child of God. You belong to the family of God now."

Ralph sat there thinking, *I don't feel any different at all; it must not have worked for me.*

The second program came on and at the end of the program another invitation was given and a prayer for salvation was spoken, and once again Ralph got down on his knees in front of the TV and prayed the prayer. Again he thought, *this is too easy, there has to be more to this.* By now the third program was on, and lo and behold, at the end an invitation and prayer were given. In front of the TV, on his knees, once again he prayed something like this simple prayer:

"Father, I've come to a place in my life where I need You. I can't go on without You any longer. I know I've been lost and that I have done things in my life that have not been pleasing to You. Please forgive me for those things. I want to grow in the love and knowledge of You. Please come into my heart Lord and make me a new creature in You. Thank You, Lord, for hearing my prayer. Amen."

At the end of the prayer, still not feeling any bells, whistles, or fireworks go off, Ralph lifted his eyes upward and said out loud, "Lord, what am I doing wrong?"

And at that moment Ralph's entire life began flashing through his mind. The abuse that he had shown his wife and family for the last twelve years was running at full speed before his eyes, and with tears rolling down his face he exclaimed, "How will they ever forgive me?"

He felt physically shaken and totally drained, but most importantly, he knew he was saved! And when that assurance settled into his heart and mind, *then* he suddenly felt different.

He had asked Christ into his heart, so now he was what was referred to as born again. He barely had time to dry his tears and find something to do when his family returned home. The kids ran to their rooms to change their clothes, but they also ran to their rooms out of old habit, because it was always a good place to be in case their father was in one of his moods. Jeanie went to the kitchen figuring it wouldn't be long before she heard, "I'm starving, when can we eat?" As soon as Ralph got his face back in order he walked into the kitchen and said to Jeanie,

"Guess what I did today?"

Jeanie, who was standing with her back to him and while she was working at the counter preparing food, said, "I give up; what?"

"I asked the Lord into my heart today"

Jeanie never moved a muscle and just kept doing what she had been doing, and then she answered blandly, "Oh, that's nice."

Ralph could tell by the tone of her voice that she wasn't impressed or that she just didn't believe him at all. He had just asked the Lord how his family would ever forgive him, and he knew in his heart it was going to be a long, hard road ahead.

He continued, "But now I need a new Bible, because my old King James is too hard for me to understand."

The entire time this conversation was going on, Stephanie, who had been standing outside her bedroom door listening, turned and went back into her room. Then holding something in her hand she came running down the hall.

"Here, Daddy, you can have this." As she stretched out her hand Ralph could see this tiny, red Bible being handed to him.

"They gave me this in Sunday school, but you can have it, and it's really easy to read."

Now Ralph was a pretty tough guy and his family had never seen him cry, but it took every ounce of strength he had to fight back the tears. His throat had closed up so tight that he could hardly speak. The Bible was so small it looked lost in his hand, but to him this was a precious gift. As Stephanie turned and ran back to her room, Ralph managed to croak out the words, "Thank you, honey, thank you so much."

The little red Bible was just the New Testament, but that was all he needed as a brand-new baby Christian.

Jeanie never showed any emotion over his salvation experience, and Ralph figured he had to prove it to her, but she did tell Bonnie, who told Mike, who told the pastor at the Baptistown Baptist Church where they were members. The next day Ralph received a phone call from a pastor, Richard Kollmar, who asked if he could come over and talk to him. Ralph couldn't believe it, but he said sure, and they set a time on the following Saturday when they would meet. Saturday came quickly and a man came knocking on the back door of the house. He introduced himself as Dick Kollmar, pastor of the Baptist church. Ralph invited him in and they went into the family room to sit down.

Pastor Kollmar said, "I understand you just accepted Christ as your Savior?"

Ralph answered, "Yes, last Sunday"

"How about you tell me about that?" Ralph and the pastor talked for almost an hour, and when they had finished the pastor stood up and said, "I'd like to meet the rest of your family. Why don't you come visit us at our service tomorrow?"

Without hesitation Ralph answered, "I will, thank you." On January 11, 1980, Ralph had accepted Christ as his savoir, and eight days later on Stephanie's eleventh birthday, Ralph, Jeanie, Stephanie, and Rodney went to church for the first time together as a family.

* * * * *

Early in January Gid found his interest focused on a series of seminars in Florida being given by Jack Miller and John Schaub. The seminars caught his attention because of the phrase, "Making It Big With Little Deals." They were explaining how to buy homes with little or no money down.

Gid was thoroughly fascinated with the idea, and after attending a number of the lectures he thought Betty should listen to some of them also. Betty was still working full-time for BioServe in Frenchtown, so to attend these seminars meant going to Florida for the weekend, which they did. By the spring of 1980, Gid decided to give this method a try back in New Jersey. His first purchase was a multi-family home in Flemington, and he quickly had Betty and the children helping him with the maintenance, painting and cleaning, and so on, getting it spruced up to rent. In all he wound up with five multi-family homes to rent out in New Jersey.

This was quite an adventurous enterprise and it took up a lot of Betty and Gid's free time. With repairs and tenants coming and going, there was always plenty of work to do. Gid's flight schedule was a busy one that kept him on the go a lot, which left Betty juggling the new career of property manager. This new title didn't mean just sitting behind a desk, which she did as well, but it also meant cleaning, painting, scheduling repairs, collecting rents, and interviewing prospective new tenants, all of this on top of managing her own home, property, and family. The amazing thing about this scenario is that you would expect to see a very frazzled women if you ran into her, but on the contrary, Betty was always the picture of perfection, always quiet and well–mannered, and she always looked like she had just stepped out of a magazine ad — that is, unless she was painting.

Karla was in her senior year at Lancaster Mennonite High School and Mike was in his freshman year at Plumsteadville Christian Academy. Since Karla was living away from home for school, this meant she couldn't help with the rental properties on the weekends, which left Mike and his mother to do whatever work had to be done with them. The rental business was really exciting to Gid, and he couldn't wait to expand it even more. His idea was for this business to be their nest egg, eventually leading to an early retirement. He wanted to be able to travel the world and show his family all there was to see, and he believed these rentals were the key to his dreams.

* * * * *

The drive to church only took fifteen minutes, but for Ralph it seemed to take forever on that morning in January, his first time going to church as a new Christian. His mind was racing with questions. He hadn't gone to church or Sunday school for about twenty-five years. He really felt inadequate in Bible knowledge, but he knew it had felt right when he had asked Christ into his heart. When they pulled into the driveway of the church, they parked the car and waited for a while to see where everyone was going in. Then they left the car and headed for the building.

Mike and Bonnie were there to meet them at the door and took them to the church office so they could find out what classrooms the children should go to. After the children were taken care of, the four adults went to an adult Sunday school class where they were welcomed by so many people, too many to remember. This was an entirely new experience for Ralph, but he noticed with a great sense of relief that he felt totally at ease around them all. After class was over they just followed the crowd to the sanctuary, picking up the children on the way. The children were very talkative and excited because they already knew some of the other children from school. Ralph thought the service was great, and he couldn't stop talking about it all the way home. The children were each trying to tell about their new friends, and Jeanie seemed very interested in everything they were saying.

The following weeks were filled with excitement for Ralph. He had been going to work early every morning and sitting in the truck reading the little red Bible. He read it from cover to cover again and again and each time would discover something new that spoke to his heart. Now all he wanted to do was be at the church all the time. He even started to go to prayer meetings on Thursday evenings. They would start out with a Bible study then go to prayer. The prayer part was a little new to him, and he didn't really know how to start. For the first few times he just listened and prayed silently, but it wasn't long before he ventured forth with some short two- or three-sentence prayers. He soon learned that prayer is the way God communicates with us. We have an open line of communication to God through Jesus Christ. This communication works both ways: not only can we speak to Him, but also if we listen, He will speak to us through His Holy Spirit. Our speaking should be in response to what the Holy Spirit is convicting us about. There is so much to learn about prayer, and the Bible has so much in the scriptures that can teach us. Some of the helpful places for Ralph were found in these verses: Matthew 6:9-13; John 14:13; Luke 11:5-9; 1 Timothy 2:1-4; and Hebrews 4:16.

On the job Ralph was getting a lot of flak from the men he had worked with for years. He wasn't afraid to let them know he didn't like it when someone used the Lord's name in vain. He always told them he found it offensive and that using the Lord's name as a curse word wasn't acceptable. They would usually respond by saying they didn't mean it as a curse word, and that it was just an expression. Ralph would respond, "It's still wrong." And then he would quote to them from Exodus 20:7: "You shall not take the name of the Lord your God in vain, for the Lord will not hold him guiltless who takes His name in vain." Then at lunchtime Ralph would bow his head inconspicuously and silently give thanks for his food. There would naturally be someone close by who would catch a glimpse and start yelling,

"Hey, bless this," or "hey, holy-roller," or "hey, preacher man!"

There were plenty of jokes at his expense, but he would just let them slide by. When he was offered a beer and refused, someone would always say this would never last, especially when Ralph told them he had dumped all his beer and liquor down the drain. Then when he told them he'd stopped smoking his box of cigars cold turkey, they would just throw up their hands and walk away. Sometimes, though, his changed behavior did lead to some of them asking questions, which gave Ralph an opportunity to share Christ with them. This was all new to him, and lots of times he would have to say, "I don't know the answer to that, but I'll try to find out for you."

Even if he never saw that person again, he loved the challenge of researching the question in search of the answer, or if he had to, asking the pastor for help.

One day Ralph had just started a new job on the home of a young married couple. They had just built an addition onto their house and had hired Ralph to do the drywall. The house was an older home, and they had added new bedrooms to the upstairs. When Ralph arrived on the job that morning, they hadn't left for work yet, as it was still pretty early, so they all took some time to talk. Gary was an insurance salesman and his wife, Gayle, who was pregnant, was in her last days of employment due to the upcoming birth of their baby. Now Ralph, being a new believer, was always eager to share about his faith. He asked them if they went to church, and they began to tell him they had a little problem. One of them was Jewish and the other was Catholic, and their families were in turmoil over how the new baby would be raised. One family wanted the child raised Jewish and the other naturally wanted it raised Catholic. Ralph thought to himself, *what I have gotten myself into now*. They went on to say they just didn't know what to do. They didn't want to hurt either family any more then they already had. Then Ralph blurted out, "Just come to the Baptist Church where I go; it's neither

Jewish nor Catholic, and everyone is welcome there!" They just smiled politely and said they were running late for work and had to leave.

So they left and Ralph went upstairs to work. The rest of the time while he worked there he was burdened by the helplessness they were feeling. As he was working, the impression that he should tell them about Christ was overwhelming him. Before he knew what he was doing, he was looking for something to write on. The only thing he could find was the tape that he used for spackling. It was only two inches wide, so he tore off a two-foot piece and wrote about the love of Christ on it. He explained about salvation. Then he wrote, *Gary you're an insurance salesman, I want to tell you about the greatest insurance policy there will ever be written. It's an eternal life policy, and the best thing about this policy is that it's free to you — that's right, free to you! This policy has already been paid for, in full, by Jesus Christ. He went to the cross and paid the price for our sins. All we have to do is accept His free gift of salvation. Gary and Gayle, I'm giving you this Bible. It's all I have right now, but I'll get you a better one soon. Your friend, Ralph.*

Ralph ran out to the truck and brought in the little red Bible from the dashboard. Then he put the note and the Bible on the kitchen counter. After that he picked up his tools and headed for home. All the way home he thought about what he had done. First he had given away his precious little Bible, and secondly, he knew he had to go back there tomorrow and face them. The next morning as he pulled into their driveway, he was a nervous wreck. But when he walked up to the door and knocked, a voice yelled out, "its open, come on in!"

The buckets of spackling compound that Ralph was going to use upstairs were sitting in the dining room directly across from the kitchen, so he had to stop there to mix up the compound. As he was mixing he could hear Gayle saying to Gary, "Go ahead — tell him"

Then he heard Gary's voice coming from behind him, saying, "Ralph, we just want to say thank you for the Bible and for what you wrote. That was the nicest gift anyone has ever given us."

Then they left very quickly and Ralph went upstairs to try to work, but his hands were shaking too much. He just looked up and said, "Thank you, Lord." But he had one more thing he needed to know. Where was the little red Bible? He opened the door to their bedroom, and there it was lying on the nightstand next to their bed. He felt a little sad that he had given away the Bible that his daughter had given him, but he was excited that someone else who needed it had it now. That Sunday in church they sang the praise song, "Pass It On." It seemed like confirmation to Ralph that God wants us to do this, to just pass it on. God's Word is too great a gift to keep all to ourselves; it needs to be shared, and we need to keep passing it on. We will never be too new or too old a believer to share God's Word with someone. If we truly love our Lord and Savior, it is our honor to share it with those who don't know of His amazing love for us.

Friendships were starting to form now for Ralph. He had never had any close relationships with other men before, but now with his brothers in faith, he felt that special bond of friendship that had been lacking in his life. One particular man became a special friend to Ralph in his new walk of faith; his name was Gene Hale. Gene owned the local hardware store in Frenchtown, and Ralph would often stop in at the end of the day to chat and sometimes ask for advice. Gene was an elder in the church. He and his wife, Debbie, had four daughters, Marcy, Emily, Colleen, and Elizabeth. Gene was a good Christian man who was not ashamed to share his faith with those he came in contact with. Mark 8:38 says: "For whoever is ashamed of Me and My words in this adulterous and sinful generation, of him the Son of Man also will be ashamed when He comes in the glory of His Father with the Holy Angels." (NKJV)

One day Ralph stopped in to see Gene concerning a problem that was weighing heavily on his heart. When he had first walked up to the counter and begun telling Gene about it, the store had been empty. After hearing Ralph's concern, Gene immediately said, "Let's take it to the Lord in prayer," and he began to pray right there and then. Ralph was still relatively new at this type of thing. Actually this was a first for him, praying in a public place of business, but Gene continued. Not too long into the prayer Ralph could hear the footsteps of others behind him, and he began to feel nervous and embarrassed. When Gene had finished, he said, "Amen."

Ralph said, "Thank you," and stepped aside. As he did he noticed that three people were standing in line behind him. No one said a word; they all took their turns checking out, and some even looked at Ralph and smiled. Gene Hale became the standard of a Christian man in Ralph's life. Not only did he talk it, but he lived it also. Gene was a very humble man and who was also very generous in the giving of his time. If ever someone had a need, Gene would usually go the extra mile to help out.

Two times a year the church held a work night or a work weekend, where the members would come to the church and help with the maintenance of the buildings and grounds. Having always been a hard worker, Ralph asked if he could help in any way. "Of course, everybody can help," came the response. So this particular evening he showed up ready to do his part, and he quickly joined in the activities. One of the jobs they were doing was stripping the floors and putting down a new coat of wax. The man who seemed to be in charged was named Dick Emmons. Ralph quickly noticed that Dick was a very meticulous worker, but loved to have fun with all the other men working there. Dick always had a smile on his face, and when he was around there was always a lot of laughter. Dick once said, "Just because you're a Christian doesn't mean you can't have fun."

Another man caught Ralph's attention that first night. His name was Steven Zedepski. Steve was an older gentleman who had been in the construction business too. Steve was in a class by himself. Now in his retirement he did fine woodworking, making things like grandfather clocks, chairs, cabinets, and jewelry boxes. He was out of Ralph's league, but the interesting thing about Steve was that he was a teacher, and he would share his knowledge on woodworking with anyone who wanted to know. Steve not only taught how to work with your hands, but he was a godly teacher as well. He wasn't afraid to pass on his wisdom of the Scriptures, either. On this particular work night Ralph was busy working in the kitchen when the pastor came in and said, "Ralph, I'd like you to meet someone."

"Ralph, this is Jeff DeRoche."

"Jeff, this is Ralph Walls."

They shook hands and greeted each other.

"Ralph, Jeff just became a new believer like you." Then he began to explain how Jeff was working for the road department but having a hard time practicing his faith with the working conditions there. The swearing, dirty jokes, and drinking were taking a toll on his new faith, and he was looking for new employment. Then he asked Ralph, "You wouldn't be looking for any help, now would you?" Actually, the pastor already knew Ralph was looking to hire some workers, because they had talked about that just a week ago.

"Yes, as a matter of fact I am" Ralph responded. Then the pastor tried to move them closer together so they could talk, but soon realized he wasn't moving Jeff. Jeff was quite an imposing figure, and he was built like a linebacker. He stood about six foot three and probably weighed in at about two hundred fifty pounds. The only way Jeff was going to move was when he wanted to. Ralph and Jeff spent a lot of time talking that night, and by the end of the evening Ralph had a new friend and work partner and Jeff had a new job. The thing that Ralph would soon discover about Jeff was that his heart was the biggest part of him.

There was one more person whom Ralph met that night, but it was just a passing introduction. This one particular blonde-haired lady had been scurrying around there all night, carrying a ladder, a paint pail, and a brush. As she was about to pass him in the hall she stopped, put out her hand and said, "Hi, I'm Betty Miller, I was meaning to say hi earlier but I didn't get the chance."

"Hi, I'm Ralph Walls; it's nice to meet you." It was the end of the night, so she had to run and clean up her tools.

Within a couple of weeks Ralph and Jeff were hanging drywall together on a job in Flemington.

Jeanie was still working at the dental office and really enjoying it. Drew and Mary Ellen had become more then just employers; they were really good friends. Life at home was much improved, but Jeanie wasn't quite sure how long this new Ralph would last. But for now the yelling, fighting, and crazy demands that Ralph had put on his family had stopped, and everyone was quietly thankful for this. As the weeks went on, though, the one thing that bothered Jeanie the most was that the people at church just didn't know the old Ralph. They didn't have any idea what she had put up with for the last twelve years. All they could see was this wonderful man that they were so impressed with. *They haven't lived with him and felt the hurt and pain that he's inflicted like I have done*, she thought. Jeanie was filled with bitterness over this but she covered it up. She decided that she would do her best to put on a happy face and be polite.

Easter was approaching and the pastor asked Ralph if he was ready to be baptized. Ralph asked what all that involved.

The Billy Graham Training Center Bible NKJV says this: "Baptism represents what God has done through Christ on your behalf. Jesus Christ paid the penalty for your sins by dying on the cross and rising from the dead. When you are baptized in the name of the Lord, you publicly acknowledge that you are sinful and have accepted Christ as Lord and Savior (Acts 2:38; 8:16; 10:48). Baptism publicly signifies you're cleansed from sin, and it sets you apart for service to Christ. (Matthew 10:32, 33.)

Through baptism, you are identified with Christ. Though baptism is important to the Christian faith, it is not a means of salvation. Only acceptance of Christ's sacrificial death can save you. Baptism, however, is symbolic of your new life in Christ — washed clean from your sin by Jesus' death on the cross. "Or do you not know that as many of us as were baptized into Christ Jesus were baptized into His death? Therefore we were buried with Him through baptism into death, that just as Christ was raised from the dead by the glory of the Father, even so we also should walk in newness of life" (Romans 6:3, 4). The act of baptism represents the death of your sinful nature and the new life you have in Christ. Jesus Christ is honored when you obey Him and show this public acknowledgement of your faith in Him."

Easter morning was overcast, and Ralph was a little fearful of being up in front of the church and standing in a tub of water in the baptistery. Ralph had never even seen a baptism before; he had seen the sprinkling kind, but not the full blown dunking. In school he would turn ten shades of red if he had to stand in front of the class to give a book report, and then he would always say it had taken years off his life. Now at the age of thirty-four he was about to be baptized in front of a whole church full of people, plus his wife and children were watching. The time in the service for the baptisms had come, and Ralph had been waiting in an area behind the pulpit. The door opened and elder Frank Dalrumple took him by the arm and led him to the baptistery where pastor Kollmar was standing waist deep in water. He reached out his hand to help Ralph down into the water. Then he turned to the congregation and spoke for a little while explaining baptism. Above the baptistery there was a skylight, and after asking Ralph if he had accepted Christ as his Savior, he leaned him back. As Ralph was going down into the water he could see the clouds passing overhead through the skylight. Then as he was lifted out of the water the sun broke through the clouds and the rays shown directly on him in the baptistery. Then the pastor turned to Ralph and asked him if he would like to give a testimony (say something about his salvation experience). Ralph, as we stated before wasn't a public speaker, and now he was standing there soaking wet with a spotlight from the heavenlies shining down on him. Believe it or not, he moved to the front of the baptistery and spoke without hesitation. It wasn't long, maybe ten sentences, but all fear was gone and he wasn't ashamed to confess his trust and faith in the Lord. Frank came over and yanked him out of the water, and with his suit and tie on gave Ralph the biggest hug he had ever received from a man in his life. Frank was a contractor who had became one of Ralph's dearest friends. After the service when everyone was greeting one another, Jeff came up to Ralph and said, "I've got to tell them not to dump the water out, because I want to be baptized next week." And so he was – but they did give him fresh water!

Summer was coming and the kids had lots of new friends. All their friends at church were talking about going to camp. The camp was Spruce Lake Retreat and Conference Center and had been recommended by Gid and Betty Miller. While at church one day Jeanie and Betty had met one another and soon discovered that they were both from a Mennonite background. Then they discovered that they were also distant relatives. Jeanie couldn't wait to tell Ralph.

"You won't believe this, Ralph, I met this lady at church today and we are related."

"Really, who is it?'

"Her name is Betty Miller."

"You have to be kidding; I met her at work night. She was scurrying around carrying paint pails and a ladder as I recall!"

"You never told me about her."

"No, I guess I didn't, probably because it was right before everyone was going home, and we just passed in the hallway as we were putting away our supplies. She just quickly stopped and introduced herself. I guess I forgot to tell you because it was such a quick introduction.""Well anyway, her husband is a pilot and they live on Tinsman Road. She told me to stop over sometime."

"That's great, Jeanie."

"She is also the one who recommended the camp for the kids; she said they have a wilderness camp for them. So I think we should send them."

"Sounds good to me."

That summer Ralph and Jeanie helped take a group of children to the Spruce Lake Camp. The following week when they went to pick them up, Stephanie and Rodney told them they had asked Christ into their hearts. The ride home was filled with nonstop chatter, with all the kids sharing their stories at the same time. One of the kids would start telling a story, and then someone else would interrupt and tell their version. It was obvious that they all had a great time. A total of thirteen children from the church accepted Christ as their Savior that week at the camp.

Each year in the fall the church held a special service for giving thanks. It was always held the night before Thanksgiving. It was a totally unprepared service; in other words, you came in and sat down, and if you wanted to give thanks for something the Lord blessed you with, you would stand up and share it. After you spoke you could select a hymn that was meaningful to you, and everyone would sing it. The service would usually run about an hour, or until there was no more sharing. Ralph had so much to be thankful for, but he was a little nervous about standing and sharing. He kept looking at his watch and realizing that the time was flying by, and if he didn't stand up soon it would be over and then he would probably regret it forever. Finally he stood and began to speak.

"I have so much to be thankful for this year. First of all I want to thank God for loving me so much that He sent His Son to die for me. I truly find it amazing that someone could care for a wretch like me. I thank God for being patient in waiting for me, and that's something I need to learn, patience. Most of all I want to thank God for my wife and children who put up with me for so many years. I want to publicly tell them that I love them and that they mean so much to me. Thank you, Lord." Ralph picked his favorite hymn, *Pass it On*, and sat down. Before he sat down he glanced at his family; Jeanie just had a blank look on her face, Stephanie gave a quick smile, and Rodney was looking around the church. Ralph felt peace within himself after sitting down, not a proud feeling, but a feeling of being truly thankful to God for even being able to acknowledge Him publicly. Jeanie, however, was having deep feelings of bitterness over the whole thing. She sat there fuming, *how could a loving and just God allow Ralph to come in here and say all those things in front of these people? What about what I've been through for twelve years? They haven't any idea what he was like. All they see now is this man telling everyone how much he loves God and his family. It just isn't fair.* Ralph could tell she was a little upset, but he figured she was just embarrassed because he stood up and said those things, and now people were looking at her.

The next day was Thanksgiving, and Jeanie had her whole family over for dinner; this was the first time Ralph had ever asked the blessing in front of his mother-in-law and her family.

* * * * *

Karla was now a senior at Lancaster Mennonite High School and was testing the dating scene. Once in awhile she would bring a boyfriend or some friends to her home in New Jersey for the weekend. Her family enjoyed meeting her friends. In the spring of her senior year there seemed to be one boy in particular that she talked about a lot. His name was Wil Esh. It seems they had been paired up together in one of their classes and had to pretend they were husband and wife. This had lead to them getting to know one another better, which gave Wil the courage to ask Karla out. Well, kind of ask her out. You see, he had asked her if she would give him a perm first, as curly hair was suddenly all the rage, and then he would take her to dinner. This turned out to be their first date.

Gid and Betty's rental business was doing so well that he thought they should expand it to Florida. So without hesitation they started buying homes in Sarasota. One of the houses they purchased was built in such a way that they could put an apartment in the rear of the house, thus creating a place for them to stay while in Sarasota. With Gid's flying schedule increasing greatly, Betty found herself managing rental homes now in two states. But by having the small apartment in Sarasota it made things much easier when they came into town for business.

* * * * *

Ralph and Jeanie had decided to sell their home once again; they'd had their house on the market for a while now and were getting no action. Ralph was getting a little depressed about that. Jeanie asked him if he had been praying about it. He said he hadn't thought about asking God for something like that. He thought God had better things to do than to help with the sale of their house. Jeanie assured him that God wants us to bring all our cares and concerns to Him no matter how unimportant we think they are. So Ralph began to pray for the sale of the house. The whole reason for selling was so he could build his family a new house that he would design himself. Also, they were still carrying two mortgages with the Benton farm they owned.

After church the following Sunday, Jeanie was finishing up the dishes when the phone rang. Ralph had just gone into the living room to catch the end of one of his favorite gospel programs. He heard Jeanie talking on the phone but figured it was one of her friends. A few minutes later she came into the room and said, "You won't believe this, Ralph; here, you better talk to your Uncle Jim." Jeanie laid the phone down for Ralph to come pick it up. Ralph figured something bad must have happened to someone in the family, so he jumped to his feet and ran for the phone. "Hi, Uncle Jim, What's happening?"

"Nothing much. Hey, I've got some friends here and I was just telling them about your farm out in Benton, and they were wondering if you might want to sell it?"

"Well, Uncle Jim, I've been trying to sell *this* house, actually. But I have never even thought about selling the farm. Have they seen it already?"

"Oh no, I was just telling them about it, and they asked if I thought you might sell it. So I said, 'Well, let's call him and find out.'"

"I've never even given it any thought, but can I call you right back?"

"Sure, Ralph, take your time."

"Ok, talk to you soon, Uncle Jim; bye."

"Bye"

The farm meant the world to them, and they thought that someday they would move there permanently. Ralph turned to Jeanie and said incredulously, "Can you believe that?

"Maybe we're not supposed to have the farm. Maybe God is trying to tell us something," Jeanie said.

"What do you think?" Ralph asked.

"Well ... what do you think?" Jeanie responded, wanting to know his mindset so they could be in agreement about it.

"I think I'll put a high price on it and see what happens." Ralph said decisively, and the picked up the phone and called his uncle right back.

"Hi, Uncle Jim, it's me again already."

"Yes, Ralph?"

"I've got an asking price I want, and if they pay that price then they can have it."

Ralph then told him the price. There was a moment of silence on the other end as Uncle Jim told the couple what Ralph had just said.

"They want to know if they can see it today."

"Really? Well, let's see ... it takes two hours from here, and you are another half hour farther away."

"Let's go, then!" Jim responded enthusiastically.

"Ok, we'll be on our way soon!" Ralph replied, smiling over at Jeanie.

They decided where to meet and then drove to Benton, Pennsylvania that very afternoon. They pulled in the lane, drove down past the pond, and parked the vehicles. When the couple got out, they hugged each other excitedly and said, "This is just what we have been looking for! When can we close?"

Ralph and Jeanie were shocked, and the kids kept asking, "Are we really going to sell the farm?"

"I guess so," Jeanie responded.The couple spent about an hour and a half looking at the house, the barn, and walking the property. Then they all shook hands and headed for home. As they drove back no one spoke for the first half hour, as they all were thinking about what they had just done. When the shock finally wore off, Ralph said, "Well, I guess it was meant to be." They had just sold their precious farm.

Two weeks later on a Sunday afternoon a realtor sold their home in Delaware Township. Ralph asked Jeanie later on that evening, "So now what does this mean? First He cleans my heart, then He cleans house. It's like He is giving me a totally clean start."

Jeanie just simply said, "I guess we just need to trust Him."

They had three months to find a place to live, but that wasn't enough time to buy a lot and build a house, so they decided to rent a house for a while.

Ralph said, "Whether we rent or buy, it has to be close to the church."

Jeanie came home from work one day and informed Ralph that Drew and Mary Ellen were planning on building a new home, and they wondered if he would be interested in sitting down with them and working up a price. Ralph was glad for the work and told Jeanie to work out when and where they could meet. Business was really going well. Ralph had a number of offers to build homes and several additions as well. The drywall business was also going strong. Jeff had proved to be a valuable asset to Ralph in that regard.

Jeanie was making new friends at church, and one of those ladies was Carol Lyons. Carol was married to Ollie and they had three sons, Scott, Doug, and Matthew. She loved creating things, decorating, and had a gift for growing flowers. Jeanie and Carol soon became great friends and did a lot together. The thing she valued about Carol was that she could share her feelings with her and know they were safe with her because Carol never gossiped. Carol had a great sense of humor and kept Jeanie laughing all the time. They were perfect for each other; when one was down the other could always lift her spirit. Jeanie was still harboring a lot of resentment towards Ralph, but he never new it. She had become very skilled at hiding her true feelings over the past twelve years from having to walk on eggshells around Ralph before he'd become a Christian. Carol was a good listener, and Jeanie felt like she could tell her anything. At home everything seemed to be going great. To Ralph it seemed like he was having good quality time with the kids and his marriage seemed to be going well. As far as he knew, Jeanie had forgiven him for all the years of abuse he had inflicted on her.

The meeting with Drew and Mary Ellen went really well. They had already picked out a house plan and had purchased a building lot in Pattenburg. Ralph was really impressed with Drew's knowledge of Scripture, and it was very obvious that they knew the Lord. The only thing left to do was to come up with a price.

Jobs were starting to pour in; within days Ralph had received a call from a couple at the church who wanted him to take a look at a major renovation job. Their names were Bob and Diane Carboy and they had purchased a home in Fanwood, close to where they both worked. Their plan was to completely gut the inside and restore the home back to its original condition but with modern updates. Upon arriving at the job Ralph quickly noticed that it had just received a new roof.

When he entered the front door, the second thing he noticed was that it was already gutted. He then pushed the door open and took one step in and suddenly felt the urge to run or fall straight ahead. Then Ralph decided he needed to bring in his carpenter's level, which he did. The new roof outside looked true and straight, but inside there was definitely something wrong. After checking the floor out with the level, Ralph and Jeff discovered that the floor was sloped nine and a half inches from front to back. They wondered how that could be possible when the new roof outside looked perfect. Then they saw what the previous owner had done. He had known how bad the house was sloped, but he needed a new roof put on in order to sell the house. So what the roofers had done was to remove the entire roof structure and reframe a new roof system on top of jacks (2x4's) cut from zero inches in the front to nine and a half inches in the rear of the house.

No one had noticed because the home wasn't gutted when he sold it. By doing this, it made it impossible to jack the house up and fix the foundation. If you did then the roof would be on an angle. Ralph decided the only thing they could do was build the floor up nine and a half inches from front to rear. By doing this all the walls would then be the same height. Bob and Diane hired them to do the job and told them they weren't in a rush, which was a blessing. The Carboys became very special friends to two fairly new believers, and they contributed greatly to Ralph and Jeff's growth in their new faith. The one trait that Ralph always remarked that he admired about them was how they handled adversity. They always had a positive outlook in every situation. It was a joy working for them and knowing them. The smiles on their faces always made him feel welcomed to be around them. This home ended up taking two years to complete, and upon completion the Carboy's dubbed Ralph and Jeff the "Miracle Workers."

Back in Pattenburg, Drew and Mary Ellen's home was underway. The plan they had chosen was a saltbox style home, which was one of Ralph's favorite designs. The house went up quickly due to the fact that Ralph had to hire more subcontractors than usual. His drywall business had grown to the point that he needed subcontractors to help get the work done, because he didn't want to lose any of his regular builders due to slowness in completion.

Jeanie had been looking for a house to rent that wouldn't be too far from the church. Someone told her about a house in Milford and when she saw it, she told the owner that they would take it. The house was a cape cod that sat right on the main road, and behind it was the Delaware River. It also had a detached garage for Ralph to store equipment in. During the same time period Ralph found a piece of property on Hilltop Avenue in Frenchtown that they bought for their future home. Jeanie had learned from much experience that when Ralph made up his mind to move, nothing was going to stop him. They had always done every move by themselves, so after work, Ralph would move anything he could to the new location. In a couple of weeks they were settled into the rental home in Milford.

One of the things that Ralph and Jeanie did well together was draw and design houses. They had no intensions of starting their house until the following spring, but they wanted to make sure everything was completely ready by then. Ralph never liked renting for very long because that was just throwing money away when you could be building up equity in a house. Ralph wanted to build a house that looked like a barn, especially on the inside. For years he had taken old barns and converted them into homes for other people, but now he wanted to make a new house look like one. They designed a house with all the upstairs bedrooms separated by a twenty-four foot catwalk, with the children's bedrooms on one side and the master suite on the other. The whole design gave the barn effect that they were trying to achieve, and they were very anxious to start it. As it turned out, calls were pouring in for new projects that people wanted started in the new year, so they decided to start their new home as soon as possible to get it done before then. They broke ground before year's end and had the deck completely done and covered before the first snowfall.

* * * * *

The new year was off to a flying start. Mike and Bonnie had decided to build a new home in Kingwood Township and had asked Ralph and Jeff to build it. With Drew and Mary Ellen's house completed and the Carboys' house moving along, they began construction in the spring on Mike and Bonnie Hudock's new home. Ralph had also received from his friend Gene Hale plans to bid on a job to renovate an old car dealership building, a job that would separate it into four stores, including Gene's new hardware store. During this year Drew sold his practice, which meant Jeanie would need to find other employment. It was during this time when the video craze was sweeping the nation, and Jeff wanted to get in on it. So Ralph and Jeff decided to get their feet wet in the video rental business. They knew this would probably be frowned upon by some church individuals, but they had a plan. There would be no x-rated movies in their store, and they would offer Christian video rentals for free. They started by renting a small store in Frenchtown, and since Jeanie needed a job she could run the store during the day and Jeff would run it at nights. Jeanie had also begun to build up a wallpaper business, so when she had a wallpaper job to do, Jeff would mind the store.

* * * * *

Karla had been dating Wil Esh since she was a senior in high school at Lancaster Mennonite High School. They had been secretly engaged for over a year, and in the spring of 1983 they told Karla's parents that they would like to get married in the fall. Gid and Betty felt they were a little young to be making that commitment, but they also knew that they were mature and hard-working young people. Due to scheduling conflicts, they set the date for July 30th, 1983. Betty was busy making Karla's wedding gown, two of the bridesmaids' dresses, and the flower girl's dress. They were married at Mellinger's Mennonite Church near Lancaster, Pennsylvania, with the reception held at Bird-in-Hand Restaurant. After their honeymoon to the Bahamas, they set up housekeeping at Redwood Lodges near Strasburg, Pennsylvania. Wil continued to work for his father, Jonathan Esh, in the paint business, and Karla worked at the New Holland Farmer's Bank near Smoketown.

* * * * *

The pace was hectic that year with all the construction jobs and trying to squeeze building their own home in also. Ralph added two new employees to his roster during the summer, his son Rodney and his son's best friend, Kyle Burke, who was also their neighbor. Sometimes Ralph had to pinch himself because it seemed like only yesterday when he was just a teenager working for his dad. *Like father, like son*, he would think as he watched his son working hard for him. If it wasn't for those two young men working their tails off that summer, the work wouldn't have been completed on time. When they went back to school in the fall they were greatly missed. However, they were offered Saturday employment whenever they wanted to work. Stephanie had graduated from the Baptistown Christian School and was ready to start high school at Delaware Valley Regional.

By the fall, construction had been started on Gene's project and the Hudock and Carboy jobs were in their final days. Ralph and Jeanie's house was also nearing completion, and Jeff had purchased a building lot on Creek Road to build his own house. Jeff's plan was to do the same thing Ralph had done, which was to get the foundation in and covered before winter. Jeanie was picking up more wallpapering jobs, which meant Jeff would have to run the video store during the day. That also meant Ralph needed to hire more subs to help him complete his jobs on time. During this busy year the drywall work had never slowed down, either, and all this was adding to Ralph's ever-growing feeling of being overwhelmed.

By year's end, Jeff's foundation was in and covered and Gene's project was moving right along with completion expected by the spring.

The new house had turned out just the way they had planned it, and the catwalk in the center of the great room was a real eye catcher when you walked in the front door. Ralph was happy with his oversized garage that suddenly had become full overnight. The kids were happy with their cool, new rooms that looked down into the great room, and Jeanie was pleased with her kitchen that she had designed herself.

It was March of 1984 and time to start some new projects. Jeanie wanted to visit with Betty in Sarasota, so she made arrangements to spend four days with her in Florida. Jeanie stayed with Betty in their apartment. They had a good time doing girlie things and of course managed to get sunburned while at the beach. A few days later she returned home and was back to work wallpapering.

Plans had been made to start framing Jeff's A-frame house when a call came in from Florida that his father had passed away. Ralph had only seen Jeff's father on two different occasions, and he knew from the very first that he was a special man. With all the work they had right now, Ralph felt there was no need for Jeff to rush into anything at this time, and whenever he felt up to it, they would start his house.

Ralph's father also was not doing very well. The last time he had seen him Ralph thought he was acting a little different. He had asked his mother what was going on with Pop, and she wondered what he meant. Ralph hadn't been around his dad for a few months, and so he was able to notice a change that everyone who was with him regularly couldn't see. His mother and brother were with RH every day and didn't see what Ralph had noticed. He just had a faraway look about him and was a little slow in reacting to things. His mother said that she would get him to the doctors to have him checked out. Ralph suggested to her that he thought that Pop might have had a stroke. Sure enough, after some tests were done, it was determined that his father had indeed had not only one, but they believed a number of mini strokes. He was still working, but he was just doing smaller jobs now, and if he did take on a bigger job Ralph and Jeff would come and help get it started.

Gene's new hardware store was completed, and Ralph helped him move into the new location. The location was in such a busy area that Jeff and Ralph decided to rent one of the stores from Gene and move their little cramped video store into this new and much larger space. It turned out to be a very good spot between a pizza restaurant and a pharmacy. Jeanie was getting a lot of wallpapering jobs and loving it, so Jeff took over the daily running of the video business, and Ralph stayed busy with the construction and drywall business.

* * * * *

Gid and Betty were spending more and more time in Sarasota taking care of their rental properties and making new friends. Jan and Elmer Ebersole convinced them that they should take some time off to have a little fun, considering they were in Florida, no less, and invited them to go to Bird Key to do some sail boarding. They thought they would at least like to first watch and see how this was done. Some other friends, Steve Handrich and Sam Kurtz, were there also. First Gid got the courage to try it and was doing pretty well, but Betty was a little more reluctant. But when she saw Jan and Elmer's eleven-year-old daughter, Alicia, sail boarding, she decided to give it a try, too. They always joked that it took a hundred falls before you actually learned to sailboard, so when someone would fall, someone from shore would yell out a number like "Forty-five!," keeping count so the surfer knew that he or she only had fifty-five more falls to go!

Betty was gradually building up confidence, but she soon learned to gain a lot of respect for the wind. She was about halfway between Bird Key and City Island when the wind seemed to change direction, plus she was using Steve's board which had a larger sail and was harder for her to control. Elmer came out to help her, but they finally decided to stop fighting the wind and just let it carry them to City Island. Gid drove to City Island with the station wagon to pick them up.

Gid and Betty soon bought their own boards, and whenever they were in Florida, they would go sail boarding with their friends. One afternoon Elmer, Gid, and Betty sailed around Bird Key.

* * * * *

By summer Ralph was swamped with work, but thank goodness for those two, strong young backs eager to make some spending money, and just in time to help in the construction of Jeff's A-frame. The construction of Jeff's house turned out to be a lot of fun, especially when it came to the roof. Watching the expressions on the boy's faces when they were told to climb out there to help sheath the roof was priceless.

It wasn't long though, before they were like cats running about up there. The neat thing about an eighteen-inch pitch is that you are practically standing straight up instead of bent over, which makes the work a lot easier on everyone's back. Since Jeff's father had been in the plumbing and heating business, he was familiar with doing this phase of the job himself. With Jeff doing his own plumbing, the job was able to move along at a much quicker pace, and the entire job was completed in a shorter time period.

Fall meant the kids were back in school, so Rodney and Kyle would only be able to work on weekends, so Ralph had to be careful how much work he was booking ahead. Up until this point he had always been able to keep his word and not hold his customers up, and he planned on continuing in this same manner. He continued to get jobs from his church family, including two major additions and some roofing and siding work. But with winter just around the corner he needed to make sure he had sufficient inside work to carry him through the cold months when he couldn't work outside as frequently. This was their second Christmas in the new house, and it was time for the annual finding and cutting of the tree. This year everyone wanted the biggest tree they could possibly find. Ralph wasn't about to drag a tree in the house that was tall enough to touch the cathedral ceiling. He reminded them it had to be decorated, which meant he would end up being the one on the ladder doing the top part of the tree, as usual. They settled for a thirteen-foot tree which still caused quite a bit of trauma. The kids were into videoing everything and they wanted to film their father putting up the tree, which he always turned into a circus. They joked that he had this other personality named Icky that always came out at Christmastime.

Icky was only three years old, but stood 5' 11" tall and weighed 200 pounds, and he talked with this hideous little voice and did the most ridiculous things. The kids loved it and always egged him on, but Jeanie would get a little tired of it after a while and want Icky to go away so she could get some things done. Christmas was a great time of year. In the video store they convinced Ralph to be Santa Claus and wear a costume all day, passing treats out to all the little ones and a few not-so-little ones. Overall, the year ended well with a lot having been accomplished. Jeff was living in his new home on Creek Road and was constantly busy between the video store and helping at church. Ralph was also helping at the church; he had been asked to serve on the board of deacons eleven months earlier and was really finding it important in his walk of faith. The church had become his second home, and he was always anxious to help in whatever way he could.

13

Keep It All

January 11 started out like any other normal day. The kids were off to school and Ralph was heading out the door for his first job of the day. Jeanie, however, said she didn't have a wallpaper job that day so she had planned to go to the mall and shop. The whole family knew that tonight they had to be at the church to serve a dinner. That afternoon when the kids got home from school, they did their usual routine chores but failed to notice a note on the counter. When Ralph got home he asked the kids where their mother was. They responded that they didn't know. It was a short time later when Ralph noticed a note on the counter that Jeanie had written saying she would be late getting home, and so she would just meet them at the church. They all got ready and headed for the church.

With the tables set up and people arriving, but still no sign of Jeanie, Ralph was starting to get really concerned.

People started to ask where Jeanie was, and Ralph said she went to the mall today and that she would probably be running a little late. Halfway through the serving of the meal, there was still no sign of Jeanie, and Ralph was getting really anxious and upset. Jeff came up to him and said, "Ralph, I'm going to travel the route to the mall that she would have taken and see if maybe she had an accident." Rodney wanted to go with him because he was really worried about his mother, so they both left to search for her. On the way Jeff stopped at a police barracks and asked if there had been any accidents that day reported involving a blue van. The officer checked the records and said not yet, so Jeff and Rodney continued on. They drove all the way to the mall and then drove through every single parking lot, but there was no sign of Jeanie's van. Jeff started back for the church, but this time he slowed down at every curve, looking over the embankments to check for a wrecked vehicle. By the time they arrived back at the church the meal was over and things were cleaned up. There was a small group of people still there waiting with Ralph for any news of Jeanie. They all decided to go back to Ralph's house in case Jeanie or someone else called with any news. One of the couples that went back to the house with Ralph was Carol and Olie. Everyone was deeply concerned and trying to calm Ralph down. Ralph had noticed that Carol had been acting a little nervous all evening, but he had just chalked it up to the fact that she and Jeanie were such great friends, and so naturally Carol would be the most worried about her. It wasn't too long before Carol came forward and whispered something in Ralph's ear.

She whispered, "Ralph, I think you should call this phone number," as she handed Ralph a scrap of paper with a number scrawled on it. Then she said, "I think he will know."Ralph had no idea what she was talking about, but it didn't sound good to him, so he said, "What do you mean, you think he will know? And who is he?"

"I think she has been seeing this guy," Carol whispered nervously, looking into Ralph's eyes with an almost apologetic expression.

"What?" he whispered loudly.

"Just try the number, Ralph."

Ralph went in another room where he could make the phone call out of the earshot of everyone gathered at the house, and when he dialed the number, and a lady answered.

"Hello?"

"Hello, my name is Ralph Walls, is my wife there?"

"I'm sorry, you must have the wrong number," the woman replied.

"Ma'am, I was told that my wife might be with your husband," he said bluntly. Ralph believed in getting down to the bottom of things quickly.

"Sir, my husband is out of town." The woman spoke matter-of-factly, but there was now a trace a nervousness in her voice.

"Do you have his number so I can call him?" Ralph's voice was growing more demanding by the minute.

"He is in Florida."

"I don't care where he is, but do you have his number so I can find out where my wife is?"

"Ok, his number in Florida is xxx-xxx-xxxx."

"Thank you." And with that Ralph slammed down the phone.

Carol had been pacing the floor the whole time Ralph was on the phone. Ralph didn't waste any time making the next phone call. "Hello?"

"Jeanie?"

"Yes..."

"What's going on?"

"I'm leaving..."

"What do you mean, you're leaving? And why?"

"I'm not coming back, and don't worry; I don't want your money, your house, or the kids. You can keep it all."

"Jeanie, why? What did I do wrong?"

"You didn't do anything wrong, Ralph, it's just me. I left the van in Flemington behind the bank. You can keep that too. I'll stop back during the day sometime and get my clothes while the kids are in school. I've got to go now."

Ralph heard a click on the other end of the line, and just like that Jeanie had hung up.

Needless to say, Ralph hung up the phone completely dumbfounded over the events that had just transpired. Everyone gathered there was speechless, and Carol was still pacing back and forth, wringing her hands as she paced. "I'm sorry," she said, "I didn't think she would really do it, Ralph."

"What do you mean?" Ralph demanded to know.

"She had been saying that she was going to leave you, but I didn't think she would really do it."

Everyone started to filter out saying that they would be praying for Ralph and the children. Carol kept saying she was so sorry, over and over. Jeff had tried to keep the kids distracted during the whole episode, but they still heard everything. It wasn't long before everyone had gone home. Stephanie lay in her bed that night listening to the crying coming from her father's room. The next day was Saturday and everyone tried to act as normal as possible.

* * * * *

In January of 1985, Gid had a scheduled flight to Cairo with a two-night layover, so he twisted Betty's arm to go along with him, but he didn't have to persuade her too much. Even though these layovers were short trips, the two of them treasured every moment together. Holding hands while walking among the pyramids and touring the Sphinx was just what they needed to escape the real world of work and more work. To stand there and gaze upon the enormous size of those structures made them wonder how a civilization without modern tools or technology could accomplish such a feat. When they stood there they couldn't help but think they were standing where kings, slaves, and prophets once stood. The thought sent chills up their spines. After doing some sightseeing, they tried their hand at bargaining in the market place and felt like they had done a good job of it.

Soon the trip was over and they had to get back to reality. Gid continued making his European flights and Betty went back to staying ahead of the fifteen rentals they had by then. She felt like a business commuter traveling back and forth between New Jersey and Florida. The frequency of the trips had really increased. There was always a new tenant to interview or a house to paint or clean. The flight from New York to Tampa, Florida, was always late in the evening and she had a long walk to the employees' parking lot (where she was able to park because Gid was employed by an airline)). She would usually wait until she saw some crew members walking in the same direction and she would join them.

One night her car broke down in a very dark area of town and she needed assistance. She called AAA, and while she was waiting for them some people offered to help, but she really didn't know them. Luckily she was able to get through to a friend in Sarasota who came to her aid and got her safely to her apartment in Sarasota after AAA towed the car to a car repair shop. These little incidents didn't slow Betty down, though. Bright and early the next day she would be up and ready to work. If there was work to be done, Betty was going to make sure it got completed.

* * * * *

After Jeanie left the family, Stephanie went into take-charge mode. From the start she had determined that everything was going to run smoothly even if her mother had abandoned them. Laundry, food, lists and more lists; she was a great list maker. Ralph tried his best to act normal, but his mind raced continually as he tried to figure out what he had done wrong. He just couldn't put his finger on it; if he could he knew he could make it better. Each day came to an end quickly it seemed.

He knew that Sunday would be a rough day, going to church and facing all those people who by now most likely knew everything. The next day they all got up, got ready, and went to Sunday school and church like they had done on any other Sunday, as a family. They could feel people looking at them to see if they would show some kind of emotion, but they acted as normal as anyone else that day. A few people came up and said if there was anything they could do to just give them a call. The following week was a little hectic, and as the days passed by it became more evident that Jeanie was gone for good and was not planning on coming back.

Friday night there was supposed to be a birthday party at their house for Stephanie and another girl from school, who were both going to be sixteen just days apart from one another. Stephanie got off the bus that afternoon and noticed a little red car sitting in the driveway that she didn't recognize. At first she was hesitant about going in, thinking someone might be robbing the house, but just then someone started coming out the front door. It was her mother carrying a suitcase and trying to get away undetected.

"Stephanie, you startled me."

"What are you doing?" Stephanie demanded, feeling protective of their home in her new role of woman of the house.

"I thought I could get my clothes out before you got home." Jeanie had a hard time making eye contact with her daughter.

"Where are you going, Mom?"

"I don't know, Stephanie, I'm just going, that's all I can tell you right now."

"Well take me with you then," Stephanie blurted out, taking Jeanie completely by surprise with this request. She hesitated a moment before looking back up at her daughter.

"No, you can't go, Stephanie, I'm sorry," she stated flatly.

"Why?"

"Because you just can't, that's all!" Jeanie yelled a bit too loudly as she looked around the neighborhood quickly to make sure no one heard her shout.

"But I don't want to stay here, Mom, I want to be with you."

"You have to, now get out of my way; I don't want your father to see me."

With that Jeanie pushed past Stephanie and headed for the car. Stephanie bent down, quickly gathered up some stones from the walkway and hurled them at her mother yelling, "I hate you!" Then she stood there stunned and sobbing as her mother pulled out of the driveway and took off down the street, never looking back or waving goodbye.

Ralph was on his way home wondering how he was going to get ready for a teen girls' birthday party tonight, knowing he has no idea what to do. When he got home and was sorting through the mail in the kitchen, Stephanie walked in a casually announced, "Mom was here today."

"She was?" Ralph turned around quickly to face his daughter, trying to read her facial expression because she sounded so blasé about it.

"How do you know?"

"I caught her trying to sneak out with her clothes," Stephanie replied blandly.

"Well ...Did she say anything?" Ralph felt desperate to know details, something, anything, especially if Jeanie had asked about him.

"No, she didn't say anything at all, she just had a piece of luggage in her hands."

"Where is she staying?"

"I don't know, Dad; I tried to find out but she wouldn't tell me."

"That's it?"

"Oh, and she was driving a little red car."

Just then there was a knock at the door and when they opened it, there stood Carol with a birthday cake, decorations, and everything else to have a party. The party was a success thanks to Carol and the other birthday girl's mother. It was a good thing Carol showed up, because Ralph and Jeff just stood there acting dumbfounded, as Stephanie joked about later.

To quote Ralph, "Who wouldn't with a basement full of screaming sixteen-year-old girls?"

Weeks turned into months, and Jeanie never came home. Ralph had made regular attempts to contact her, but to no avail. He heard that she was staying very busy with her wall-papering business and was doing fine.

The video store was doing well and Jeff had given a lot of young people the chance for some part-time employment by offering some sales positions at the store. Sundays were usually the toughest day for Ralph since he had nothing to do in the afternoons, so he would go down to the store and try to help out, but mainly just so he wouldn't have to be alone. Jeff was really into computers and was trying to find a software package that would run the store. One day he had been talking to Gid about computers and software, and Gid suggested that he let his son Mike have a try at creating a program for him. If it worked well then they could market it to other video stores. While Jeff, Gid, and Mike were in the back room talking computer talk, Ralph stayed at the counter and helped.

Up till now Ralph had only thought about getting Jeanie back; nothing else had even crossed his mind. But as he stood there in the store day after day, he began noticing a lot of single girls coming and going from the store, which would lead him to think, *why should I stay single now? Maybe I should start looking for someone to date.* It was almost the end of March now, and Ralph started thinking realistically now about facing the future without Jeanie. There were a few interesting girls out there, but he decided he better sleep on this awhile and think things through. About a week later he ran into Gid and Betty after church, and they asked him if he could come over later that afternoon to visit.

He said, "Sure, when? "

They said, "How about three o'clock?"

"Fine, I'll be there."

What on earth do they want to see me about? He wondered. But at three o'clock he pulled in their driveway and walked to the door. Betty answered the door, saying,

"Hi, Ralph, come on in!"

"Hi, Betty."

"Ralph I'm really sorry, but Gid just got a last minute flight and has to rush off."

"Oh, I can come back another time."

"Oh no, that's no problem." Just then Gid came into the room with one arm in his jacket and grabbing his bag with his other hand.

"Sorry there, Ralph, I got to fly."

"That's ok, Gid, take care."

"You're in good hands with Betty." Gid said to Ralph cheerfully.

"Bye, honey" he said, as he gave Betty a kiss on the lips and headed out the door.

"Ralph, we can sit here at the table."

"Ok, but are you sure you want me to stay?"

"Sure, relax ... Gid and I have been thinking and praying about you a lot and we just wanted to see how you're doing."

"Thank you, I've been managing." They talked for a little while about their children and Ralph's work, and then Betty changed the subject.

"Have you had any contact with Jeanie since she's been gone?"

"Not really, she won't take my calls."

"Do you want her back?"

"Yes."

"Do you love her?"

"Yes, of course I do."

"Then don't give up, Ralph; keep trying, let her know you really care for her."

"I am trying, but I guess there is always room to try harder. If she would only talk to me then I would know what I need to do or stop doing, but she just won't take my calls."

"Don't give up; I really believe she will come back."

"I hope you're right."

"Do you know if she has spoken to an attorney?"

"I'm not totally sure, but I heard a rumor that she has."

"Ralph, I would like to give you the name of a Christian attorney in Flemington; if you feel you need to talk to someone, give him a call."

"Ok, thank you for all your advice and concern. I really appreciate it, Betty. I really do."

"I hope and pray everything works out for you."

"Thank you."

They said goodbye and Ralph drove home more determined then ever to win Jeanie back. He went home and made some phone calls around, asking friends if they knew where Jeanie was staying now. Finally that evening he learned that Jeanie was now staying at her mother's house and sleeping in the basement. That night he called his mother-in-law's house. Evelyn answered the phone.

"Hello, Mom."

"Yes?"

"This is Ralph!" *Has she forgotten my voice so soon?* Ralph wondered wryly.

"Oh, hi." Evelyn's stilted tone was not lost on Ralph. Suddenly this phone call was bringing back a flood of memories from many years ago when they were only 14 and 18 years old.

"Is Jeanie there?"

"Yes, but she said she didn't want to talk to you if you called."

"What do I need to do to get her back, Mom?"

Evelyn started to cry. "I don't know … she won't listen to me."

"I still love her, and I want her to know that," Ralph choked out, holding back tears.

Through her tears Evelyn answered, "I know you do, but I think she needs time to realize that."

"Please tell her I called, OK?"

"I will, Ralph. Bye now."

"Bye, Mom, and thanks."

Evelyn had told Jeanie not to date Ralph all those years ago, because he wasn't a believer and that it would only lead to trouble. But when the inevitable happened and they had to marry, she had continued to pray for Ralph that he would come to know the Lord. Five years ago she had seen an answer to her prayers. Now she so desperately wanted to see them work this out. She was hurt terribly over their separation and grieved over it continually, but she continued to pray for them.

The next day Ralph called again, and this time Jeanie answered the phone. Ralph asked her, "Jeanie, is there something I can do or change so that you'll come back to me?"

Jeanie responded, "Ralph, it's not you; you haven't done anything wrong. For the last five years you have been great to me, but I just don't have any feelings for you any more. I've spoken to an attorney, and maybe you should do the same."

For a moment Ralph sat there stunned and quiet, holding the phone to his ear, because Jeanie sounded so calm about it all. This was so different from how he expected her to sound whenever they would finally speak again.

Working up his nerve, Ralph took a deep breath and said, "I still love you, Jeanie," and then all he heard was a click when she hung up the phone.

After Ralph hung up the phone, he didn't know what to think. *Maybe,* he thought, *I should go speak to that attorney that Betty Miller told me about.* The attorney's office wouldn't be open until tomorrow, so for now he had a lot to think about.

The following day Ralph was working near Flemington, so on his lunch hour he stopped in at the lawyer's office to schedule an appointment. The receptionist was very pleasant and inquired what Ralph needed to see Mr. Smith (not his real name) about. Ralph told her his wife had left him and she had told him to get an attorney. She then told Ralph that they could see him tomorrow. With the meeting set for tomorrow afternoon, he went back to work, but he had a hard time concentrating on what he was doing. He had only ever used a lawyer for contracts and closings; this was going to be something he wasn't very sure about. Ralph really didn't want to get a divorce, but it seemed like there was no hope since Jeanie wouldn't even talk about it and since she had already spoke to an attorney herself. Ralph's mind was spinning trying to guess what this attorney was going to suggest he do. It had been about four months since Jeanie had left, and the children seemed to be handling this a lot better than their father. Stephanie was doing most of the cooking and laundry and had to yell at Rodney on a regular basis for not picking his things up off the floor, but otherwise things seemed to be going well. They still went to church and Sunday school every Sunday, and they both were doing great in school.

Tuesday afternoon Ralph showed up at the attorney's office about fifteen minutes early and was told that Mr. Smith would be with him in a few minutes. About ten minutes later a smartly dressed man about age forty appeared.

"Mr. Walls," he said, almost like an announcement as he walked toward Ralph with his hand outstretched.

"Yes," Ralph replied as he stood up to greet him.

"How are you today?" Mr. Smith asked, sounding a bit too jovial for Ralph's nerves.

"I'll let you know in a few minutes," Ralph replied humorously with a wry smile.

"Oh, don't worry; it's not going to be that bad." Mr. Smith reassured Ralph as he motioned for him to go into the office.

"My secretary informs me that your wife left you, and that your wife has advised you to get an attorney."

"That's correct."

"Why don't you tell me a little about what happened?"

"How much time do you have?" Ralph was thinking of all the years of his bad moods and verbal abuse."Don't worry, take all the time you want."

Ralph then began to tell Mr. Smith how he had treated his wife and family for the first twelve years of their marriage. He told him how he had asked the Lord into his heart in 1980 and had tried to be a better husband and father ever since. He told the attorney that he had tried to call Jeanie repeatedly but to no avail, except for a few minutes the other night. He told him also how she kept saying that it wasn't anything he did, that it's just her. They continued to talk for quite some time, and then Mr. Smith looked Ralph straight in the eye and asked, "Mr. Walls, do you still love your wife?"

"Yes I do sir, very much."

"Then I suggest that you don't give up, keep praying and trying. As long as she hasn't given you any papers, there is still hope. If she does hand you papers, we can take care of it then. Until then keep trying to make contact with her, and let her know that you still love her, Ok?"

"That's all?"

"That's all."

"Ok, thank you very much sir, and what do I owe you?"

"Let's wait and see what happens first."

Then they shook hands and said goodbye. As Ralph left the office he was truly amazed.

That's not how it happens on TV with lawyers and clients. They are usually trying to figure out how they can get the upper hand on the other spouse. This guy wants us to try and save our marriage, I like that, he thought. That night when he got home Ralph wanted to call Jeanie in the worst way, but decided he should give her a couple of days to think about it. Thursday evening after prayer meeting he felt the time was right, so he called his mother-in-law's house again. Evelyn answered the phone and Ralph asked if he could speak to Jeanie. She told him that Jeanie had told her she didn't want to talk to Ralph if he called.

He told Evelyn, "I still love her and it doesn't matter to me what she's done, I just want her to come back."

Then he asked Evelyn, "What should I do?"

Evelyn started to cry and then said, "I don't know, I've tried talking to her, but she won't listen to me. Just keep trying and praying, Ralph. I have to go now. Bye." And with that she hung up the phone.

It was the middle of June now, and Ralph had called Jeanie three times a week for the last month with the same response. And then one day when Ralph pulled into his driveway after work, there sat Jeanie's red car. His first thought was, *oh no, she probably came to get something out of the house and didn't expect me home yet or maybe this is it, she's delivering the divorce papers in person to me.* But he really didn't care what the reason was as long as he could talk to her. When he walked into the house he could tell that someone had just cleaned; it just plain smelled good and fresh. When he walked into the great room he saw Jeanie standing by the couch, and it looked like she had been crying. Ralph asked cautiously, "Is everything all right?"

"No, I've really messed things up. I've hurt you really bad and I'm sorry." Jeanie really started to cry then. Ralph walked over toward her and embraced her, saying, "I'm sorry, too, Jeanie." They just held each other for a long time without speaking. Then through her tears Jeanie asked, "I would like to come back if you'll have me."

"I love you and I have never stopped loving you, Jeanie, of course you can come back."

They embraced each other again, both crying now, and then when they'd had a chance to wipe away their tears, Ralph gave Jeanie a long, loving kiss.

"So what do we do now?" Ralph asked hesitantly, feeling almost like an 18-year-old again, starting all over.

"Why don't we go for a ride and talk, like we used to do in the old days, because the kids will be home any minute and I don't want them to hear us," Jeanie answered.

"Let me leave the kids a note so they know where I am, because when they see my truck in the driveway but find I'm not here they'll be wondering what happened."

"Good idea." Ralph scribbled a note and left it on the kitchen counter.

"Ok, let's go." They got in Jeanie's car and drove off. Ralph was afraid to say anything at first, hoping Jeanie would start the conversation. Ralph finally started by asking her if she was still doing her wallpapering business, just to get the conversation going. They talked about everything they could think of. Then Jeanie pulled into a parking lot and stopped the car. She sat there for a minute with her eyes filling up, looking for the words to say.

"Ralph, I am so sorry for what I've done to you and the children. I don't know if you will ever be able to forgive me. This is the hardest part; I feel I have to tell you everything that I've done." Ralph reached over quietly and put two of his fingers on her lips and said,

"No, you don't have to tell me anything, I don't want to know. All I care is that you've come back to me. I love you, and that's all that matters."

"But I've done such bad things." Ralph hushed her with his fingers again and said, "I put you and the kids through hell for twelve years; you can't even come close to that. So let's just end it there. What's done is done; let's just start fresh from right now with our new lives. Let's not bring up the past; we can't change what's already happened."

"But how can I show my face at church, Ralph? I've embarrassed you and the children."

"I'm not embarrassed; I'm proud to have you back. Just hold my hand and walk right in by my side. A lot of them have been praying for us, and the ones who want to talk, let them talk. That's their problem, not ours. Let's just take one day at a time. I know there will be problems, but let's just face each one as it happens. For now, let's go home and tell the kids and just love each other." Ralph leaned over and gave Jeanie a tender kiss to confirm all his words to her.

"I hope you're right." Jeanie said, and she started the car and they drove home together.

At home Stephanie had already suspected something was up involving her mother. She, too, noticed her mother's touch in the house immediately when she walked in. Then, remembering that she'd seen her father's truck in the driveway, she figured that they were together. Even though she was only sixteen, Stephanie had pretty much run the house for the last five months, and with the way she and her

mother had parted from their last meeting, she wasn't feeling too thrilled knowing her mother had come back and then gone off somewhere with her Dad.

Once they returned home, Ralph helped carry Jeanie's things in. Stephanie and Rodney were both there anticipating their mom's arrival. Stephanie said, "I had a feeling you two would be coming in together," and Rodney gave his usual, "Hey, Mom, what's happening?" Jeanie walked toward the children to hug them.

"I'm sorry for what I've done."

"Don't worry about it, Mom." Rodney replied sweetly, giving his mom a big hug.

Stephanie made herself busy for the moment and Jeanie sensed a little tension there, so she decided not to push it.

"Stephanie, I'm sorry for hurting you."

"Yeah, ok," Stephanie shot back over her shoulder as she stomped across the room, acting busy even though there was nothing to clean because Jeanie had gotten the house spotless while they'd all been gone.

"Look, why don't we all go out for pizza or something so we don't have to cook tonight?" Ralph asked trying to lighten the mood.

"Sounds good to me," Rodney spoke up enthusiastically.

"I don't know," Jeanie said, thinking she didn't want to be seen or gossiped about yet.

Stephanie picked up on her mother's concern and said, "I think we should go."

Ralph sensed what was going on, and so he offered, "Honey, if you would rather, I could just go pick up some pizzas and we can eat here at home."

"That might be a better idea," Jeanie replied.

Ralph called the pizza parlor and placed a to-go order for two pizzas. When he left to pick up the pizzas, he hoped and prayed the whole drive there and back that mother and

daughter could spend a few minutes together and make peace.

The next few days seemed to be going ok until Stephanie approached her father and informed him that the other man had been calling and that Mom had been talking to him. Now, the old Ralph would have been off the wall in a fit of rage, but the new Ralph calmly asked Jeanie if this was true. Jeanie admitted that it was true. Ralph then asked Jeanie if he could go and talk to the other man. Now Jeanie was thinking, *I know Ralph has changed, but has he changed that much that he will just talk calmly to him?* Ralph assured her that he meant the guy no harm, and he asked her to call the other man and tell him that Ralph wanted to talk to him. The other man didn't trust Ralph because of all the stories he had heard about him. The meeting date was set and Ralph went to the man's place of business to see him. When Ralph walked into the store, the man was hiding behind some equipment in such a way that Ralph could only see his face and chest. Ralph just walked in and calmly said, "Hello, I'm Ralph Walls."

The man responded by calling out, "Don't come any closer, I have a knife." In fact, he had quite a large knife.

"You don't need a knife." Ralph said reassuringly, laughing and shaking his head a little. "I'm not here to hurt you; I just want to talk to you." Ralph could tell that the man was actually shaking in fear.

"It doesn't matter, just stay by the door."

"No problem, sir, but you need to calm down." Ralph knew he needed to calmly take the upper hand in this conversation. "I just want to talk to you man to man. I understand you have a wife and a little boy. Is that right?"

"Yeah, so?"

"I just wanted to know how your family is handling this," Ralph asked, putting his hands in his pockets as he waited for an answer.

"What do you mean?"

"What's your wife think about you having an affair?"

"I don't think that's any concern of yours."

"Well, actually it is my concern, because not only have you ruined my family's lives, but I'm sure your family will never be the same again, either. Did you ever think about all the children that are involved, yours and mine? Did you ever think about all that? You know you're a pretty lucky guy."

"Why's that?

"Because the man standing in front of you is a new man now."

"What do you mean, a new man?"

"I mean I've changed; the old me would have come in here charging, and no knife would have stopped me from getting to you. But now you see a changed man. I've come with my own weapon." The man tensed up thinking Ralph might have a gun.

"Here's my weapon." The man wasn't sure whether to run or duck as Ralph lifted his arm up, holding a book.

"I've brought this for you; it changed my life, and it can change yours, too. It's a Bible. I think you should read it."

Ralph laid the Bible on a piece of equipment and started to turn around to walk out.

"Oh, and one more thing, you don't have to walk around looking over your shoulder expecting me to jump out of some dark corner and get you. I'm not going to do that. What I am going to do is forgive you as best as I humanly can. Now, I can't say all my friends and brothers-in-law will do the same, so I think it would be best if you kept your distance from my wife. Have a nice day!" Ralph walked calmly out of the building and went home to Jeanie.

* * * * *

God be praised, Jeanie had come back home to Ralph and they never even had to contemplate divorce proceedings. If you are facing a similar situation in your life, however, and you're wondering what the Bible has to say about divorce, the following scriptures provide some excellent guidelines:

The Causes of Divorce (Matthew 19:8)
Allowances for Divorce (1 Corinthians 7:12-15)
The Cure for Divorce (Philippians 2:3, 4)
(Billy Graham Training Center Bible, NKJV)

* * * * *

By now, Gid and Betty had used the "no money down method" quite often and had accumulated approximately twelve rental properties in the Sarasota area. Commuting to Florida to manage the properties was getting very time consuming and costly, especially for Betty, so one day she had the idea of selling their home in New Jersey and moving to Florida. She didn't think Gid would agree since this was the home they'd always dreamed of having — in the country with some acreage, a large house to entertain friends and family, a barn/hangar for Gid to store his collectibles and an adjoining airstrip. This had been their home for fourteen years. But when she mentioned her idea to Gid, she was surprised at his reaction. He was ready to relocate. Soon there was a "For Sale" sign in their front lawn.

* * * * *

The remainder of that year Jeanie became really involved with her wallpapering business. She had built up a good reputation from her quality workmanship, and she was in high demand. Her good friend Carol joined her on the jobs, which made for many exciting times together. Carol had a real gift for making people laugh, and was just the right medicine for healing that Jeanie needed at that time in her life. Their relationship grew so strong that it spread to their husbands as well, and before long the four of them would be spending many memorable times together. Ralph always said Carol and Olie were the only two comedians he knew who didn't get paid for entertaining people.

Jeff had gotten interested in racing radio-controlled cars, and soon he had bought Rodney and Kyle their own cars too. They got so good at it that they would enter competitions and frequently win. The boys were also interested in music, and since Rodney had become quite good on the piano, Jeff bought him a keyboard for Christmas. Kyle owned a drum set, so they would set up their equipment along with some large speakers in the basement and make really loud music together. Another friend of theirs in the neighborhood named John Schaible soon joined them. He was very good at playing drums, which moved Kyle to guitar, vocals, and some of the craziest dancing you ever saw. Kyle was the comedian of the group and without a doubt kept everyone laughing. The boys were very considerate and always knew when to stop so the rest of the family could have some peace.

It always seemed that the winter months made Ralph think about building a new house. Probably because he had less to do outside and had too much free time to dream during those cold winter months. His idea this time was to take the barn-style house design they had built for themselves and expand it by more than twice its size. Ralph reasoned that since they were basically starting a new life together, why not start over with a new home?

For anyone reading this book that already knows Ralph, you know that when he gets excited about something, his volume increases as he is expressing his passion about an idea. He figured he would have to sell Jeanie on this one, because she already had a new home and loved it, and probably didn't want to part with it. So he carefully planned his strategy, making sure he could sell her on his concept of "a better house than what you have now" on the first try. He started out quietly by asking her to sit on the couch because he wanted to present an idea to her. Jeanie had been married to this man long enough to know there was a sales pitch coming, and it usually meant a move was involved, but she didn't say a word because she knew these sessions were usually a lot of fun. As soon as he started to promote his plan and explain the design he had in his head, his tone would pick up and he would talk faster; he was sure she would stop him before he could finish, so he spoke fast to get it all said quickly. But Jeanie sat there and listened to the whole thing.

There were, however, a few times when she thought he was done, because he had paused for a tenth of a second, only to then start again with another thought that had just entered his mind. She sat there for about twenty minutes listening to her husband try to tell her why this new house would be just perfect for them and be the cap on their retirement. When he finished he just stood there and looked at her, waiting for a response, expecting the worst. Then she spoke.

"Can I help you draw this house?" A big smile went across Ralph's face.

"I don't want to do this without you, Jeanie. I need your input."

"When and how do you plan on doing this? It sounds very costly."

"Well, I already talked to Jeff and he said we could move in with him when we sell this and while we build the new one."

"Where do you plan on building this house?"

"Well, Pat told me about a piece of land along the river that looks very promising. And we could probably get three or four lots out of it. (Pat was a local realtor who was married to Ralph's cousin, Debbie.)

"Do you want to go see it now?"

"Let's go; I know I won't have any peace till you show me," Jeanie said laughingly.

They drove out to the property where Ralph showed her the land and pointed out the spot where he thought their house would be perfectly situated on it, and she said, "Go for it."

Jeanie had been making some plans of her own, which involved going back to school. She had been looking into some courses on decorating and design. She had selected Trenton State College since it wasn't that terribly far for her to commute to. Ralph already knew she had artistic abilities and thought she should go for it, also.

The next several months were tied up in buying the land and getting subdivision approval. Jeanie stayed busy with the courses at school and still managed to squeeze in some small wallpapering jobs on her days off. By June they had all the necessary building permits and the next step was to put their house up for sale. Ralph thought this would be a fast sale, but everyone else said it wouldn't be. In four days the house was sold, and of course Ralph figured he must have sold it too cheap. Once they had a contract they started the moving project into Jeff's house. When the closing day came, Ralph asked the new owner how much he would have paid for his house. The couple said they looked at a lot of houses and there was nothing on the market that compared to this house. They remarked that it was one of a kind and they would have paid anything to have it. Ralph really needed to hear that, now that he'd sold it too low! But at least he could consider it a compliment to his design.

Ralph and Jeanie could concentrate on their new home to be built now that they had sold their existing home. The two of them spent a lot of time together working on this new house plan and loving every minute of it. This was what they did best and it always seemed to bring them closer together. Jeff allowed them to use the balcony master suite, and it was covered with drawings, books, and magazines that they were using to create their dream home.

*　*　*　*　*

Gid and Betty got a contract on their home and now faced the big question: What were they going to do with all this "stuff" they had accumulated over the past fourteen years? Karla and Wil had been married for two and a half years, and Mike was living in Lancaster County working in construction. Perhaps they would want some things - well, not much! It was decided that on April 22, 1986, the date of their twenty-fifth wedding anniversary, they would have an auction and sell everything they didn't want to take to Florida where they would have a much smaller house with no basement and no barn in the backyard. It took the auctioneer from 9:00 am to 6:00 pm to sell everything. Gid's remark was, "Well, you wanted to do something different for our anniversary, didn't you?" It was a lot of hard work, but they both felt good about downsizing.

Meanwhile they were trying to have a house built in Florida. They decided on a floor plan and found a lot in Sherwood Forest with some nice big oak trees, and it was only about a mile from the Bahia Vista Mennonite Church where they attended when in Sarasota. The closing in New Jersey happened before the house in Sarasota was completed, so they lived in one of their rental properties until the new house was completed.

While all this moving preparation was taking place, something very exciting was happening in Lancaster County. Karla and Wil were expecting their first child, which, of course, was also Gid and Betty's first grandchild. When Karla first told Betty that she was pregnant, Betty was very excited, and then she realized that she would be a grandmother and that sounded "so… old," but she soon got over that and could hardly wait to see their first grandchild. Christopher Jon Esh came into this world on July 18th, 1986. Betty was in the delivery room to comfort Karla in case Wil passed out, but he did just fine. However, Betty was the first to notice that the baby was a boy. Gid was on a flight and couldn't see his first grandson until he was three days old. He couldn't help wondering if he would grow up to be a pilot.

* * * * *

By fall of 1986 Ralph had all the necessary permits and was ready to break ground on what they now called the "River House." Because of the design of the house, the foundation had to be done in two phases. This enabled the well driller to reach the back of the property before the upper foundation went in. It was quite an undertaking, and they were in no hurry to rush this job. From the beginning Ralph had promised he would only work on this house as a fill-in job, in other words, when he wasn't busy with the drywall business, which he was very busy with.

By midwinter they had the entire house framed and under cover. Then they were just going to wait till spring of the following year to begin work again.

By March Jeanie was in big demand for her wallpapering services, and some of the jobs were so big that they required the use of scaffolding, and then she had to have Ralph help her, which he was glad to do. There was one particular job that everyone on the crew had to help with, and on that one the walls were over 26 feet high. She had to order special rolls of paper for that job, and Ralph and Rodney stood on the scaffolding at different levels as she dropped the rolls from the top. That was one job everyone was glad to see finished. That house was quite the house; for example, the master bathroom was 32 feet wide and 40 feet long with 26 floor-to-ceiling windows around the entire room. That's not a misprint; you read it right, that was the size of the *bathroom.* Oh, and the ceiling was sixteen feet high, all wood with skylights.

By spring they were back at work on their river house and hoping to have it completed by the fall. In May Jeff received a call informing him of the passing of his mother. After the services he took some time off to fly to England to spend time with some family members who lived there.

In June Stephanie graduated from Delaware Valley High and Rod completed his junior year. Work had really increased and Ralph had to hire some more help, one of which was his brother Glenn. Ralph's father had taken a turn for the worst and was unable to continue working.

Ralph's mother felt she could take care of his dad at home by herself rather than put him in a nursing home, but Ralph and Glenn thought that was too big an undertaking for her to do by herself. But how do you tell someone to put their spouse into a home when they still want to be with them? It's hard to let go after so many years together. There is always that hope that they might get better, and what would they think if they did and you had put them in a home? It would seem like you had given up on them. That's what the two brothers were thinking was going through their mother's mind, so they didn't push the issue.

In October Stephanie had decided on a travel career, so Jeanie and Carol drove her to Pittsburgh to the school where she had chosen to study. With their first child leaving the nest, things felt a little different at home. The river house was completed now, so Ralph, Jeanie, and Rod moved in and set up Stephanie's room just the way she would have wanted it. This was the first time one of their children wasn't with them when they moved into a new house and it was a strange feeling. To make things worse, Rod was now driving and spending more time away from home also. His interest in music had peaked, and he and his friends had moved their practice sessions into the Schaible's basement, where they were spending a great deal of time. Occasionally Ralph and Jeanie would run up to see how the band was doing and would be impressed with the effort they were putting into all their practicing. The boys had also added three new members, Bret and Billy Palleria, and Mark Cyphers. In addition they had come up with a name for their group, Point Blank. The music was loud, but Ralph remembered how his parents thought the music of the sixties that he'd loved so much had been too loud!

* * * * *

It was November 2, 1987, and Karla and Wil were expecting their second child who was now two weeks later than the doctors had calculated. Karla was at the doctor's office where they did a stress test on the baby. They told her to go home and get a good night's sleep and then come back in the morning and they would induce labor. Apparently the baby didn't like that idea at all, and during the night Karla's water broke and they were on their way to the hospital after dropping CJ off at his Grandma and Grandpa Esh's. On November 3, 1987, a healthy little girl, Kari Amanda Esh, was born into their family. Betty arrived the next day to help take care of her new granddaughter and entertain CJ so that his mother could spend more time with his new baby sister.

* * * * *

Settling in at the river house was quite an experience. The house was so big for basically just the two of them that it seemed silly for them to be living there, but Ralph reminded her that this was an investment for their future. Despite the size, Jeanie made quick use of one of the three large loft areas and turned it into a studio. Jeanie had always been interested in antiques and loved using them in her decorating themes. Carol was also very good at finding great sales and auctions to go to where they could find treasures to bid on. This had become one of the girls' favorite pastimes, and they always came home with a story of how they just found the most amazing bargain. One of the finds was an antique easel that Jeanie purchased and placed in her studio loft. Even Ralph thought it was gorgeous. He commented that the layers of paint were so thick on it that it looked like it belonged to Michelangelo. She really did have a gift for putting the right thing in the right place. Carol and Jeanie had become quite a team, and Ralph could always tell by the smiles on their faces that they enjoyed each other's company very much.

* * * * *

In January, Gid and Betty were heading back to Africa. Jay Lehman was taking a tour of about thirty people. This time Nelson and Ruth Brunk, and Chet and Reba Nolt joined the Millers and the Lehmans on their trek through the African plains. This was the dry season, but they experienced some unusually heavy rains in Ambeselli, which made travel very difficult at times. They got the van stuck on a couple of occasions, which made for some humorous moments. One particular time one of the young men was standing on the bumper of the van to give it more weight while several other men were trying to push the van out of the mud puddle. As the van lurched forward, it threw him backwards, landing him firmly on his butt in the mud. All the onlookers had a good laugh because it was so comical, but Betty felt sorry for him because everyone was laughing at his expense. The man was a good sport about it, though, and he laughed right along with them.

The safari wasn't quite as good this time, in regards to animal viewing. The weather had been so wet that the animals could get water at higher locations. Nonetheless, the trip was once again a memorable experience. While they were in Nairobi, the Brunks and the Millers met up with their friends, Mark and Jeanie Martin, who were teaching there at Roslyn Academy. Nelson thought he would have some fun with Jeanie, so while they were walking around he would throw his voice in a manner that made her keep turning around to see who was calling her name. This went on for some period of time until she asked if anyone else heard someone calling her. By then they all couldn't hold it in any longer, and began to laugh. Nelson had a lot more things up his sleeve, one of which was making up sayings to make you think and laugh at the same time. An example would be, "I feel more like I do now then I ever did before" Gid quickly caught on and adopted this practice as well, and whenever he had the opportunity, he would hit you with one. And, I might add, he became very good at it. This completed another successful trip to one of their favorite destinations.

* * * * *

In February of 1988, Stephanie returned home from completing school and quickly got a job at a travel agency in Trenton. She really loved being on her own and thoroughly enjoyed the benefits of being in the travel agency. Occasionally she would be sent to a beautiful resort so she could better sell that particular vacation package to someone else.

As always her parents were very busy with their work, but not too busy to spend time together with each other. In the last two years they had become much closer and stronger in their relationship with one another. Work was the only thing that kept them apart now.

In June of that year Rodney graduated from high school and began working full-time for his father. Kyle also joined the team, but before they started work Ralph had a little surprise for the two of them. They had given him all their summers and Saturdays while in high school so he thought it only fitting that he reward them. Ralph and Jeanie had discovered that they loved going on cruises, and so they thought, why not send the boys on a cruise by themselves for their graduation present. They had gotten this idea before Stephanie started working at the travel agency, so they had booked it through a friend at church. The cruise was a four-day cruise, but days before the cruise was scheduled their friend, Mary Ann, called and said the cruise had been over-booked. Ralph and Jeanie's hearts sank, but then Mary Ann said, not to worry, they are going to give them an upgrade at no additional cost. Then she said it was a singles cruise and it was for seven days. Guess who was cheering and who wasn't? Ralph and Jeanie were a little worried. But everything was wonderful, and when the boys came home, they thanked Ralph for the greatest present anyone could have ever given them. They started off by telling their parents they had hit it off immediately with five Italian girls, all sisters. The girls told the boys that their father had put them on the cruise and told them not to come home without husbands. The boys had the time of their lives and, thankfully, they came home single!

* * * * *

Gid and Betty had been talking to their friends, Jake and Bonnie Beachey about going on a trip together. They finally decided they'd go to San Francisco in August. They were surprised at how cool the ocean breeze was and it was very comfortable for a hot summer day. They traveled south along the coast to Big Sur and north over the Golden Gate Bridge to Sausalito and the wine country. Betty knew about this area from some books she had read. Fisherman's Wharf was also a favorite.

* * * * *

On a sadder note Ralph's mother was finding it much harder to continue taking care of her husband at home. The decision was made to have him admitted to a nursing home that was close enough for her to continue seeing him regularly and to assist in his daily care. Her decision was a difficult one to make, but both of her sons supported her in making her choice. They had been really concerned over the physical toll that caring for him at home was taking on her, especially when she had to lift or move him during the day.

* * * * *

Gid was now Captain on the 727 that he flew regularly, and he was commuting to Europe to fly the Boeing 727 between different European cities. He usually flew out from the same city for a month at a time. In November of 1988 he was flying to Berlin, and since Betty had never been there, she decided to go along. It was interesting to walk along the wall and see all the graffiti, Check Point Charlie, and the Brandenburg Gate. The military provided a bus to take you to East Berlin to go shopping, and Gid and Betty decided to take the trip. The bus went through the wall at Check Point Charlie. Everyone had to hold up their passports by the window so the security guard could see them. It was rather sobering driving to the other side of the wall.The buildings were so drab and there were guards with guns on almost every corner. However, with the money exchange so good, Betty made some good purchases including cut crystal water glasses and a nice doll. It felt good to be back in West Berlin, but before leaving they visited the museum at Check

Point Charlie. They learned how many of the people escaped from East Berlin to West Berlin.

* * * * *

Toward the year's end Jeanie was having a little discomfort in her stomach area and went to the doctor's to have it checked out. She had always been a stickler about getting her yearly checkups, and she always hounded her girlfriends to do the same. The doctor said Jeanie's discomfort was just due to bloating and to take some antacid tablets.

Jeanie was always into healthy foods and thought good nutrition was important. She was always trying to get her family to try something natural or organic. Her cooking was the best you could find anywhere, bar none, and once in a while she would slip something into a meal without them knowing it, and then when they finished and said how delicious it was, she would tell them what was in it. Most of the time they would just make faces, but on some humorous occasions Ralph would spit it out saying, "I can't believe you let me eat that without telling me." And Jeanie would always say, "You sure thought it was good when you didn't know what it was; how come all of a sudden, now it's bad?" Ralph loved it of course, but he just had to put on a show to get the kids to laugh.

* * * * *

A trip to Hawaii sounded real good to Betty, especially after the continuous parade of rental homes to collect late monthly payments from, then to clean, and then to repaint whenever someone would move out and new tenants were moving in. Just the thought of laying on a beach in a romantic paradise made her day. Gid and Betty asked their friends, Jan and Elmer, to join them for a week of fun in Hawaii, and that's just what the boys were going to have. They were no sooner there than Gid and Elmer were wind surfing the biggest waves they had ever seen. In fact, from where the girls were laying on the beach it looked like the guys had completely disappeared from view behind those enormous waves. This was a little frightening to the girls, and even though they eventually would appear on the other side of the wave, they let them know they would rather they spent more time on shore with them. Boys will be boys, but eventually they would come ashore to spend time with their honeys. The girls finally convinced them to take some time touring the island with them, and they all had a wonderful experience. At one point they were standing very near an active lava flow and saw the huge pillar of steam as the hot lava flowed into the ocean.

* * * * *

A new year had begun, and everything continued as usual; Ralph and Jeanie were both very busy with work. By now Rodney and the boys in the band had started to take their show on the road, playing music at different locations. When they were playing one gig in particular, a popular band in the Allentown area had noticed what a good musician Rod was. It just so happened that they were in need of a keyboard player, and they asked him to join their band. The band was called the Armadillos, and they had quite a following already. Rod talked it over with his band and they gave him the go ahead. The days that followed were days of little sleep for Rod. Playing to all hours of the night and getting up at 5:30 am to work for his dad became a real effort. One day they found Rod holding a hammer and leaning against the wall. Apparently he had fallen asleep while nailing up the drywall.

* * * * *

Wil and his brother, Titus, were ready to give up the painting business and move on to different interests. There was an opportunity to receive management training for 84 Lumber Company, so Wil elected to pursue it.

During this same period of time Gid had become interested in building a Grease Monkey franchise. The Grease Monkeys were a chain of automotive quick lubes. Art Sensenig, who was the president of the company, was married to Betty's cousin, Edith, and he helped Gid to get started with his new venture. Gid bought the land and hired a contractor to build the building. As the building was nearing completion, Gid realized he needed someone reliable to run the business, so he offered the job to his son-in-law, Wil. Wil accepted the challenge and turned out to be the perfect man for the job.

Wil's talents didn't go unnoticed, and it wasn't long before Grease Monkey offered him a job as a regional manager, and he and Karla and the two children moved to Fort Wayne, Indiana. It was very hard to see them go, but Gid and Betty knew it was a good opportunity for Wil.

* * * * *

In December Stephanie started a new job working for Club Med in Port St. Lucie, Florida. Her contract ran through the end of May 1990. She loved travel and this also gave her a chance to use her dancing abilities while performing in shows during the evenings.

In February Jeanie went back to the doctor's still experiencing discomfort in her abdominal area, and again the doctors said it was nothing but gas. Jeanie had a hunch it was more than that and thought they should run more tests, but they told her she would be wasting her money and that there was nothing wrong.

* * * * *

In 1990 Gid was flying to Berlin again. The wall was now down and Betty decided to go with Gid on one of his trips, hoping they would have time to go see the wall again. Once they were in Berlin, they and one of the other pilots took a taxi to see the wall. As they walked along they picked up some souvenirs to take home. The two pilots actually had found some quite large pieces. When they arrived back at the airport and were walking down the airport in uniform carrying their large pieces of Berlin wall on the end of some rebar, Betty noticed the ticket agents smiling.

Another thing Betty will always remember about that trip is that she was allowed to sit in the extra seat in the cockpit with Gid because the flight was so full. She wore earphones and listened to the pilots converse with the air traffic controllers and found it to be a fascinating experience with her husband.

* * * * *

By April Ralph and Jeanie had made the decision that the house was just too much for them, and so they decided to sell it. The clincher was the yearly property tax bill, which was over $7,000. When Ralph saw the latest tax increase he said it was time to leave the state of New Jersey and head to Pennsylvania. They put their house on the market and began looking back in the Benton area where they had owned the farm they were so happy at.

Stephanie had completed her tour with Club Med in Florida by the end of May, and a week later went to her second assignment in Zihautanejo, Mexico.

The river house sold in June, and Ralph and Jeanie still had not found a place to live. The closing was scheduled for August and they both were getting a little anxious.

* * * * *

Mike decided to work on the wheat harvest the summer of 1990 before starting college at Montana State University in Bozeman, Montana. He would be majoring in wildlife management and ecology. He started in Oklahoma and ended up in Montana leaving his truck in Oklahoma. Now he was in Montana and needed his truck, so Gid and Betty flew to Oklahoma City and drove his truck to Montana.

In June, Gid and Betty flew to Salt Lake City, did some sightseeing there and drove up through Wyoming to Yellowstone National Park where they met Mike. After taking in all the beauties of Yellowstone, they went to Bozeman to see Mike at the University. There was a rodeo at the university so they watched that, enjoying the western atmosphere.

Next the three of them headed towards Glacier National Park. It was beautiful, too, but in a different way than Yellowstone. There was still a lot of snow in the Park and the roads weren't plowed through the high elevations, so they had to go out the way they came in. They decided to drive up through Canada and come in the east entrance to the park.

Gid's brother-in-law, Elam Ebersol, had told them of an Amish settlement near Rexford, Montana, where his niece and nephew lived, so Gid, Betty, and Mike decided to look it up on their way to Canada. After getting a motel in Eureka, they drove through Rexford and across Lake Koocanusa and north to the northwest corner of Montana. It was beautiful country with open range cattle and lots of log homes. They soon found the Amish community with its log store, school and Post Office. It was Sunday evening and they were having a hymn sing. This is where they found John and

Lydia Algyer, Elam's niece and nephew. It was getting late, so they made plans to come back the next afternoon. It was great getting to know them, and they walked to the Canadian border where there was a fence that could be seen for miles through the cut in the forest.

* * * * *

Time was running out for Ralph and Jeanie to find a new home to live in, and so they decided to make one more trip to the Benton area to find a house. But once again nothing was found. As they were returning home Ralph made one last stop in Cunningham, Pennsylvania, to pick up some real estate magazines for Jeanie to check out. Within a couple of days Jeanie had found them a place to stay for a while. Ralph notified all his builders that he was leaving. They asked him who was going to take care of their drywall needs, and he told them that nineteen-year-old Kyle Burke had said he would take it over. Kyle had turned into quite a good contractor and was completely able to handle their work if given the opportunity. Glenn had decided to leave the construction business and move on to something else. He eventually began working for the High Bridge School. Before they left town to move away, Jeanie made one more trip to the doctors, and this time the doctor called Ralph at home and told him that his wife was a hypochondriac. Ralph was furious and wanted to go and confront the doctor, but Jeanie calmed him down and told him to let it go.

On July 8, 1990, Jeanie received a call from Ralph's mother telling them of her husband's passing. Ralph H. Walls was 69 when he died and had served ten years on the Clinton township town council, six of which he was the mayor. Many came to pay tribute to the man who had served his township and country faithfully throughout his years. The news of his father's death put a little more of a damper on their departure from New Jersey. But Ralph's mother assured him that everything would be fine; Glenn and her sister, Eleanor, didn't live that far away and could come to her aid if she needed anything.

14

RINGTOWN

Moving day was very emotional and yet exciting at the same time. This was the kind of thing Jeanie and Ralph had always talked about doing one day, but had never thought of it actually happening. As the two big rigs pulled out of the driveway with all there worldly processions in them, a feeling of the end of an era came over them. Their church, friends and families were all being left behind.

They were moving to a place they knew nothing about and where they didn't know a single person. Jeanie had the Jimmy filled with personal items and Ralph had the van packed to the ceiling with construction tools. They had prayed about this move, and both of them felt this was what they were meant to do, but now this convoy of vehicles heading down the road made it suddenly very real, and that was a scary feeling to Jeanie. Ralph, on the other hand, kept saying, "We just have to trust God, I just feel He has something special for us. He is with us no matter where we go." Ralph had the spirit of adventure in him, and couldn't wait to start exploring the surrounding areas of their new home.

Late that afternoon they pulled into their destination. Ralph didn't want to keep Paul and his crew there late into the night, so he told them just to take the heavy things into the house and leave all the small stuff in the driveway or garage. He didn't plan on renting in Sugar Loaf for very long. In fact, he had already told Jeanie that starting Monday they were going to begin driving circles around this location and expanding them after each lap was completed. That way they wouldn't miss any hidden treasures that might be for sale. She new exactly what he was talking about, because he did the same thing every time they were looking for a new place to live.

That evening they said goodbye to their good friend Paul, and his trucks pulled out of their driveway and then disappeared from view. It was official, they were alone, and now they only had each other. As Jeanie looked around she was overwhelmed with how much stuff Ralph had told them to leave sitting out. But Ralph told her not to worry; he would take care of it all. By 10:00 that evening he had kept his word, and the driveway was empty. It was easy falling asleep that night, because they were both so exhausted, but by morning Ralph was raring to go.

"Times a wasting, let's get breakfast and start looking for a place."

"You have to be kidding. You said we would start on Monday, and this is only Sunday. Isn't this supposed to be a day of rest?"

"You're right. Plan Number Two. Let me find my Bible and I'll read some Scripture, and then we'll have breakfast and head out. We can rest while we're in the car."

"You're pathetic. It's going to take me a while to find all the kitchen stuff, though."

"Plan Three. I'll take you out for breakfast and that will save time."

"Like I said, you're pathetic."

"I'll take that as a compliment."

The day they had found this place in Sugar Loaf was just sheer luck. They were returning from a trip to Benton in hopes of finding a place out there, but they had been unable to. Riding home that day they remembered how they had always said Sugar Loaf looked very attractive from up on Route 80, and that some day they needed to stop there and explore. So after no success in Benton and time running out to find a place to live, they took the exit ramp into Sugar Loaf. It was 5:00 in the evening and all the real estate offices were closed. Jeanie was feeling down and getting a little tense about not having a place to live. Ralph kept saying don't worry about it we still have three weeks. Then he thought, *I'll pull into this diner, they always have those racks with real estate books, and I'll grab a few.* He came out with a handful, which kept Jeanie occupied all the way home. When Ralph had come home from work that following Monday evening, Jeanie had good news. She had called one of the realtors in the book and told her the situation. The realtor said, "Let me make a call and I'll get right back to you." As it turns out the realtor had a client who had a house on the market that was willing to rent it for up to six months. When she told Ralph he thought it sounded great and to go ahead and make the deal.

With the Bible reading over and breakfast completed, they began their adventure in finding their new home. While Ralph was driving Jeanie had the atlas on her lap tracing their route. They drove all day. It was such a beautiful area, but they didn't see anything that interested them. Ralph pulled the Jimmy over and asked Jeanie to show him on the map where they were right now. He pulled the map up close to his eyes and studied a minute. Then he said, "Let's try this place. It's got a nice ring to it." Jeanie took the map back and looked to where he was pointing.

"Funny, aren't you the clever one?" The name of the town was Ringtown.

"Well it does. Don't you think?"

"That's probably another eight miles from where we are right now."

"So, we've got nothing else to do." This was still their first day of looking and they both were getting pretty tired. The approach to the town was on an uphill grade with trees on both sides of the road, and then it opened up to an open field on the right. Right in the front portion of this field sat a big, beautiful home with a stone wall along the front of the property. Farther to the right were barns. The trees on the property were huge and beautiful, and in the front yard, smack-dab in front of them, was a FOR SALE sign.

Their mouths were hanging so far open that neither one could speak. Simultaneously, they knew what they were going to do. The place looked empty and there was no driveway that they could see. Ralph knew there had to be a way into it, so he drove into town, turned right and pulled into a lane between a church and a house. Jeanie exclaimed. "What are you doing? You can't just pull into someone else's drive."

"I'm not. This has to be the drive to that house." Behind the church was a barn, and sure enough, behind the barn the driveway turned left, and there sat the bank barn and the walk to the back of the house. Ralph stopped the vehicle and opened the door.

"Ralph, what are you doing?" Jeanie asked, nervous that they were here uninvited.

"Checking this place out."

"You can't just look around."

"The house is for sale, that's what you're supposed to do when something is for sale. Besides, I don't think there is anyone living here. Come on, let's look."

"Ok, just give me a minute to get out of the car." It appeared that there were three barns and two homes. It was terrific, and they spent an hour walking around and looking in windows. Ralph started to run down the front lawn, and Jeanie yelled, "Now where are you going?"

"To get the phone number off the sign." They got back in the car and took a quick drive through the town. It was a very quaint little town, and they could tell that people loved it, because everyone's place looked well taken care of. The ride back to Sugar Loaf was non-stop chatter about the property; they were so excited. Ralph couldn't wait to call about it, but Jeanie kept reminding him that it was late Sunday evening, maybe not the best time to call. It could wait till tomorrow, she told him. Early Monday morning Ralph was already pacing the floor.

"When do you think would be a good time to call that real estate office?"

"Would you just relax, honey? Did you do your devotions yet?"

"Yeah, an hour ago."

"Why don't you go do them again, and maybe that will calm you down."

"I can't."

"Why can't you?"

"I already did a week's worth while waiting for you to get up."

Jeanie laughed out loud at that comment. Ralph always could get a good laugh out of her. "You could be a little more help around here, then. I still haven't found all the cookware the way you boys packed things."

"Oh, it's right over here." Ralph took about five steps and picked up a box marked "kitchen" on the top.

"When did that get put there?"

"I did that this morning after I finished my week's worth of devotions."

Jeanie busted out laughing again and said, "Well, at least now I can start to cook something." Rod finally came in to see what all the talking was about. They all sat down and had breakfast, and then Ralph and Rod started helping Jeanie look for boxes she needed to unpack. Around 10:00 a.m. Ralph couldn't wait any longer, so he called the real estate office. The lady who answered was named Lois Nolte; she knew everything about the listing and was eager to show them. They agreed to meet her at the property by noon. It only took twenty minutes to drive to Ringtown, but Ralph insisted they leave by 11:00 at the latest. So they threw the camera in the Jimmy and drove back to Ringtown. They both loved the property and figured the price had to be out of reach, but it would be fun to look at it anyway. At 11:50 Lois pulled into the driveway and got out to greet them. They spent over two hours with her going through every nook and cranny. Then they started to talk price, and they had bought enough properties to know how to react when a price was given. But when something that would be selling for thousands more in New Jersey was offered in Pennsylvania for probably half the price, it was hard to contain themselves. But they did, and Ralph even asked if the owner was motivated to sell.

"Make an offer and let's see what happens," Lois said. Ralph said that he would like a minute to talk to Jeanie first. They turn and walked away, and when they'd gotten far enough to be out of earshot, they started to talk excitedly.

"Do you believe it?" Jeanie said.

"No, pinch me. Are we dreaming?"

"What are you going to do?" Jeanie asked.

"I'll offer $10,000 less and see what they say."

"I'd give them just what they're asking if I were you, Ralph."

"Me, too, but let's try this first." They walked back to Lois and presented what they thought was a good offer. Lois asked if they were willing to put up some money to make the offer enticing. They said sure, and agreed to follow her back to the office to draw up the papers.

As soon as they got in the car Ralph turned to Jeanie and said, "This is our house, Jeanie; there is no way we're going to lose this property." Jeanie was glad to hear that. Most people wouldn't even consider living in that house. You see, it had been a funeral parlor for the second generation that lived there, which explained why the inside was so beautiful. The second home could be used as a rental or a studio for Jeanie. There were twelve acres of beautiful hay fields and all those barns for Ralph. The paper work was finished and now the waiting game began. This was always the part that Ralph wasn't good at. In a day Lois called with a counter offer from the owner. Ralph and Jeanie didn't want to fool around, so they said fine. Lois said the owner would like to meet them at the property first, which they quickly agreed to. The date and time was set and the celebrating began. Ralph already had plans for what he wanted to do with the property. His idea was to cut a driveway in on the lower side of the house that would go back to the bank barn. Then he wanted to continue the stonewall all the way back to the barn also, remodel the barn, and start a nursery and landscaping business. Jeanie could have a craft store inside along with all the nursery and greenhouse items. Ralph thought the location was perfect for such a thing. Jeanie loved the idea and then became even more excited, adding her ideas into the mix. They were scheduled to meet the homeowner tomorrow at noon, which meant they had a whole twenty-four hours to kill. There was no way they wanted to stay at home, so they hopped in the Jimmy and decided to explore the area around Ringtown further. The countryside was so pretty it just reminded them both of their childhoods and where they had grown up. Beautiful farmland and truck patches dotted the land, just like a postcard. They decided to search for a church that would be close to their new home, and it had to be either a Baptist or a Mennonite church. The church next to their house was a United Church of Christ and it looked very tiny. It seemed like a very nice church but they had made up their minds on what they were looking for and continued on. Jeanie kept telling Ralph not to worry, that they would find something. The day came to a close without finding a church, but they knew God already had one picked out for them. The next day's meeting with the owner was enjoyable. Mr. Barrow, who was actually the owner's son, was helping his family sell the property. Their mother was recently moved to a retirement home, and the children needed to help her with the disposal of her real estate. The meeting went very well and Mr. Barrow supplied them with lots of information about the history of the property. They ended their visit by shaking hands. The closing date had been set and once again it was just a matter of waiting.

In the weeks that followed Ralph and Jeanie continued to explore the area around Ringtown, but they still hadn't found a church. One day Jeanie had been talking to her mother on the phone, catching her up on all the exciting news, and when she hung up she told Ralph that her mother said there were some Mennonite churches up toward the Danville area. So they got the atlas out to see how far that would be from their house. It looked like it was going to be quite a ride, but since they had nothing else to do they decided to take a nice Saturday drive and check it out. Once they got to Ringtown Ralph said, "OK, you watch the time and I'll watch the mileage." They drove through the little town of Aristis, then on to Mt. Carmel where they turned right onto Route 61 and headed for Danville. After about forty minutes of driving, Ralph said, "This isn't going to work; this is too much driving," and he turned the car around and began heading back. They had been driving back for about twenty minutes and Jeanie could sense that Ralph was getting a little upset.

"Well, I guess I'll just watch TV church for the fifth week in a row again tomorrow," He said, with a little disgust in his voice

"You know, Ralph, maybe we should expand our choices. Mom said you might want to consider a Bible Fellowship Church. Mom said that she thought they were started by Mennonites and Baptists."

"Did you say Bible Fellowship?"

"Yes, why?"

"Just as you said that we passed a brick church on the right, and I'm pretty sure the sign said Bible Fellowship." Ralph checked his mirror and spun the car around and drove about two hundred feet back down the road. Sure enough the sign said Bible Fellowship. He pulled in the driveway, stopped the car and ran to the door, but there was no sign telling what time services were held. As he walked back to the car to tell Jeanie, he noticed there was a sidewalk connected to the parking lot, which lead to a brick home.

"I'll bet that's the parsonage next door. I'm going to go over and ask about the church."

"Are you sure that belongs to the church?"

"No, but what's it matter? Do you want to come?"

"No, I'll wait." Ralph ran down the sidewalk, up to the front door, and promptly knocked on it loudly. A petite lady answered the door.

"Yes, may I help you?"

"Yes, Hi. My name is Ralph Walls. I'm not from around here and I was wondering about the church next door. Do you know anything about it?"

"Yes, I do. I'm Laura Cassel and my husband, Alva, is the pastor."

"Oh great, what can you tell me about what you believe?"

Laura Cassel had a big smile on her face as she began to explain their beliefs to Ralph. After a few moments she asked, "Would you like to come in?"

"Oh no, my wife is waiting for me in the car."

"She is? Well, have her come in, too." She then started to walk down the sidewalk with Ralph toward the car. When they got to the end of the walk, Laura saw that her husband was walking down the hill toward them.

"Here comes my husband and grandson now." Ralph looked up the hill and saw a man wearing a cowboy hat and carrying a gun coming toward him. There also was a young boy with him.

"Alva, this is Ralph Walls, and he wants to know about our church. Ralph, this is my husband, Alva, and my oldest grandson, Luke.

"Pleased to meet you, I think." Ralph said with a grin on his face, nodding slightly toward the gun while reaching over to shake the pastor's hand.

"So, you want to know about the church, do you?" Alva asked as he slung the gun over his shoulder. It was all Ralph could do to keep from laughing. *This guy is a gun-toting pastor*, he thought to himself; this was something Ralph wasn't quite familiar with. Meanwhile Laura has made her way to the car as Jeanie was getting out; they exchanged greetings and walked toward the men. They talked about their faith and their church and invited Ralph and Jeanie to join them for dinner after church tomorrow.

"That would be great; we would love to." They returned to the Jimmy and started their drive back to Sugar Loaf.

The next morning they were up early and ready for Sunday school and church. When they arrived at the Bethany Bible Fellowship Church, they were greeted by a lot of people. A man by the name of Hal Snyder was one of the first to greet them. Another man was the Sunday school superintendent, Bob Scott. Both men showed an interest in their visit that day and lead them to the adult class that was being held in the sanctuary. Ralph and Jeanie took quite an interest in the man who was preaching that day, since it was only the day before that they'd first met him wearing a cowboy hat and shouldering a gun. Alva was a kind and loving man of God, which was completely obvious, from the way he spoke to the mannerisms he portrayed. His style of preaching was such that it kept their attention focused on the message he was delivering. They both felt like this was home for them, and the people seated around them were their new church family. After the service many people came up to meet them and welcome them, and they couldn't wait till the time came when they would know them all by name. Eventually they made it over to the parsonage and enjoyed a delicious meal that Laura had prepared for them. It just so happened that it was Ralph's favorite meal, pork and sauerkraut. Ralph took this as a sign from God, that this was where he was supposed to be. They also got to meet one of the Cassel's daughters, Joanna who was there along with her husband, Tony. Tony and Joanna Murrin were missionaries for the New Tribes Mission and were preparing to go to the field to serve in Bolivia. Tony was a pilot and Joanna would be teaching while they were there. A friendship had begun that day that would become very special in the years to come.

* * * * *

This particular month Gid was flying out of Oslo, Norway. What a beautiful country! He would take a short flight each morning and be back to the hotel by early afternoon. This was his schedule for three or four days, and then he would go home for four days and then go back to Europe and fly a few days again. Betty had never seen Norway, so Gid asked her to go along. They were having some kind of big celebration in Oslo, and after Gid and Betty went up to see the mountains, they took in some of the festivities. There was lots of food and confetti and spray string everywhere. Soon it was bedtime even though it was still light outside because Norway is so close to the Arctic Circle. It didn't get dark until after 11:00 pm, but Gid had to get up early the next morning to fly.

Betty slept in and then went for a morning walk. She was admiring how quickly they had the streets and everything cleaned up already when she heard some loud voices. To her surprise she looked ahead and saw three men coming towards her wearing no clothes. She figured they'd had too much to drink the night before. Plus, the practical side of Betty thought, *it isn't warm enough to be without clothes!*

* * * * *

The next few weeks were filled with excitement leading up to the closing on the Ringtown property. When the big day came they were anxious to move all their things in, but they decided to paint a couple of rooms first, which didn't take long. As usual, they did the moving a little at a time. Stephanie had just completed her last Club Med assignment and planned to stay with them until she'd decided where she wanted to live and work. Rod was still playing nights with the band, but he helped his parents during the day with some of the moving. His eventual plan was to move back to the Allentown area to be closer to the rest of the band members, which would make the practicing times a lot more convenient. All the band members agreed on sharing a rental house, and the move to Allentown was finalized. Stephanie thought that sounded like a great idea and asked if they had room for one more person, which they all said yes to. She signed a one-year lease and moved in with her brother.

With a new home and church all taken care of, Ralph and Jeanie needed to make some decisions on what to do with their time. Ralph didn't think he should start the nursery project yet; Jeanie wasn't in the mood to start tearing up the property so soon. One day they were riding through Mahanoy City when they saw a store for sale, so they stopped in to take a look at it. The architecture was beautiful, and the store reminded them of stores they had been to as children. This store was such a vintage treasure that it even had a cable running from the upstairs to the front cashier. The wire had a canister on it that you put the money for the purchase in and sent it to the upstairs for the correct change. The walls were lined with huge and fancy mahogany cabinetry. The aisles were lined with glass and mahogany cases. Pressed metal ceilings were all throughout the building. It looked as though one day it had been a very high-class clothing store. When you entered the store you entered between two very large glass display windows. The present owners were selling crafts and ceramics. Ralph and Jeanie both thought this would be a great place to showcase all their collectables and antiques, plus they could continue selling the crafts and ceramics. They talked to the owner and worked out an agreement. They didn't actually buy the store, but were just testing the waters to see if it was right for them. If they decided not to go through with the purchase, they would pay the owner for any merchandise of hers that they sold along with a rental fee. It sounded good for starters, so now they were merchants.

As time went on Jeanie began to sense that something was wrong within her body again. They immediately found a new doctor, and Jeanie had tests done to determine what was causing her discomfort. Once again the doctor came back saying that the bloating she was experiencing was a gas problem and gave her a prescription for something that would help. This was the sixth time a doctor had made the same diagnosis.

* * * * *

Betty's good friend, Shirley Grace, whom she'd met on Long Island in 1965, had been fighting cancer for five years. They had so much fun together raising their children and traveling together and meeting at Spruce Lake Retreat every July with their other New York friends. When a mutual friend told Betty that she didn't think Shirley was going to get better, it really hit her hard. She felt she wanted to spend a few days with her in her home in Long Island and give her husband, Carl, a break. He had been taking care of her with some help from friends. Carl was good at making things easier for Shirley like putting blocks of wood on one of the kitchen chairs so that it would be easier for her to get up from the chair. It was planned that Betty would go to Long Island for a few days in March. It just so happened that some of the other Spruce Lake friends were going to be in the area, too. It finally worked out that all eight ladies from the Spruce Lake Group were there. What a blessing to spend a day together with Shirley! It was the last time that Betty saw her alive. She died on April 13, 1991, and was buried at Maple Grove Mennonite Church in Belleville, Pennsylvania. Betty had lost a wonderful friend, a friend she could count on; a friend who loved the Lord, loved her family and people, a friend who loved to have a good time. Her son-in-law, Joe, said that she was the only person he knew who deserved to have the word "Grace" in her name twice. You see, she was given the name Shirley Grace Yoder when she was born, and then she married Carl Grace, so she was Shirley Grace Grace. Wouldn't it be funny if her first name had been Grace?!

Gid was still commuting to Europe to fly the Boeing 727, this time from Vienna, Austria and Stockholm, Sweden. Vienna was a favorite city of theirs, and Betty went with him several times. They enjoyed the sightseeing, the beautiful gardens, and concerts. They found this a very comforting place to be while grieving the loss of their dear friend Shirley.

* * * * *

By late spring of 1991, Ralph and Jeanie had decided not to purchase the store, and so they moved their items back to their house in Ringtown. One of the main reasons for this decision was that Jeanie was not feeling like herself and seemed to tire very easily. Once again she went to a doctor, and once again she was told the same thing. They were thankful to have found a home church so quickly, and they really enjoyed all the new friends they were making and were actively involved in most of the church activities. Ralph had decided that he wanted to get back into construction, and one of the church members asked him if he would be interested in helping him start a new project. Within a week Ralph was helping a man named Rick Cantino convert an old garage into a restaurant. Ralph worked as a subcontractor for Rick and really enjoyed getting to know him and his family. Eventually Ralph started to buy some homes to fix up and resell, and on those projects Jeanie would work right along side of him. Before long others in the church were asking for estimates on some of their construction needs as well, and Ralph was back into full-time business. He was doing everything you could think of, including roofing, siding, window replacement, drywall, framing, and plumbing.

* * * * *

One of Gid and Betty's favorite mission projects was Habitat for Humanity. They had a large presence in Sarasota under the leadership of John Schaub, one of their favorite real estate lecturers. One summer Habitat for Humanity was doing a building blitz when they built six houses in one week. The foundations were poured ahead of time. Gid was off flying, but Betty and Susie Schmucker decided to help for a day. It was a hot day in June, and they were asked to direct traffic. However, there were so many people assigned to directing traffic that they were getting relieved every fifteen minutes, so they asked if there was something else they could do. Soon they had learned to measure and cut aluminum window trim and were nailing it on. It was a great day and a lot had been accomplished.

* * * * *

In the fall of that year, Alva asked Ralph and another man from church, Dale Kahler, if they would like to accompany him to Maine to work on his cabin and do some fishing. The three of them had five days of fun roughing it in the forests of Maine. On the way back they filled coolers with live lobsters, and just before they got home they called their wives and had them put on kettles of boiling water. Needless to say, they all ate like kings that night.

Christmas in Ringtown was beautiful once again. Jeanie loved to decorate and especially with this big old house she could really do her thing. It was a given that she would be entertaining, and this year she wanted to have an open house for the whole church. Not everyone could make it, but there was a steady flow of people all afternoon. Shortly after the first of the year Stephanie called asking her father to help her move out of the band's house and into her girlfriend Tara's house. Ralph and Jeanie drove to Allentown to help with the move. It had only been a couple of weeks since Stephanie had seen her mother, but when she saw her she commented that she didn't look well. Her mother said she didn't feel well and that as soon as they got home was going to get a second opinion. Jeanie was feeling really tired and had gained a lot of weight. She was sure that something was wrong with her so she asked some other friends if they could recommend a different doctor. A new doctor was tried and again the same thing was said, discomfort due to bloating.

By March Jeanie couldn't take it any more and was willing to try anything to get an answer. Someone recommended an iridologist, a person who looks into your eyes and can tell if there is something wrong with any part of your body. Jeanie made an appointment, and the lady told her not to tell her anything that was wrong with her. Jeanie went for her scheduled appointment and had her eyes read. After the exam the lady told Jeanie that her eyes were telling her that something was wrong in her reproductive area, but she couldn't pinpoint exactly what was the problem. She advised that Jeanie should have someone check that area for her. Jeanie thanked her and started to leave but paused to ask her if she could recommend a good doctor. The lady gave her the name of one in Bloomsburg and said he was a good Christian man.

* * * * *

TWA was awarded flights into Moscow in 1992. This was the first airline in the United States to fly into Russia, and Gid and his crew flew the first flight. Sightseeing in Moscow was very interesting and Gid took lots of pictures to bring back home to show Betty and the family. He also bought quite a few authentic Russian hand crafted souvenirs. On one particular trip he bought a beautiful glass wine carafe from a street vender. He bargained with her and got it for quite a bit less than the asking price. Afterwards he was feeling guilty, thinking that this may have been a family heirloom and she had to sell it so she would have money to buy food for her family, and he had convinced her to sell it to him for a cheap price. But he felt better the next day when he saw her on the street again with quite a few more carafes.

* * * * *

Jeanie met with Dr. Russell Hoch in March of 1992. The first thing the doctor did was to examine her, and upon putting a stethoscope on her back said she had fluid in her lungs and they needed to get her admitted to the hospital for tests. Jeanie was sent to the Geisinger medical center in Danville, Pennsylvania where they discovered she had ovarian cancer. They suggested immediate surgery on Friday the 13th. Ralph sat in the waiting room with a few of his friends from the church, Ed and Judy Scoick, Rhoda Fetterolf, and Rosie Cantino. Alva was there, but then he got called away on another emergency call. Three hours later Ralph was told the doctor would like to speak with him, and he asked if his friends could come in to the room with him also. The doctor came right to the point.

"Mr. Walls, I'm going to be very honest with you. Your wife has stage four ovarian cancer. When I looked in there I could see it was everywhere. I tried to scrape some of the nodules off but there were just too many of them, so we decided to stop the surgery and instead treat the cancer with chemo when she is strong enough. I'm sorry to give you such terrible news." Ralph just sat there motionless, the ladies were crying, and Ed put his arm around Ralph's shoulder.

"So doctor, what are you telling me? How much time does she have?"

"Mr. Walls, it's really hard to tell. It could be as quick as six weeks or it could be as long as six months. It's in its final stages."

"Thank you for being honest with me."

"If you have no other questions, I need to go. Once again I'm sorry to have to be the one to tell you this. Feel free to stay here as long as you need to." The doctor stood up and started to leave.

"Sir, how soon before I can see her?"

"She'll be in recovery for at least another hour, and then I think you can go in." The doctor left the room and everyone began to say, "Oh, I'm so sorry" all at once. Ralph turned to everyone and asked a favor of them all.

"What you just heard the doctor say about how long she has must not be told to her. I will tell her when I feel the time is right. If she hears that she might give up, and right now she needs to be strong and heal from the surgery. I'm also going to make sure the doctor doesn't tell her what he just told us." They all agreed, and then asked Ralph if he wanted them to stay with him at the hospital. He thanked them all for being there with him and said that he would be fine and that he knew that Alva would be coming back soon. They all hugged him and said goodbye. A little later Alva arrived back at the hospital and Ralph filled him in on the morning's events. They sat there and prayed, then walked for a while. Later that day Ralph and Alva were able to go in and see Jeanie. See saw them coming and had a slight smile on her face. Before anyone said a word Ralph could see that Jeanie's eyes were darting back and forth between Alva and Ralph trying to read their expressions. But neither one of them gave a clue as to what they knew.

"Hi, Honey, how are you feeling?" Ralph leaned over to look right into her face, smiling as he held her hand.

"Ok, I guess. How are you doing?" She was still looking for a sign in their facial expressions.

"Don't worry about me, honey." They stayed with her for a while, but could tell she needed to rest. She had nodded off a couple of times while they were talking, so they just all held hands as Alva prayed, and then they left the room. Ralph told Alva not to hang around, that he'd be ok, and he planned on staying till visiting hours were over. The remainder of the day Ralph stayed close to Jeanie's side. At one point Jeanie woke up and said she was sorry for causing so many problems and thought Ralph should leave and go get some work done. Ralph assured her she didn't do anything wrong and that his work could wait. He told her that she was more important than any work that he might have to do and she should just be still and rest. She did ask if the doctor had talked to him and he replied that he did. Then she asked if the doctor had given him any indication on the prognosis. Ralph told her that the doctor said she would be going through some follow-up treatments that were yet to be determined. When the time came for saying goodnight, Ralph kissed her and told her he would be back first thing in the morning. The ride home seemed to take longer than usual. Ralph's mind was spinning, thinking about their future and what would lie ahead for Jeanie. It was too hard to hold the tears back now that he was alone. During the day he hadn't wanted any signs of emotion to show on his face to indicate to Jeanie that there was any major concern, but now he was alone and the reality of what the doctor had told him was just too much to bear. He knew that nothing was impossible for God, and that if he turned this over to Him and prayed harder than he had ever prayed before God might lengthen her years. She was just too young to die, and Ralph had fought too hard to win her back. God had answered those prayers, so he was not going to throw in the towel and give up. All Ralph could do was pray; it was Jeanie who had to do the fighting, she was the one who would have to go through the suffering that was to come. Ralph had made his mind up that no matter what it cost or how much time it took, he would be by her side, even if it took every penny they had, he would not quit supporting her or getting her any treatment that was needed. In a short period of time Ralph had determined that nothing else in his life was more important then fighting with every bit of strength he had to save his wife. He would give it all up if it meant they could grow old together. Penniless, poor, it just didn't matter, just give me my wife back, is what he pleaded to God.

In the weeks that followed Jeanie quickly regained her strength and seemed to be doing great. Jeanie told Ralph that she felt well enough to travel, and would like to go and visit Gid and Betty in Florida; he couldn't help noticing that she added "this might be the last time I ever get to see them." Ralph told her not to say such things. But he also thought a trip to Florida would be great. The arrangements were made and they made the flight to Sarasota, rented a car and were at the Miller's home in Sherwood Forest in practically no time at all. Ralph couldn't believe how hot it was and he asked Betty if this was normal for April, and Betty said it seemed about right to her. The thermometer was reading 93 degrees. Ralph said this is ok for a visit, but how could anyone live here full time? As he was standing there the sweat was running down his face. After Ralph got over the initial shock of the heat they began their visit. For the days they were there they thoroughly enjoyed themselves. They had long chats and were taken to many different places. Betty was an exceptional hostess and her house was always spotless, that is except for Gid's office. One of the highlights of the trip for Ralph was when Gid and Betty took them to a Thai restaurant named the Siam Orchid. Ralph had never experienced hot or spicy food in his sheltered life before, so Gid wanted to have some fun with him. First he told him the hot sauce was good and to try some, but just take a drop. Ralph did, and it was hot, but he loved it. Then Gid offered up a challenge, and Ralph was never one to back down from a challenge. Gid suggested they see who could eat a forkful with the most hot sauce drops on it. The contest began, they had already had one drop so now each forkful had to have two; it was hot, but not enough to make Ralph quit. The contest continued, three, then four, Ralph was drinking a little more water after each bite now, five then six. They both grabbed their glasses and quickly asked for more water. They had a good laugh, and the ladies said they were not going to take them to the hospital or feel sorry for them if they got sick. Ralph liked it so much that he asked the owner if she could sell him some, and she said she wasn't allowed to do that but before they left she gave him a small bottle as a gift. Ralph thanked her and said he knew exactly who was going to get this as a gift the next time he saw him. He was talking about Olie Lyons, who could never find anything too hot for his taste. The visit was a much-needed break and seeing their special friends made it a time they would cherish for a long time to come.

15

MAHANTONGO

When they arrived back home it was time for Jeanie's chemo treatments to begin. Stephanie had been calling constantly checking on her mother's condition, and during one phone call she had some news that she was excited about. At first they were both afraid to ask, but then Stephanie laughed and said, "You two are silly, it's about Rod. He met a girl and I think this is the one. She is real pretty and works for a modeling agency in Allentown. Her name is Peggy Cummings."

When Jeanie heard this she said, "I think I better stick around here a little longer." She had read everything she could get her hands on about ovarian cancer. Books and articles were scattered all about the house. She had a great positive attitude about everything. She had even ordered ahead of time two wigs to use when the appropriate time came. That kind of pushed Ralph over the limit and he broke down, but Jeanie told him not to give up on her, she wasn't about to die. She had too much to do yet, and grandchildren to meet someday. When she said that, Ralph had to leave the house. For the last few weeks he had found the barn a place where he could hide and let his emotions out without Jeanie seeing him sobbing. This had become his sanctuary, his meeting place with his Lord; it was a place where he could talk out loud and lift his prayers up to God.

* * * * *

It was time to take another break from flying, cleaning, painting, and finding new renters, so Gid and Betty decided to take a trip to visit Mike in Bozeman, Montana. They loved Montana, especially in the summer. They flew into Seattle, Washington, this time, rented a car, took a ferry across to Bainbridge Island and then drove across the northern part of Washington State through Idaho and on to Glacier National Park. What a difference in Glacier National Park from last year at this same time. Last year they couldn't even drive through the park because of snow. The lodge had been almost buried in snow then; this year there was no snow, and the grass was green with lots of yellow glacier lilies blooming, and there were even some long horn sheep grazing with their lambs!

The Meyers/Aero Commander that Gid specialized in had a fly-in each year, and it was held alternatively in the western part of the U.S. and then the eastern part of the U.S. Some of the fly-ins that Gid and Betty had attended were held in Bohn Mt., Michigan; Los Angeles, California; Eugene, Oregon; and Kalispell, Montana. It was a great opportunity to meet other Meyer's owners and talk airplane talk. This year the fly-in was held in Kalispell, Montana, which made it convenient to visit with Mike again.

When they arrived in Bozeman, Mike, as always, found lots of fun places where they could get out in the natural world and enjoy God's creation. There was Cottonwood Canyon with lots and lots of wild flowers, climbing up Bridger Divide and watching Mike's dog, Bo, sliding down the patches of snow, hiking around Fairy Lake high up in the mountains, sitting on the front porch of an old saloon in Virginia City, and driving through Turner Ranch. It was a great trip!

* * * * *

Karla and Wil were expecting their third child in August 1992, and Betty thought they probably had enough experience with newborn babies by now and she wouldn't have to go up to help until after the birth. The baby was a little girl, and they named her Kalicia Elizabeth. Kari picked out the first name, and her middle name was in memory of her great-grandmother, Elizabeth Herr.

* * * * *

Ralph stayed right by Jeanie's side through all the chemo treatments. Sitting there next to her he tried not to let it be obvious that he was staring at all the other people getting their treatments. There were people in so many different stages of cancer receiving chemo; some had kerchiefs on, some had their heads shaved, and some had clumps of hair missing, as if they were in the stage when their hair was just starting to fall out. It was obvious that Jeanie was a first timer. The treatments made Jeanie sick and caused a lot of discomfort. It seemed like they went on forever, but eventually they came to an end. Jeanie wore either a kerchief or a wig depending on where they were going that day. Ralph kept telling her that he thought she looked very pretty, and in his usual good sense of humor he said he thought maybe she should keep the shaved look, because that was his favorite. He just loved to bring a smile to her face. In fact, he wanted to shave his head also, and he pleaded with her to let him do it, but she said she didn't want any more attention brought to her than was necessary. A few months later she had her scheduled follow-up appointment where they took blood to check the PSA levels. The results were startling in a good way; Jeanie was told that everything looked great, and that her blood was like that of a completely well person, free of cancer. Jeanie turned to Ralph, who was already mopping the tears, and she began to cry also.

"See, I told you not to give up on me," Jeanie said when they had both managed to stop crying. They thanked the doctor profusely and left for home. Ralph was determined that now he wasn't going to waste another moment without her by his side. He reminded her of the plans they first had for making the farm into a nursery business. They both agreed that this was what they wanted to do now, to work side-by-side together forever.

Ralph had already drawn the plans for the project and they had selected the name of Apple Alley Farm. They began filing all the necessary papers and in no time were ready to begin the project. Jeanie had renewed strength and energy and was eager to start. Once the permits were secured Ralph hired an excavator by the name of Bruce Rarrick to cut in the new driveway entrance. Bruce was a very friendly and helpful man. He gave Ralph a lot of pointers on how to construct the stone wall that would run the full length of the driveway as well as the steps leading up from it to the house. He even found the correct stone to match the existing wall. Bruce seemed like a man of faith and Ralph always enjoyed talking with him. He was one of those people that you wished you could spend more time with and get to know better. But since Ralph was also a contractor, he knew how precious your time was during the day when you have a business to run, so he tried not to talk Bruce's ear off too much.

The stone wall turned out to be one of the most fun things Ralph had ever built. The whole idea was to try to make it look as old as all the rest of the existing wall. Jeanie was very good at adding the little plants and vines that were already growing in the original wall to the cracks and crags of the new one. Jeanie thought this was too much of a project for Ralph to be doing alone, so she gave Rod a call and he came right over to help his dad. This turned out to be a precious time for them to be together, and Jeanie loved to look out the window and see them working side by side. By the time the wall was done it matched completely. You couldn't tell where one started and the other had stopped. The next project was to connect the new steps with a walk, and then add a picket fence to surround the new flowerbeds and landscaped gardens. Ralph had also planned a sunken patio as a surprise for Jeanie. When the project was done Jeanie was elated, because it was something she had always dreamed of having. Seeing the joy on her face was all Ralph had hoped to achieve. Jeanie spent all her free time in those gardens. Ralph added the special touch of a garden shed at one end, and when Jeanie stood there with her straw hat and gloves on with dirt smeared across her face, it melted his heart to see her so happy.

* * * * *

Jay and Ella Mae Lehman were good friends and part of the Miller's Spruce Lake Group. Gid had taught Jay to fly a small, single engine plane, but Jay had always wanted to fly with Gid in one of the big TWA planes. A trip was planned for February 1993 to Rome and Athens, and Gid was the Captain of the flight. It was arranged to move his two special passengers into First Class where Betty would be seated also. What a fun time they had together sightseeing. The Roman architecture, fountains, the Coliseum, the Catacombs, and the good Italian food and shopping were all things they enjoyed.

A short flight to Athens was next. Here they saw the Parthenon, dancers in native costumes dancing in the street, did some shopping, and they even got caught up in the Greek Mardi Gras celebration. The walking street was full of people with confetti flying, spray string going everywhere, and plastic bats to hit your friends with! A little of this went a long way and they were soon heading back to the hotel.

* * * * *

That winter Jeanie and Ralph decided that they would start to grow from seeds as many perennial flowers as they could. In the basement Ralph set up lots of tables and bought some special growing lights to hang above the trays holding the tiny seeds. They received loads of good information from Alva's youngest son, Matt, who ran a nursery business for someone. Matt was quite a hard-working young man, and he wasn't afraid to get dirty. His dream was to someday have his own nursery business. Jeanie loved talking with Matt about flowers, as he was like a walking encyclopedia on plants, and whenever she saw him her face would light up. If she was having a down day and Matt showed up, her whole attitude would change. She used to say, "we all should spend more time around flowers; they just bring the best in you and make you happy." It turned out to be hard and continuous work; as the plants grew they had to be transplanted into bigger trays. Four thousand plants for beginners was a big job, but by spring the fruit of their labors was evident. The plants were getting very big and needed to be moved out to the porch so they could harden before setting them out. Ralph had prepared an area for the plants, and it wasn't long before they had them in the ground. Now whenever Jeanie needed plants to achieve a desired effect in one of her many flowerbeds, she simply went to the big garden and dug up whatever she wanted.

* * * * *

During this period of time Stephanie moved into the rental house on the property and began working in the Habband store at the Schuylkill Mall. While she was working there, a coworker who was also a friend of hers recommended that she meet a certain guy by the name of Mark Broda and it wasn't long before they began to date.

* * * * *

Calls were starting to come in for construction work, and Jeanie decided that Ralph should slow down on the nursery project and help some of the people who needed to have work done.

She assured him that she would be fine at home alone. It wasn't long, however, before Jeanie was starting to feel weak and tired again. After a trip to the hospital it was discovered she was in need of a blood transfusion, and after receiving the transfusion she felt much better again. This burst of energy proved to be short-lived, though, and a few weeks later Jeanie was back in the hospital; they learned that her cancer had come back and had spread into her large intestine and was causing an obstruction. The surgeon needed to make an incision in Jeanie's abdomen and bring the intestine to the surface forming an artificial opening allowing for waste to be discharged. This procedure was called a colostomy. This would mean that a lightweight bag would need to be fastened to her skin. The thought of this happening to his wife was hard for Ralph to handle. *Why did she need to suffer like this?* He kept thinking. During her time of recovery they both received lessons on the care and management of her new way of living. The equipment was very costly, and Jeanie was upset that they had to be spend so much money to help her stay alive. Ralph kept telling her not to worry and not to give up. Once they got home the problems started immediately; no matter what she did she couldn't get a new bag to seal properly to her skin, and she would become very distraught over the amount of money she was wasting each time one failed to work. Ralph reassured her every time not to worry about the money, that it was worth every penny if it kept her alive and able to function. Finally Ralph called a friend who called another friend named Mary who worked at a different hospital. Mary called the house and told them to meet her at the other hospital. At that time it was already after nine o'clock in the evening. The wing of the hospital where they met Mary was closed, but she was waiting there nonetheless to let them in. She worked on Jeanie for quite some time and had Ralph practice attaching one also. She freely provided them with a good supply of the necessary items they needed, and she told them where they could purchase replacements at a discounted price when they needed more. Ralph offered to pay for all she had done but she refused. They left the hospital after midnight that night exhausted but relieved that everything was working properly now. On the way home they thanked God for bringing Mary into their lives. Truly He had sent an angel to them that night. A couple of weeks later Jeanie was strong enough to start another round of chemo, but she didn't even want to think about going through it all over again. She just dreaded the thought of it. The first surgery had been fifteen months ago and she was well past the time that the doctor had given her to live. Ralph still hadn't told her what the doctor had shared with him, and he didn't think this was the time to do so now. She eventually got up the courage to start the treatments, but they took a lot out of her. While she was getting them she would put on a good face and talk with the other patients who were getting their treatments. Sometimes it was hard to believe that it was the same person who just moments before was really feeling down and now was this bubbly lady giving others encouragement. Ralph would usually leave the room when she started to talk about her cancer with other ladies, not because it bothered him but because they usually were more open to share with Jeanie their troubles if a man wasn't present.

* * * * *

July, 1993 Banner Elk, North Carolina

Rhoda and Ora Mast, who were friends of Gid and Betty and also part of the Spruce Lake Group, lived in Marietta, Georgia. Gid and Betty were spending one of their timeshare weeks in Banner Elk, North Carolina, and they asked Rhoda and Ora if they would like to join them for a couple days. They visited and ate dinner at the Mast Farm Inn, which was quite unique. It was also a charming Bed and Breakfast inn, which Rhoda and Ora went back to later for a special weekend.

Karla and Wil were building a new home in Reynoldsburg, OH and they had already sold their home in Ft. Wayne, Indiana; since they were homeless for a few months, they decided to also come to Banner Elk along with their three children, CJ, Kari and Kalicia, and the whole group went to Grandfather Mountain. There was a swinging bridge stretched high above a canyon and Betty, knowing that Rhoda hated heights, decided to just keep talking with her as they walked along and maybe they could get across the bridge without her realizing. But no such luck; at the last moment Rhoda realized what was happening and came to an abrupt halt. She stayed planted on solid ground while the rest walked across the bridge and came back again!

Karla and the children spent some time in Pennsylvania with the Esh grandparents and then went to Florida with the Miller grandparents, and soon their house was finished. Karla's Grandmother Herr had always done a lot of quilting, and Karla's interest was growing in learning how to quilt. Betty said she was waiting till she got old enough to quilt, and that happened in the winter of 1993-1994. Her mother had patched her last top and gave it to Betty, so she set to work quilting it and found that she actually enjoyed it!

* * * * *

In August Jeanie was finished with her treatments. This month they were to celebrate twenty-five years of marriage, but Jeanie wasn't up to having a party so they planned a nice quiet week at the shore. They had planned to leave on the last Sunday of the month, right after the church service. After church they drove home thinking they were going to load up the Jimmy and drive to Long Beach Island, but when they pulled in the driveway, Ralph could see that the lower driveway was filled with cars. And as they walked to the porch they began to hear shouts of "Surprise!" Stephanie had planned this for months in advance and had some of their special friends and family come to celebrate their anniversary. A little while later a whole lot more people showed up from Bethany, where they had just been thirty minutes ago. It was a very special day. Stephanie had outdone herself this time and didn't miss a detail. There were all kinds of memorabilia displayed everywhere, starting with their prom/engagement picture, which she had made into an invitation and sent to everyone. It was a total surprise and greatly appreciated. When the party ended they loaded the Jimmy and headed for the shore, where they enjoyed a week of relaxing.

When they returned home from their trip, Ralph went back to work and Jeanie tried her best to do all the things she loved to do, but she was finding it increasingly difficult all the time. She just didn't have the strength she once had. Ralph had noticed her decline in stamina and decided that this was just too much house for her to think about. If she saw that the flowerbeds needed weeding, or if she contemplated all the other chores that needed to be done outside, she would make every effort to work on them even if it would cause her pain or wear her out. The only solution, Ralph thought, was to move her out of this environment. Even though this was their dream house, it didn't matter; he decided he would start looking for a smaller house without her knowing about it. One day when he said he was going to work, he decided to drive through the countryside on the other side of the mountain. When he went over the mountain it opened up to the most gorgeous valley; the view was breathtaking. In the middle of the valley there sat this little Cape Cod home with an auction sign on it. It was perfect; now all he had to do was convince Jeanie to give up her dream home. He drove straight home and found Jeanie resting on the couch.

"Hi, honey, how are you doing today?" Ralph asked with concern as he sat down in the easy chair next to the sofa.

"Why are you home so early? Is something wrong?"

"No, nothing is wrong. I just want to show you something."

"What? Where is it?" Jeanie looked perplexed, but her expression revealed that she wondered what could be up Ralph's sleeve – she knew him very well!

"It's not here; we have to drive to it." He then explained to her what he had been thinking about. At first she didn't want to hear it, but soon she realized he was right. They went out and got in the Jimmy and drove to the Mahantongo Valley. When they got to the crest of the hill just before the house came into view, Ralph said, "OK, the house is the next one on the left. You're going to love it, Jeanie."

When the house came into view Jeanie exclaimed, "This is where I want to die."

It wasn't the house that was so special, but the views that surrounded the house on every side were outstanding. They stopped and walked the property and copied the number off the sign, and then they drove back to Ringtown. On the way home Jeanie started to cry and said,

"Ralph, I am so sorry for bringing so much trouble into your life. You have so many plans for the farm and now you won't be able to accomplish them. If I weren't here you would be having a great life," she said through heart-wrenching sobs.

Ralph's eyes filled with tears as he told her, "Honey, the farm means nothing to me; you know that the time I spend with you is the most important thing in my life, and if selling the farm is what it takes to keep you around, then we're selling the farm. And besides, if you weren't here I'd only be half a man, because you complete me, Jeanie."

Ralph then shared his thoughts with her concerning what to do with the farm and this new property. The new property was not a sure thing yet, because it was going to be auctioned off, which meant someone could want it more than they did and pay more for it, winning the auction. Their nursery farm didn't have to be sold that quickly. The one idea Ralph was leaning toward the most was to subdivide the property where the new driveway had been put in, leaving the house on one acre and turning the remaining eleven acres into one large lot or three. The other idea was to hold a mortgage on the place, which would give them some income. Regardless of what happened with the auctioned property, Ralph felt strongly that they should go ahead with the subdivision of the farm.

Jeanie thought this all sounded good and agreed with him, but her only concern was what they were going to do with all their stuff. They had a house three times the size of the new one and three barns that were filled as well. Ralph said not to worry about that right now, because if they were lucky enough to purchase the Mahantongo house, then they'd have a huge auction and sell it all. Jeanie liked that idea, because over the years going to auctions had become one of their favorite activities. In the weeks that followed they began the subdivision work on the farm and also contacted the people who were auctioning off the Cape Cod home. They made arrangements to preview the house before the auction and found out all the particulars of the property. As it turned out the property sat on nine acres of land. As soon as Ralph heard that, he wanted that property more than ever. It was all frontage property, which meant that it would be easy to subdivide into building lots. He figured he could get four building lots plus the one the house sat on. Now he was really excited. They examined the property and found it to be acceptable, but they knew that if they were the ones to win the auction, they would be doing some remodeling work before they moved in.

The day of the auction arrived, and it was a small crowd. When the bidding started Ralph figured he would just be quiet. It took quite some time to get the numbers up; it just seemed like there was no one interested in it. The bidding got up to $50,000 and the auctioneer was saying, "Going once." Jeanie looked at Ralph and wondered if he had changed his mind. Ralph had made his way up the hill behind the crowd so he could see who was bidding. The auctioneer said, "Going twice. Do I hear $52,500?" Ralph put his hand up. Everyone in the crowd was trying to see who made the bid, but couldn't because he was standing behind them. Ralph had got the auctioneer's attention now so he kept moving around. For the next twenty minutes the bidding went between only two bidders. In the end Ralph and Jeanie had the winning bid at what they thought was a good price.

Jeanie's condition had stayed pretty much the same; she was able to work around the property and house but she just had to take it slow. The subdivision plans for the farm were approved, and Ralph had begun work on the new property. Jeanie felt that she could still wallpaper if she just took her time. Ralph put in a new kitchen and was replacing the windows, a few at a time. They had decided not to move in until the spring, so this was going to be their last winter at Ringtown. That winter they put the farm land only up for sale and got a buyer instantly. The couple wanted the whole eleven acres so they wouldn't have any neighbors. When spring 1994 came, Ralph and Jeanie made arrangements for holding their own auction, and they sold an enormous amount of items. When the auction was completed they had the closing on the farm and then they moved into the Cape Cod and began their new life in the Mahantongo Valley.

* * * * *

Two of Betty's friends, Nancy Yoder and Treva Kurtz, thought that Betty should learn to snow ski. It was something that she had always wanted to learn, but it looked scary! However, they talked her into it, and they all went to Betty's timeshare unit at Beaver Creek, Colorado, for a ski vacation. It was snowing when they got to Denver, so they let Nancy drive the rented SUV since she was more used to driving in snow. They had a little trouble with the SUV, but finally made it.

Treva was sick during the night with altitude sickness, so Nancy said she would go with her to the doctor in the morning and that Betty should take the bus up to the ski school where she had planned to take a lesson. She went out front to get the bus and thought, "How could they let me do this by myself, I don't even know where to put my skis on the bus!" She watched the others and figured out what to do, and soon they were up the mountain at the ski school. Betty did pretty well with her ski lesson, but was very tired at the end of the day. The next day Nancy and Treva thought Betty should go to the top of the mountain taking the ski lift all the way up; Betty kept thinking, "Are we ever going to get to the top? I have to ski back down this huge mountain!" Finally it was time to get off the ski lift only to find out that they were getting on another lift to take them even higher up the mountain. By now Betty was almost in tears, especially after she looked down below and saw that someone had fallen and was screaming in pain. Betty managed to ski back down that huge mountain, but not without a few falls! But thankfully her good friend Treva was very patient with her, while Nancy went off to ski the black trails with her son, Jeff.

* * * * *

By spring Jeanie was anxious to get outside and start some new flowerbeds, so Ralph tilled some ground up for her and prepared the soil. They had a favorite place where they liked to go to purchase their plants, bulbs, and all their landscaping needs. Trail Gardens in Pottsville was where they had done their shopping for the Ringtown property and had great success, so that's where they continued to go. It seemed no matter how bad Jeanie was feeling, when she was at Trail Gardens, wandering among all the gorgeous plants and flowers, she felt good, and that's all Ralph cared about. It had been two years since Jeanie's cancer diagnosis, and on this particular trip to Trail Gardens Ralph decided to tell her what the doctor had said, because by now she had long outlived the doctor's timeline for her life expectancy.

When he had finished telling her the story, Jeanie's only comment was, "I guess I proved him wrong." Ralph didn't pursue the subject any further, but felt that she must have had an idea from the very beginning. The day her eyes were scanning Ralph and Alva's faces for some indication of her condition was when she probably knew. Ralph knew she was a strong individual and would fight for all she was worth. She loved life too much to just roll over and die. She did, however, make one comment that day that she was done with chemo treatments. She was never going through that again. Jeanie had been doing lots of reading and decided that she was going to look into alterative medicine from here on out. Ralph knew better then to question her on her decision; after all, she was the one who had gone through the suffering of having those chemicals pumped into her body and not him. Once again their trip to Trail Gardens was a success, and with a van full of plants they drove home to begin the process of getting them planted. This usually meant that Jeanie would say where she wanted each plant perfectly placed, during a dry run, and then once she was absolutely sure it was in the right position he would dig a hole and plant it. It hadn't always been like this, working together in her garden; before her cancer Ralph wasn't even allowed in her flower gardens, but now he insisted and she appreciated the help.

* * * * *

One morning in April of 1994, Gid woke up feeling a little funny and was experiencing shortness of breath. Betty immediately decided to take him to the emergency room, where the doctors determined there was nothing wrong and sent him home. The next day while doing his morning walk to the restaurant, his shortness of breath came back again. After a call to the doctor, Betty got the car and drove him back to the emergency room a second time, knowing they had to be wrong; there must be something they had missed. After checking his heart and lungs completely, the doctors had a mystery on their hands.

Finally, after two weeks of suffering, Gid was still having breathing problems and no diagnosis had been made, so they called in the infectious disease specialist. Betty had spent the whole day waiting for the specialist and was becoming discouraged, as Gid seemed to be getting worse. Around 8:00 pm her good friends, Earl and Shirley Beachy, came to see how Gid was doing. It was just what Betty needed! The specialist finally arrived at 8:30 pm. After Betty voiced her concerns about how Gid looked, the doctor said he didn't look so bad after what he had seen all day. He had been working with AIDS patients. After more tests it was discovered that Gid had pericarditis, an inflammation of the pericardium (the membrane that encloses the heart), leading, in many cases, to chest pain and fever. In addition to inflammation, there may be effusion (increased amount of fluid) in the pericardial space, which separates the two smooth layers of the pericardium. This excess fluid may compress the heart, restricting its action (Reference: The American Medical Association Home Medical Encyclopedia).

On Sunday they decided to do emergency surgery to put a window in the pericardium to drain the fluid that was restricting Gid's heart. This required open chest surgery. Jan and Elmer Ebersol and Gerald and Connie Minninger came and sat with Betty in the waiting room during this difficult time. While they were praying at the hospital, back at Bahia Vista Mennonite Church the congregation was praying also.

A few hours later the surgeon came out and told Betty that the pericardium was so hard and diseased that they had to remove the entire lining. Betty asked the doctor what that meant and what the prognosis would be for Gid. The doctor responded by saying that Gid could have a normal life, but he couldn't play any contact sports. Betty was very relieved to know that she wasn't in any danger of losing her husband, and she thanked the Lord and the doctor for all they had done.

Betty was spending every possible moment in the hospital with Gid, and in the time she was there she crocheted three afghans for the grandchildren.

One afternoon when Gid was walking around the hospital room, trying to get his suggested exercise in, he stopped to look out the window, then turned around and looked at Betty with a pale look on his face, and then he collapsed to the floor. Betty went running to the hall screaming for help, and immediately doctors and nurses came running to Gid's assistance. After more tests it was determined that he had a short circuit in the heart, which they quickly corrected the day before he left the hospital. After this five-week ordeal Gid was released from the hospital and into Betty's great care. Time to heal was what he needed now, and walking was the main therapy suggested. The first day that Gid decided to go for a walk on the street in front of their home, Betty was peeking through the blinds with tears in her eyes, watching him struggle with every step he took. She thought to herself how he looked just like an old man who could barely move, but she knew he wanted to do this on his own. She also knew that he had the determination to make it back to the strong and physically fit man he used to be. His goal, of course, was to get back in the cockpit for TWA, no matter how long it took. Gid was not a quitter, never had been, and didn't plan on being one now. Behind every step, every day, Betty was there, encouraging him on. His children encouraged him also, as did his friends and church family. It wouldn't be long before Gid was back up at the Der Dutchman Restaurant meeting his friends for breakfast in the mornings, telling them stories and making them laugh. Betty was never far away, always keeping close tabs on him, until she was absolutely sure he was one hundred percent recovered. Gid and Betty had always been strong in their Christian faith, but through this trial, they became even closer and stronger in their walk of faith. The importance of Christian friends and the support they found in them carried them through this crisis.

The importance of faith and fellowship in a Christian's life cannot be overstated. Let's take a moment to pause in our story and look at what it says in Billy Graham's Training Center Bible (NKJV):

Faith is the foundation of salvation and the doorway to peace with God: "Therefore, having been justified by faith, we have peace with God through our Lord Jesus Christ, through whom also we have access by faith into this grace in which we stand, and rejoice in hope of the glory of God" (Romans 5: 1, 2).

When Jesus' disciples were filled with fear out in the middle of a storm, they frantically asked Him for help, saying, "Teacher, do you not care that we are perishing?" Jesus calmed the storm and then asked His disciples, "How is it that you have no faith?" (Mark 4:35-41).

When you face storms in life, do you have faith that Christ will be there to help you? If you don't have that kind of faith, the Bible is the place to look: "So then faith comes by hearing, and hearing by the word of God" (Romans 10:17).

See the following verses for more on faith:

1. Faith defined: **Hebrews 11:1**.
2. Faith developed: **Matthew 13:31, 32**.
3. Faith through trials: **Deuteronomy 8:2-16**.
4. Faith demonstrated in the invisible: **Daniel 3:16-18**.
5. Faith demonstrated in the incredible: **1 Samuel 17:45, 46**.
6. Faith demonstrated in the impossible: **Luke 1:37**.
7. Lack of faith: **Romans 14:23**.

Fellowship is an important ingredient for healthy spiritual growth, both for the individual believer and the church body. Fellowship is more than sharing coffee and donuts after a church service — true fellowship involves sacrifice and accountability.

1. Fellowship begins with God and extends to others: **John 15:1, 4**.

2. Characteristics of Christian fellowship: **Acts 2:42**.
3. Unconfessed sin hinders fellowship: **James 5:16**.
4. Proper choices for fellowship: **Luke 5:30, 31**.

* * * * *

Ralph's work was really picking up; a friend from church needed an addition put on his home and there were always drywall jobs coming in. One of those jobs was for a young contractor by the name of Richie Fetteroff. Ralph was talking to him one day about the farm property and thought this would be the ideal place for a contractor to live, especially with all the barns to store his equipment. Richie was interested and wanted to talk to his wife Karen first. Ralph said to Richie, "When Karen sees this place, it's sold." That's how confident Ralph was that Karen would fall in love with the lovely gardens, the home, and the land, just as Jeanie had done. Richie just laughed and said he hoped so. Richie called later that night wondering when they could see the farm. Ralph told him to come on over anytime. The next day they met at the house and loved it but didn't know if they could swing the deal. Ralph told them he would hold the mortgage for them. Within weeks everything was taken care of, and the last of the Ringtown property was gone.

The Cape Cod was a small house with a detached two-car garage, which never had room for a car to be parked in it, with all of Ralph's tools and equipment stored in there. The house turned out beautiful with all of Jeanie's decorating. She especially loved her brand new kitchen with a nice window seat that Ralph had built for her. She would sit there often just watching the birds feeding at the feeder that she had Ralph put up for her just beyond the large window. Jeanie was still able to do most of the things around the house by herself, but Ralph thought that driving the Jimmy was a little difficult for her, so he decided that she should have a smaller car. They soon found a Dodge Shadow that Jeanie liked, and it was comfortable for her to get in and out of.

Jeanie had purchased a good food processor and began a regimen of eating fresh vegetables everyday. She had also started taking shark cartilage, and as long as she was feeling fine and alive, Ralph was happy; he didn't care what she took. The rest of the year was pretty uneventful. There were some trips to the hospital to get some blood, but other than that, Jeanie seemed to be doing well.

* * * * *

The Millers had planned another trip to Wyoming and Montana to visit Mike. This time Karla, Wil and the grandchildren would go along. Karla and Wil were living in St. Louis where they had purchased two Grease Monkey Quick Lubes. They all met in Denver, rented a van, and drove to Estes Park and then on into Rocky Mountain National Park, but they had to turn around because the road was already closed due to an early snowfall.

Arriving in Yellowstone National Park they saw Old Faithful, several hot springs, and lots of elk and buffalo. The next stop was in Bozeman to see Mike. Mike showed them a beautiful place to hike around a clear, cold mountain lake where they ate their picnic lunch. The next week was spent at a timeshare unit in Big Sky, Montana. It was a great family week! They saw lots of wild animals including two moose, spent another day in Yellowstone National Park, did a lot of hiking, went shopping, swimming, played games and celebrated Karla's birthday. One evening Mike and CJ hiked three miles with loaded backpacks to Golden Trout Lake and camped out overnight. It was a beautiful full moon night and they remembered to hang their food in a tree at least one hundred feet from their tent. There had seen a sign warning of bears in the area!

By now Gid was recovering well from his heart surgery earlier in the year, and spending a week with the family was just what he needed. Knowing it wouldn't be long before he would be well enough to go back to work, they decided to fit one more trip into their schedule in October.

They had a timeshare week that they needed to use, so they reserved a week in Hyannis, Massachusetts, and asked their good friends, John and Marie Kauffman, from their Spruce Lake Group, to go with them. Gid and Betty flew to New York where they met John and Marie, who picked them up at the airport and chauffeured them around for the week.

They drove to Providence, Rhode Island, to visit John and Marie's daughter, Jill and her husband, Ed Misto, in their lovely home, and then they went on to Hyannis to the timeshare. The drive to the end of Cape Cod was lovely; they got to see lots of lighthouses and they climbed Pilgrim Monument. Touring the Mayflower II, Plymouth Rock, and the Cranberry World Visitor Center were all very interesting.

One day was spent taking the ferry to Martha's Vineyard and touring the island. Some sights they enjoyed were the beautiful town of Edgartown, Harbor Side Inn and Lighthouse, Chappaquiddick, Mytoi Gardens, Gay Head, and beautiful beaches.

They drove to Provincetown again and took a whale watching tour and had five sightings. Gid was having a birthday in a couple of days, so they celebrated early at the Yarmouth House. Soon it was time to head back to Kennedy airport for a flight to Florida. It had been another good vacation with good friends, good food, and seeing more of God's beautiful creation.

* * * * *

The new year of 1995 started off with several bad snowstorms; at one point the snow was piled up so deep it was over Ralph's head, and another time his neighbor, Henry Reiner, who owned the large farm across the road, showed up with his tractor and cleaned the driveway out. When he was done the snow piles were at least ten feet high. Henry had a heart of gold and always refused any compensation for his labors. He always had a smile or a wave for you when he passed by. When Jeanie was alone one day he even stopped in to check on her. In March Jeanie had a scheduled appointment at the hospital with her doctor, where they just did a routine check of all her vitals. When it was time to meet with the doctor, Ralph went in with her. This particular doctor had been seeing Jeanie from the very beginning and had become a friend as well. When she walked in he just stood there and applauded her. He then said she was a walking miracle and that honestly, she shouldn't even still be alive. He hadn't expected to ever see her again after her initial visit to him. He exclaimed, "It's been three whole years, so what's your secret?" She looked him right in the eye and said, "My faith in God." Her doctor was a Jewish man, but Ralph and Jeanie both believed he was a born-again believer. He commented, "Praise God." But he did have some bad news. "There's nothing wrong with you, Jeanie, it's just that I'm taking a position in another hospital. So I won't be seeing you anymore." Jeanie had really come to like him and would greatly miss this doctor. But he assured her that the doctor taking his place was very good. They hugged and said goodbye and left the hospital feeling good about her condition but sad that her doctor was leaving Geisinger Hospital.

* * * * *

Gid had just finished his training as captain on the Boeing 747 and his first trip was on July 15, 1995, to Madrid, Spain. He was elated, as this had always been his goal. Betty went along as she always did on his first trip on a new plane or flying a new position.

About the same time, Betty's good friend, Janice Ebersole, had decided to get training and earn her license as a massage therapist and Betty thought that sounded like something she would be interested in doing. Gid was thinking that it might be pretty nice to have a fulltime massage therapist in the house! Betty enjoyed the training course very much, and when Gid wasn't flying, she practiced her massage techniques on him.

* * * * *

Also in 1995 Ralph and Jeanie started the preliminary work to get their new property subdivided. What Ralph had figured was correct; there would be four building lots, each measuring approximately one and a half acre, and the remaining three acres would be the ones surrounding their house. The people who originally owned the property were named Miller, so they decided to name the subdivision Miller's Field. Ralph had no plans to start any building projects yet, as he was too busy with all the other projects he had going on just then, but at least all the permits were in place now, so that when he was ready to start, there would be no delays.

By the end of October Jeanie was showing signs of weakness and fatigue, and it was evident something was wrong. Another trip to the hospital revealed that more of her intestines needed to be removed. Jeanie spent a week in the hospital and Ralph stayed right there with her, refusing to go to work. On a number of occasions Ralph started to enter her room, only to stop at the door and listen while Jeanie was sharing her faith with a patient in the next bed. He never let on to her that he had heard her, but he always left feeling blessed from the strength and courage she displayed as she went through this ordeal.

The weeks that followed were difficult. Jeanie's strength was gradually dissipating, and when they traveled anywhere, they made sure they had a wheelchair with them in case she was too tired to walk. Stephanie and Mark Broda's wedding was coming up, and Jeanie was determined not to miss it. It took every bit of strength she had, but she put on her usual happy face and managed to make it through the day without making anyone aware of her discomfort. Seeing the marriage of her daughter had meant a great deal to Jeanie, and she didn't want any of the attention taken away from Mark and Stephanie. When relatives asked how she was doing she would smile and say fine, wasn't it a beautiful wedding? It was so exhausting that she remained weak for some time after the wedding, but she never complained.

When springtime came that year, Ralph did the plantings with Jeanie's direction, as always. Ralph had finished all his jobs and thought he should just stay close to home, but Jeanie wouldn't hear of it. She told him he needed to get on with his life, and that she would be fine. At church Ralph told Hal how he just couldn't concentrate on running a business anymore. Hal made Ralph an offer to come to work for him. He said he would keep him close to the phone so he would always be near if Jeanie called him. The work would be easy with no pressure, and Hal and his son Brian would do all the brainwork. He said the pay wouldn't be what he was used to getting, but Ralph didn't care about that, because he just wanted to stay close to home and stay busy. Ralph had really come to appreciate Hal as a brother in the faith, and during that time he was his closest friend. What Hal had offered him meant a lot, and Ralph accepted his offer.

* * * * *

It was April of 1996 and Gid was Captain on the 747 and flying to Europe once a week, on average. Betty graduated from Massage Therapy School in March and would be taking her state licensing exam in June. April sounded like a good time to take a little vacation, so they decided to go to Big Canoe, Georgia, in the northeastern part of the state. Their friends, John and Marie Kauffman and Grace Landis met them there for a few days of hiking and enjoying the mountains and friendship. From there they went to Callaway Gardens, southwest of Atlanta, and met up with more friends, Rhoda and Ora Mast and Dory and Cecil Grove. By now they had a large percentage of their original Spruce Lake Group together. The azaleas at Callaway Gardens were in full bloom, showing off in many shades of color and in clusters so massive they were almost like small, flowering trees. The one thing they particularly remember about that weekend was having dinner at a restaurant one night when Gid was in a storytelling mood, and he had everyone laughing so hard that the diners around them were wondering what was so funny! This would turn out to be a very special time for Gid's friends.

* * * * *

One of the first things Hal wanted Ralph to help him with was the construction of his maintenance building. It would basically be a three-car garage with a shop and bathroom area. The upstairs would be a storage area with the potential of becoming an apartment someday. Working with Hal and his family was a great experience; when everyone had arrived each morning, they would all gather around the table in the kitchen for a devotion and prayer time. This was an awesome way to start the workday, Ralph thought. Even though Ralph had just spent his entire ride to Hal's already in prayer, it was great to be gathered with other believers in corporate prayer. Once that was done, everyone would head off to his assignments. The construction of the maintenance building went very smoothly, and on days when there weren't any construction needs, Ralph would get sent on mowing jobs with Phil. Phil was really growing in his faith and was a lot of fun for Ralph to work with. During those times they became great friends and shared many special times together.

July was one of Ralph's favorite months of the year in the country; the fields in the valley were showing off their different colors of new green growth, and tractors were everywhere doing cultivating and fertilizing. Pastures were doted with the various colors of different breeds of steers or cows. Everywhere you looked there was something beautiful to see. It was also the time of year when families and friends got together for picnics and reunions. Jeanie wasn't able to have one of her all-out picnics or parties as she had done for so many years, but the family did gather for some picnic food and visiting. The children had to be wondering, along with Ralph, if this would be Jeanie's last Fourth of July. These times of visiting with their mother became very special and meaningful to Stephanie and Rod. Another special thing that would happen this year was that Gid and Betty would be stopping in for a short visit between their reunions at Spruce Lake and Charter Hall. Since Ralph and Jeanie were situated about halfway between those two locations, they decided to get together. By this time Jeanie's weight was really starting to decline, and her clothes were starting to just hang on her. Ralph had felt that she didn't want to spend any money on clothes because it would be a waste, but he suggested that they go shopping anyway. He teased her that since she had always wanted to be thin, why not show off her new thin body? After a little coaxing she agreed, and they spent a special day together shopping. Every minute together was special for Ralph, and it didn't matter where they were.

16

PARIS

The events of July 17, 1996, will forever be etched in the memories of these two special sets of friends – Ralph and Jeanie Walls, and Gid and Betty Miller — that the story is best told in the present tense, just as the events leading up to that day unfolded.

On Monday, July 15, Karla, who is in Pennsylvania with her children visiting relatives, receives a call from her mother in Florida.

"Hello, this is Karla."

"Hi, Karla, this is Mom."

"Hi, Mom, how are you?"

"Fine; well, your Dad did it again."

"Did what?"

"He changed his flight so he could go to Paris and return on Friday the 19th instead of going to Hawaii and returning on the 20th."

"Why did he do that?"

"This way he won't miss a day at Spruce Lake. You know how he likes to be at Spruce Lake for the whole weekend."

"Oh, that's great, Mom; I'd like to see him for the whole weekend, too." They continue to talk for another twenty minutes, and then Betty says,

"We'll see you there Friday afternoon. Bye!"

"Bye, Mom!" Karla hangs up the phone and informs everyone about her phone conversation with her mother.

* * * * *

On, Tuesday, July 16, the phone rings in Klingerstown, and Jeanie answers,

"Hello?"

"Hello, Jeanie, this is Betty."

"Hi, Betty, it's good to hear your voice. How are you doing?"

"I'm doing fine, but how are you doing?"

"Not too bad today. I have my good days and bad days. So when are we going to see you?"

"That's why I called. Gid has a flight to Paris and will be back on the 19th. Then we will be at Spruce Lake this weekend. When we leave there on Sunday afternoon we can stop at your place for a short visit before we go to Charter Hall, if that's OK?"

"Oh that sounds great, I can't wait to see you. So what have you been doing with yourself?"

"You know, the same old same old, just taking care of all those rental houses."

They continued to talk for about fifteen minutes, and then they parted with a cheery "See ya soon!"

* * * * *

On Wednesday, July 17, Gid had already been up for an hour working on the computer when Betty got out of bed.

"What time are you going to leave this morning?" she asked her husband sleepily.

"My flight leaves Tampa at 10:45 this morning, so I should leave here at 8:00."

"Do you want me to make you some breakfast?"

"Cereal will be fine."

A half hour later Gid comes into the kitchen, pours his cereal into a bowl, and joins Betty at the table.

"What's on your schedule today, Betty?" he asked as he crunched his cereal.

"I'm going to give Sue a massage this evening and I need to catch up on some of the office work. Say, why are you taking such an early flight out of Tampa? I thought your flight to Paris wasn't until 6:00 tonight."

"You're right, it's at 6 pm, but I want to get there early so I can get some sleep before we take off." Gid finishes his cereal and puts the bowl in the dishwasher, and then he heads back to the bedroom to get ready. It wasn't long before he emerged in his uniform, stopping to give Betty a kiss on his way out the door. Betty found herself thinking for the millionth time, *He sure does look good in a uniform.* He wasn't even out the door three minutes when he came back into the house saying he'd forgotten something in the office. In less than thirty seconds he reappeared and stopped to kiss Betty goodbye again.

"You did that on purpose just so you could get another kiss."

"Darn it, I forgot something else!" Gid starts to go back in his office and Betty says,

"Get out of here, silly!" Betty went about her day doing all the items she had on her to-do list. At 4:30 Betty gets a call from Gid.

"Hi, honey, it's just me."

"Hi, honey, what are you doing?"

"There was a flight to Rome that has been cancelled, so they are combining the flights and I won't be piloting this one."

"Who is going to fly it?"

"The Rome crew, so my crew and I will just deadhead over."

"Well at least you can relax on this one and get some sleep."

"I suppose so, but you know me, I'd rather fly then sleep. Besides, you know I only sleep in front of the TV." Gid was famous for that. When the children were little they would wait for him to sit down in front of the TV knowing it would only be a matter of time before he would be asleep. Then they would quietly sneak into the room and change the channel on him. On some occasions, with his eyes still closed, just as they changed the channel he would say, "I was watching that." They would run off giggling and laughing at how he had tricked them again. Remembering this with a little laugh, Betty responds, "You're right, I don't know why you ever turn the TV on; you're out in seconds."

"I told you, so I can sleep."

"You're silly; have a good flight, honey. See you Friday. Take care."

"Goodnight."

Betty fixes herself a light dinner, and then sets up the massage table to give Sue her massage that evening. Within the next hour Sue arrives and Betty gives her a massage. After the massage Betty and Sue talk for a few minutes, and then Sue leaves. A few minutes later the phone rings and Betty answers,

"Hello."

"Hello, Betty, this is Susie Smucker … are you watching the TV news by any chance?"

"No, why?" Betty asked as she walked over to turn on the TV.

"A TWA plane went down. They said it was the one to Paris; isn't that the one Gid was taking?"

Coldness sweeps over Betty as she turns on the TV. "Yes, he was going on the one to Paris ... oh my...." Betty's hand is shaking as she grabs the remote and backs up to the couch, not taking her eyes off the TV.

"Oh, no, Betty, Howard and I are going to come right over."

Betty is in disbelief and quietly says a very small "OK" as she hangs up the phone, but no sooner had she hung it up than it was ringing again. She quickly grabs the phone thinking it could be Gid calling her to tell her he is ok.

"Hello?"

"Betty, this is Treva, are you watching...?"Betty interjected quickly with, "Yes, I am."

"Is it Gid's flight?"

"I think so, Treva."

"Do you know the number of his flight?"

"Yes, it was 800."

There was silence on the other end for a few moments, and then Treva said, "Betty, Sam and I will be right over."

Betty quietly says "ok" and she slowly puts the phone down while staring intently at the TV. The phone continued to ring constantly the remainder of the evening. Friends were all starting to arrive, Howard and Susie, Sam and Treva, Dale and Verda, Jan and Elmer, Joy and Harold, Pastor Barry Loop and his wife Sue, and many more kept coming. Sam kept trying to call the 800 number they were showing on the TV, but with no luck. At 9:30 Betty finally got through to Karla in Pennsylvania. They had just returned with the children from playing miniature golf.

"Hello, this is Karla."

"Karla, this is mom. Are you sitting down?"

"Should I be?"

"Have you heard the news? The flight Dad was supposed to be on has gone down. I haven't gotten a phone call from him, so I'm pretty sure he must've been on it." They are both very shaken and can barely talk.

Mike, who was working on a project in Dinosaur National Park in Colorado, didn't have any phone reception and Betty had no way of letting him know. He had been camping and had no means of hearing the news as soon as it happened.

* * * * *

In Klingerstown, Jeanie has been glued to the TV watching the news of the crash.

At 9:30 Ralph arrives home from the prayer meeting at church.

"Ralph, come in here, you've got to see this."

"What is it?"

"There has been a terrible plane crash in New York, and it might be the one Gid was supposed to be on."

"Oh no, was it a TWA plane?"

"Yes, and it was going to Paris; I think that's the one Betty said he was going to take."

"Yes, I remember you told me yesterday that she said Paris." Jeanie stayed with Ralph for another hour watching the TV news, but eventually she had to go lie down and sleep.

* * * * *

Wil had been at a business meeting in Kansas City and didn't here about the crash until he saw it on TV later that evening. The phone wasn't working in his hotel room, so he ran down the street to a pay phone. When Betty answered the phone she hardly recognized his voice because he was so out of breath. He, of course, wanted to know where Gid was and Betty had to tell him her worst fears.

At 11:00 pm Betty got a call from a TWA representative. He was calling from a cell phone standing just outside her door and asked if he could come in. He introduced himself as Paul Walgren from the TWA trauma team. It was then that Betty realized Gid had been on that plane. Mr. Walgren was there to help Betty during this time and to make all the arrangements for Betty to be flown to New York the next day.

Betty's friend, Verda, said she would spend the night with Betty to keep her company, and she made herself comfortable on the sofa. Betty went to bed with the TV on, but of course, she didn't sleep.

* * * * *

Ralph stayed in front of the TV watching and praying for Gid and Betty the rest of the evening. On one of the networks they were filming debris floating in the water, and all of a sudden the camera zoomed in on what looked like a day planner. Ralph's heart sunk because it looked just like the one he always saw Gid carrying. There was no way of knowing for sure, but in his heart he felt it was. With his eyes filled he prayed for Betty and her family, trying to imagine what they could possibly be going through right then. He had to tell Jeanie what he had just seen. He went upstairs to wake Jeanie to tell her, but she was still awake, praying for Gid and Betty.

"Jeanie, you won't believe what I just saw on the TV news about the crash."

"What did you see?"

"You know that day planner that Gid always carried?"

"Yes..."

"Well, I think I just saw it floating in the water."

"You know there were probably a hundred day planners on that plane, Ralph."

"I know, but Gid's was always stuffed with things, and this one had lots of stuff hanging out of it."

"Oh no … that's not a good sign, is it, Ralph? Oh, poor Betty…Honey, are you coming to bed now?"

"No, I couldn't sleep now if I wanted to. I can't imagine what must be happening in Florida now with Betty." Ralph stayed up past midnight watching the news.

* * * * *

Thursday morning Mike got up early and was planning to head to another campsite. He threw his gear in the back of his truck, got in, and turned the radio on. The news was on almost every station about the crash of TWA flight 800, which had been headed for Paris. Suddenly Mike had a sick feeling in the pit of his stomach. He wracked his brain trying to remember if that was his dad's flight number. He located the nearest phone, which was about twenty miles away, and called home.

"Hello, this is the Miller's residence, Treva speaking." When Mike heard someone other than his mother answer the phone, he anticipated the worst.

"Hi, Treva, this is Mike."

"Oh, Mike, thank God you've called. Your mother has been trying to get in touch with you. Hold on, I'll get her."

"Mike, I guess you've heard. We were wondering how we would get in touch with you. I'm so glad you've called, son; I've been wanting to talk to you so much." Betty told him all the details that she knew, and then she put Mike on hold, and on the other phone line she called Paul Walgren, the TWA representative, to get advice on how Mike should get to New York. She was told that Mike should go to Denver Airport and they would have a ticket ready for him to fly to Newark, New Jersey. Mike said he could drive himself to Denver, but his mother thought he should have someone take him, which he did.

The next morning Mr. Walgren arrived at Betty's house at 9:00 a.m. and drove her to the Tampa Airport where they boarded a flight to Kennedy Airport. They arrived after 1:00 that afternoon, and he then took her to her hotel where she could await the arrival of the rest of her family. Her father-in-law, Jonathan Esh, drove Karla to New York, and her brother-in-law, Arlen King, came along with them, and she arrived about the same time that Wil landed at the airport. Mr. Walgren picked Mike up later that evening at Newark Airport when his plane landed from Denver, and drove him directly to the Ramada Inn where the rest of his family was waiting. Karla's children, CJ, Kari, and Kalicia, stayed in Pennsylvania with their relatives.

Prayers were being lifted up at this time from all over the world for the families of those on the TWA plane. Radio and TV coverage was continuous. Theories and speculations were coming from everywhere on what really happened off the coast of Long Island the night the plane went down. There were 230 passengers on board the 747 when it exploded and crashed into the sea, and from a bystander's viewpoint the rescue efforts were heroic. The NTSB (National Transportation Safety Board) sent investigators immediately to the scene of the crash. The banquet room at the Ramada Inn had become the place for the families to gather for updates from the crash scene. Family members were anxiously waiting for any news on the recovery of their loved ones. Betty's brother, Henry and his wife Carol, arrived to stay with her during this time. When they walked into the banquet room and witnessed the raw emotions of those grieving, it was overwhelming to them. Having so many people gathered together in one room, with all of them suffering the same loss at the same time, was a very heavy feeling. You could actually feel the heaviness of suffering in the air.

Their aunt and uncle in Pennsylvania were caring for Karla's children, and they were trying their best to keep the children entertained and not focused on the tragedy. Thursday was supposed to be a special day for CJ; it was his tenth birthday. His Pop Pop had always told him that when he reached his twelfth birthday, he would teach him to fly. With two years to go, his dreams of someday sitting next to his Pop Pop in an airplane had suddenly been dashed.

Saturday morning after being debriefed of the latest findings, Betty and her children decided to leave and go to Lancaster. They just wanted to be with the rest of their families. It was very emotional being with all the other grieving families. They found out later that President Clinton had come to the Ramada Plaza Saturday afternoon to talk to the families of the victims.

On the way to Lancaster they stopped at a mall to buy Mike some clothes fit to wear to his father's memorial service. (He had come directly from the campsite where he was doing his research.) Betty wanted to buy a dress, but she felt emotionally drained from the last couple of days and didn't feel like shopping. Their first stop was at Amos and Jane Fisher's home, Wil's sister and brother-in-law, where Karla and Wil's three children were staying and where they would be spending the night. This was important to Betty, as she so much wanted to take the time to talk to each of the grandchildren about what had just happened. Just to hold them and talk to each of them meant a great deal to her. CJ was the last one that Betty spent time with, and when she started to talk with him he told her that he hated his birthday now and didn't want to celebrate anymore birthdays again. Upon hearing what her grandson had just said, Betty hugged him all the harder and said, "Your grandfather would have wanted you to keep on celebrating your birthdays; in fact, and he would be saddened if you didn't." That comment had torn at her heartstrings as she thought about the loss these little precious lives had suffered.

Betty and Mike went over to stay the night with her sister, Ruth, and her husband, Don. It was while she was here that Betty got the message that Gid's body had been found and identified by his fingerprints which TWA had on record.

On Sunday Mike and Wil made posters of Gid's life to display at the memorial service. Karla asked her friend, Sandy, to go to their house in Columbus, Ohio, to get some pictures of her dad and send them to her for the poster. Her friend, Gail Smucker, did the lettering for the poster. They also included on the poster some of the many postcards that Gid had sent to his grandchildren from faraway places. All of them were signed, "With love from Pop Pop."

On Sunday evening Betty and family all went over to Emma and Elam's house, Gid's sister and brother-in-law, where his mother also lived, and all the other sisters and brothers-in-law had gathered there as well. It was a very sad get-together and they were all anxious to hear of any details that could be given. Gid had been his mother's only son and his seven sisters' only brother. His death was a great loss to his family.

* * * * *

On Monday Jeanie received a call from Bonnie asking if they were going to be at the memorial service in Lancaster. Jeanie told her they were going to make every effort possible to get there. Jeanie had been feeling really down lately and was extremely weak. But she and Ralph both wanted to go and be there for Betty and the family, so they loaded the wheelchair in the car and made the two-hour drive to the church.

* * * * *

The memorial service was held at 3:00 p.m. Monday afternoon at Mellinger's Mennonite Church. Over six hundred friends and family came to pay their respects, arriving as early as 1:30. The line went out the door and down the side of the church. Friends came from Baptistown, New Jersey, and even as far away as Florida. All of the Spruce Lake Group was there. They had all met at Spruce Lake Retreat that weekend; that is, all of them except Gid and Betty. They had stayed an extra day in the area before going back home in order to attend the memorial service for Gid. This meant so much to Betty and the children.

* * * * *

When Mellinger's church came into view, Ralph and Jeanie couldn't believe their eyes. There were people everywhere, trucks with news station logos on the sides, TV cameras and people walking around with microphones doing interviews. The line of people waiting to get in was wrapped around the church. As they pulled into the parking lot they could see this was going to be very difficult for Jeanie, but almost in unison they both said "poor Betty" to think she was standing somewhere inside greeting all these people. Ralph could see there was no place to park the car, but as he drove around he saw a tiny opening between two cars, not big enough to park in but big enough to drive through and park on the grass. This had put them behind the church and on the lower level. So he was going to have to wheel Jeanie around the church to the line on the side. Jeanie, however, refused to go pay her respects to Gid in a wheelchair. Ralph saw that there was a door to the church on the lower level, so he tried it and thankfully it was open. They slowly walked in and up the stairs to where the line was entering the room where

Betty and all the family members were gathered. Jeanie said for Ralph to get a chair and they could wait till the end of the line came. Ralph started to go and look, but a man heard what she said and motioned for them to cut in front of him. That's when they first saw Betty, and their eyes began to fill with tears. With all she had just been through, she was standing there with a smile on her face greeting one after the other as they passed by. It didn't take too long before they were standing there in front of Betty, and when Jeanie and Betty's eyes met, they just hugged each other and cried together. As Ralph was waiting to pay his respects and give Betty a hug, he was thinking, *this is the lady who helped me save my marriage, and here I am grieving with her at the loss of her husband.* They continued through the line, paying their respects to Karla, Mike, Wil, and all Gid's sisters and his mother. From their Ralph and Jeanie found their way to the sanctuary where the service was going to be held. As soon as they entered the sanctuary, they found Mike and Bonnie, Pastor Kollmar and a whole contingency of people from the Baptistown church sitting in the pews. They went and greeted them all and then sat with Mike and Bonnie, waiting for the service to begin.

* * * * *

Many of the 600 hundred people who stood in line outside Mellinger's church that day were interviewed by reporters.

"He was very proud to have reached the accomplishment of becoming an airline pilot of one of the biggest planes in the world. It was not typical for an Amish boy," said son-in-law, Wil Esh, with loving pride in his voice.

Jeff Hawkes, of the *Lancaster Intelligencer Journal*, interviewed Ella Mae Lehman and wrote this: "Ella Mae Lehman of Ohio, who also knew Miller through church, recalled his enthusiasm for life — how, in khaki shorts, Miller chased a giraffe across the Serengeti. She also recalled how Miller, whose one eye needed no correction, scratched his eye though the lens-free side of his glasses to see how people reacted."

Mel Glick was interviewed and told the story of giving Gid his first airplane ride, and then he added, "He went on to the airlines and I didn't. He was a very determined person, and when he set his mind on something he did it. He was a nice person and a good person" (*Lancaster New Era*, by Todd R. Weiss and Andrea S. Brown).

One headline in the paper said it best: "A friend to everyone."

* * * * *

The line of mourners was finally cut off at 3:40 so the service could begin. Betty and the family entered the sanctuary and were seated down in front. Pastors who spoke that day were Don Augsburger, Gid and Betty's former pastor in Florida, Paul Landis, Betty's cousin, and Fred Martin and Leon Oberholtzer, both friends of Gid and Betty. In the front of the church was a bouquet of thirty-five red roses, one for each year that Gid and Betty were married.

Many kind things were said about Gid, a man who had a love for life and a love for people, and who lived his life through his faith. He also loved good clean fun and always had a story to tell. One TWA pilot spoke of how the TWA employees, especially the pilots who worked with Gid, would never forget him, and that where Gid was flying now, the skies would always be clear!

* * * * *

The service was beautiful and very fitting for a man who loved the Lord and his family the way he did. There were so many stories told about a man who was a master at telling stories.

There was humor and there was sadness, and when you left the sanctuary you almost felt like Gid had orchestrated the service himself. If you thought about it, he did, because it was his life that they were all talking about, the things they all remembered about the man who could make them laugh on any given occasion and who had a very serious side when it came to faith and family. He had been a boy with a dream who became a man who loved to fly.

As they left the sanctuary and went downstairs to be with the families, one of the most significant pictures was right before their eyes. There lying on a shelf were eight Amish hats and eight pilots' caps side by side. Ralph said, "Now there's a photo for a book cover." But of course he didn't have a camera with him. That picture said it all; it represented the two worlds of Gid Miller. When they went into the reception room they were told to help themselves to some food; they did so and found a table and sat down, and it wasn't long before Betty came over and sat down with them. This was a time of remembering Gid and celebrating his life and sharing words of sympathy and encouragement. A couple of pilots shared stories about working and flying with Gid, which entertained young and old alike. His Amish sisters, brothers-in-law, nieces and nephews were all excited about hearing these stories. Gid never bragged about his work, and he usually only talked about it when asked. Betty was holding up very well, and even under the circumstances she made everyone feel very welcomed. Before Ralph and Jeanie left to head back home, they were able to say goodbye to all their old friends from Baptistown, and everyone promised to stay in touch.

This had been a long day for Jeanie; she had sadness in her heart but had been encouraged by the way Betty was holding up. She commented on the way home, "Think of those who don't have faith in God and are trying to go through this ordeal alone and unsure of the future, not knowing the fate of their loved ones. Isn't it good to know that when I'm gone, that God has promised me a home in heaven, and you don't have to be worried?"

"Yes, it is good to have our faith. But I'm sure there are still going to be those times when the sadness will overwhelm a person, whether they have faith or not."

"Of course, I know that, I'm just saying that we who believe in Christ have an eternal promise: that we will live forever in eternity with our Lord. Those who don't know Christ have nothing to look forward to."

"Oh, they have something to look forward to, and it's not pretty."

"Well, you better get busy and start telling people how to have that assurance," Jeanie said to Ralph, very matter-of-factly.

"I will, Jeanie. I think you better rest now; you must be exhausted."

* * * * *

Arrangements were made to have Gid's body delivered to the Ellis R. Bachman Funeral Home in Strasburg near Lancaster, and the burial would be Wednesday morning at Mellinger's Church cemetery. The burial was private with just the immediate families attending. All of Gid and Betty's brothers and sisters and spouses were there, and Gid's mother, and Mim and Merv Landis. When the funeral director, Mr. Murray Miller, asked whether they wanted an open casket, Betty asked him to advise her of what he thought after seeing the body. Mr. Miller said he was sure of Gid's identity from the pictures he saw, but would advise them not to view the body. Betty agreed. Some family members questioned Betty's decision, but she wanted to remember him exactly as she had last seen him, smiling jauntily in his crisp pilot's uniform as he bent down to give her one last kiss.

After the burial service, Betty and the family went to Charter Hall where Betty's family was spending five days by the Chesapeake Bay. On Friday they left for Florida, where another memorial service would be held on Sunday afternoon. Over 400 mourners attended that service. Pastor Barry Loop officiated. Earl Beachy sang "The Holy City," and the New Life Sound quartet sang "Wedding Music." These were two of Gid's favorite songs. Betty heard the New Life Sound sing "Wedding Music" many times after that and it always brought tears to her eyes.

It had only been eleven days since Gid's death, but so much had happened that it seemed longer. It was a very emotionally draining experience, and Betty was beginning to wonder how they were going to get through the grieving process. She asked Glen Denlinger from Charis Center if he would come to the house and talk to her and the children about what to expect during this time of grieving for the loss of their husband, father, and grandfather. Glen talked about the different stages of grieving, and that each person grieves differently, and that they need to allow each other to grieve in his and her own way.

Soon the children and grandchildren had to go home, Mike to Colorado and Karla, Wil, CJ, Kari and Kalicia, to Columbus, Ohio. But Betty was alone for only a couple of days. Her brother, Henry and her sister-in-law, Carol, had offered to come and help her with whatever needed to be done.

Henry helped her learn more about investments and helped her sell a few of the rental houses. Betty had been managing the rentals for quite a while, so this was not a problem, but she was ready to sell them. Everyday Henry and Betty would spend some time doing a tutorial. Carol made sure he didn't try to give her too much information in one day! Carol was also very helpful with the cooking and laundry. It was great having their company, but there were still difficult times for Betty, especially at night and in the shower. That's when the tears seemed to come. Henry and Carol were with her for about a month, and then they had to return to their home.

Gid and Betty had planned a family vacation with the children and grandchildren at one of their timeshares in Frazier, Colorado, at the end of August. Betty decided to continue with those plans since they all just wanted to be together again. They had a great time, but they missed Gid tremendously. They went horseback riding, biking, and shopping. Betty remembered one particular time when Mike's humor reminded them all of Gid.

Soon it was time for them all to head home, and Betty was returning to Florida knowing she would be living alone. Betty's church and friends were a great source of friendship and encouragement in the days that followed.

17

PLEASE CONSIDER

It had been three months since the fatal crash of TWA Flight 800, and still the television news reports, newspaper, and magazine articles were almost a daily occurrence. There were many different and conflicting stories and conspiracy theories about what really happened. As Ralph and Jeanie listened to the many differing theories, their hearts went out to all those who suffered such devastating losses. Their home was located fairly close to one of the churches where the memorials for a few of the students had taken place, so they could see all the people lining up outside waiting to go in and pay their respects to the families.

It brought back memories of the day they traveled to Lancaster to go to one of Gid's memorial services. The lines of people had wrapped around Mellinger's church and there were TV crews and cameras interviewing people everywhere. Ralph and Jeanie had never seen anything like that before and felt so bad for Betty and all of the family members who were standing there greeting the people as they passed by.

It was October now and the leaves were putting on a magnificent display of color. There was coolness to the air that was refreshing. This had always been one of Ralph and

Jeanie's favorite times of year; they loved to just put a sweatshirt and go outside to rake leaves, winterize all the gardens, and just enjoy all the activities going on as the farmers worked at bringing in the remaining crops.

This would be the first time since they were married that Jeanie couldn't physically do the outside activities that she loved so much. Ralph would help her put a sweatshirt on and then take her outside where she would walk very slowly to a flower bed to examine them and then tell Ralph what she would like for him to do. It wouldn't be long before he would get her a chair so she could sit and watch him for a while. He'd ask her if she was cold or wanted anything and she would say no, not to worry, that she just wanted to sit and enjoy the view. This was probably one of the most difficult times for Jeanie. She had always been so active and full of life, and now she had to allow others to wait on her. Cooking, cleaning, laundry, and shopping were things she had always done, but now Ralph was doing them for her. She kept telling him she felt bad that he had to do so much and that she couldn't help, but he would say don't worry about it, as soon as you get back on your feet you can do it all again. Deep inside he didn't think that was going to happen, but he wanted her to know he hadn't given up on her.

Her body was slowly weakening, and it was getting to be very difficult for her to climb the stairs to the bedroom. Ralph had suggested moving their bedroom downstairs and the office upstairs, but she wouldn't hear of it. So each evening she would make the difficult trip upstairs, resting after every step, determined to sleep in her own bed next to Ralph. Her days now mainly were spent on the couch or in Ralph's favorite chair reading a book or watching TV and the clock, checking to see how much longer before Ralph would be home. Ralph was still staying close to the phones at Hal's. Hal always made sure that either Brian or he could get to Ralph quickly if an emergency call should come in to the office.

* * * * *

On September 9, 1996, TWA Captain Lou Thieblemont got two fifteen-passenger vans and picked up Gid's sisters and their husbands and drove them to the JFK training center. Betty flew up from Florida to join them. They wanted to see firsthand where Gid had worked and what the inside of a Boeing 747 looked like. The men even got a chance to sit in a simulator and try their hand at flying one. They got to watch the planes taking off and landing, and they even got to see the Concord come in for a landing. From the reports afterward all the Amish hats were blown off as the Concord streaked by. While they were there Betty was presented with a pair of Captain's wings with Gid's name engraved on the back. That trip gave the family many precious memories to cherish for ages to come. The entire article was in the *Trans World Airlines* magazine, December 1996, vol. 1 number 4 issue. The article was entitled, "The Plain People Tour the Plane." Here is the last paragraph from that article:

> "Since then, Rachael Stoltzfus's husband Elmer cut a small runway in his corn field for me to land my Piper Cub. I fly my Cub down to his farm and try to arrive around lunchtime so as to enjoy their family fellowship and some good food. Last week I flew over the farm before landing and John, Elmer's son, spotted me from the one-room Amish school. The classroom emptied as the children hurried to see me land. Within seconds after I landed, there were 25 to 30 kids circling my plane with smiles and questions. Rachael said she had a tear in her eye whenever I

flew in to see them. "It reminds me of Gid when he would fly over."

* * * * *

Ralph's days always started out the same; the drive to Hal's took about 45 minutes, and he often found himself in a state of prayer during the entire trip there. Once at Hal's they began every day with a devotional and prayer time while gathered around the kitchen table. Then they were off to the days' assignments. Hal had become a brother to Ralph, just like how Gene had been to him in the early days of his new faith. Hal was a man of his word, devoted and godly, filled with the Spirit and always an encouragement to others.

One day Ralph was outside working in the shop and needed to ask Hal a question. He went into the house where his office was and Sandy said, "Oh, he's in his office; just go around back." When Ralph got to the door, he could see Hal sitting at his desk leaning over something. Ralph knocked to get Hal's attention, not wanting to disturb him by just walking in. Hal looked up wiping his eyes and said, "Come on in, buddy."

"Is this a bad time?" Ralph asked. It looked like Hal had been crying.

"Oh no, I get like this every month when I send out these checks."

Now Ralph thought this was a set-up, because he always used to say he cried every month when he had to pay the bills too. But Hal wasn't crying for that reason. He went on to say,

"When my Sandy and I started this business, we had nothing but a bucket and a mop. We went on in faith believing that God was going to supply what we needed. And as the business prospered, we made a promise that we would always give back to God a portion of what He had so graciously supplied us with. What you see here on this desk are not monthly bills that I'm crying over. They are monthly support checks for missionaries that Sandy, Brian, and I give to the Lord. So every month about this time I get very emotional when writing them out. Sometimes I feel a weakness in my hands as I'm writing and I start to sob. I was just praying over them when you walked in."

At this point Ralph's eyes were tearing up as well. Ralph had tried to make a quick count of the checks without making it look obvious, and he came up with seventeen checks that were being sent all over the world to support missionaries who were working on the frontlines for God. As he stood there he was also thanking God for the privilege of knowing this precious family that loved the Lord so much.

"So buddy, what can I help you with?" Hal asked.

"I have no idea what I was going to ask you, but I don't think it was as important as what you just shared with me. Thank you for that, Hal!"

"If you remember what you needed, just come back over and let me know, buddy," Hal replied, looking up with a smile. "I sure will," Ralph answered.

> "God's Word tells Christians to give tithes and offerings to God. Just as we give gifts to friends and family out of love for them, we show our love for God by such offerings. Tithing is also our acknowledgement to God that He is our provider and that all we have belongs to Him and comes from Him." (Taken from Billy Graham's Training Center Bible NKJV).
>
> Helpful verses of Scripture are: **1 Chronicles 29:12-14; 2 Corinthians 9: 6-8; 1 Corinthians 16: 2; Malachi 3: 10.**

Fall turned into winter, and the Mahantongo Valley was covered with a pure white blanket of snow, a new view for Jeanie to gaze upon from her window, which triggered fond memories of when she was dating Ralph and they would go tobogganing, sledding, and ice skating. Then another fond memory flooded her mind with feelings of great joy. She remembered the time that she and her girlfriend, Rosemary, were ice skating on Round Valley reservoir after it had frozen over. There were a bunch of boys there also, playing hockey. She knew all those boys except one, and she was curious to know who he was. He looked older then the rest of them. The boys whom she recognized were Butch, John and Mike Teets, Glenn Walls, and her brother Herbie. All of a sudden the puck came flying towards her and hit her skate, stopping right next to her blade. As she was bending down to retrieve it, the unknown skater came whizzing over causing scraped ice to fly all over her. "Watch out kid, you're going to get hurt."

Then he maneuvered the puck with his stick, sending it back into the game. That guy turned out to be Ralph. He was a junior in high school and she was in the seventh grade.

She remembered that following summer when she went over to visit Carol Jo Wurst, who just happened to live next to Ralph. Glenn, Ralph's younger brother, was showing some signs of interest in Carol Jo, so the girls would hide behind the raspberry bushes spying on the two brothers while they played ball in their yard. The boys never noticed them at all that summer.

Jeanie couldn't wait to tell Ralph that night when he came home from work about all those memories she'd had during the day. When he got home that evening she told him the whole story, and they sat there laughing, talking, and just enjoying each other's company, and then Ralph said, "Let me go get cleaned up so I can get dinner started."

He stood up and bent over, giving her a kiss as he left the room. Once he was in the bathroom the tears began to flow; he didn't know why, but he just had to let them go. He had been thinking a lot about what was going to happen if she died. They had talked once about it. Jeanie had asked him, "What will you do when I'm gone? Will you remarry?"

Ralph had responded, "No, I'm just going to go live in the wilderness and become a hermit."

"No, promise me you won't desert the children, Ralph, promise me."

"Don't worry about the kids; I won't ignore them."

A few days later while at work, Ralph got a call from Jeanie saying that she wasn't feeling quite right; she wasn't in any pain, but just felt a little strange. He said he would be right home. She told him not to rush because it wasn't urgent. When he arrived home and saw her, he thought she looked a little pale, so he decided to take her to the hospital. They said she needed some blood and proceeded to hook her up. They said she could go back home after the blood transfusion, so Ralph wheeled her back to the car and they went home. When they got home Ralph told her to wait in the car while he went and unlocked the door. Then he came back, picked her up and carried her to the house. Once they'd gotten inside the house Jeanie said, "I just want to lie on the couch." So Ralph carried her into the living room and laid her on the couch, tucking blankets around her to make her feel snug and cozy.

"How's that? You comfortable?"

"Yes, thank you, honey. And thank you for taking such good care of me — I love you."

"I love you too, honey," Ralph said tenderly, and then he turned and headed for the stairs. He had one hand on the stair railing when he heard Jeanie call out to him in a very quiet voice. "Come back, Ralph."

Ralph turned around and went back to the couch. When he reached the couch she was lying there with her arms outstretched saying, "Come here."

Thinking she wanted to kiss him, he leaned down, but then Jeanie reached out her hands and grabbed his shirt, pulling him within inches of her face. She looked directly into his eyes and said, "When I'm gone, please consider Betty; she would be perfect for you."

Ralph was totally taken by surprise. Pulling back he responded, "First of all, you're not going anywhere, and secondly, she is a princess and I am a frog." She started to say more but before she could get the words out Ralph had gently placed two fingers on her lips, saying, "There's nothing more to discuss, so stop trying to play matchmaker." Then before she could respond, he pulled his fingers away and placed a big, juicy kiss right on her lips.

As he headed back to the stairs she said, "I'm serious."

"Me too, get some rest, and quit straining your brain."

Christmas had come and gone, and before they knew it early spring was making its delicate entrance all around them. The blanket of snow was starting to pull back and new signs of life were bursting forth. The early flowers that Jeanie and Ralph had planted a couple of years before were beginning to show their beautiful colors. Oh, how she enjoyed those first signs of spring. Jeanie had lost so much weight now that no one could understand how she could possibly stand, let alone what was keeping her alive. She no longer could climb the stairs to the bedroom, and she again refused to let Ralph change the house around. She did agree to have a bed put in the office, but only if Ralph would stay in the bed upstairs. Ralph didn't like that idea because he wanted to be with her, but in the end she won again with one stipulation. He could put a baby monitor next to her bed.

Alva was making regular visits to the house now since Jeanie found it too difficult to attend church. People from the church had also started to come and visit more often. Despite her frail condition Jeanie still found the strength to go outside and show off her flowerbeds in the spring when Stephanie stopped in to check on her. She put one of her favorite dresses on and wanted her picture taken with her daughter in front of the flowers. The one thing she never lost was her ability to smile. That day she let Ralph take a lot of pictures of her, but the one picture that was the hardest to take was when she wanted one taken of her waving goodbye. A few more weeks went by fairly uneventfully, and then one afternoon Ralph came home and found Jeanie crying and in desperate need of help. She was in terrible pain and had been franticly trying to find someone to take her to the hospital. When Ralph came in she said, "Thank you so much for coming home. I didn't know what to do. I'm in terrible pain and I need help." Ralph knew this was serious because she had never in her life complained of pain.

This had to be an answer to her prayer, because he didn't usually come home this early. When Jeanie asked him why he was home so early, he just said something told him to go home, so he did. Ralph got her into the car as fast as he could and started the drive to the hospital in Danville. The drive there was very tense. Jeanie was moaning and holding herself with her arms wrapped around her body.

Ralph was trying to stay focused on the road ahead; he had never driven this fast on these back roads before. They were making great time and finally made it to the highway where the road would be a lot smoother. About two and a half miles from the hospital there is a section on the route where you need to pay close attention. As you come around a turn on the left there is a shear wall of rocks and cliffs, and on the right side a little lower down there are railroad tracks, and lower yet is the Schuylkill River. Many times you will see cars with broken windshields or dented hoods and roofs from falling ice or rocks. Sometimes vehicles had run head on into oncoming traffic while trying to avoid falling objects. Ralph was now approaching this spot and was totally focused on everything ahead of him. Jeanie was still in extreme pain when Ralph entered that area. He wasn't even a hundred yards into it when Jeanie called out, "Look!"

Ralph instantly grabbed the wheel tighter and expected the worst. Had he missed something falling or coming at him? Then Jeanie continued, "Look, look at the flowers in the crags!" Ralph looked at her and saw she was pointing to the mountainside and she had a beautiful smile on her face. Ralph looked up to where she was pointing, and just as he did the sun broke through the clouds and radiant beams of light shone down onto some beautiful wildflowers that were tucked into the crags on the mountain. There were still spots of snow dotting the mountainside in places where the sun didn't reach. But the picture looked like the hand of God had painted it just for her to enjoy. In the seconds that it took to see that picture, an entire story flashed through Ralph's mind. He turned to Jeanie and said, "You just gave me the title of the book that I'm going to write about you."

"Isn't it beautiful? You're going to write a book about me?"

"Yes I am," he answered.

For that brief moment in time, all pain was gone. God had placed those flowers there at that precise moment to comfort Jeanie in her time of need. Isn't that what our great God does for all of us who trust in Him? As we travel this road of life, through times of struggle and hardship, trial and tribulation, good times and bad, God never fails us. He always provides something or someone to help us through. Those precious people are the flowers in the crags along our journey of life. We just need to watch and listen. And at times if we are really observant, we may just catch a glimpse of something or someone that God has put there just for us. Sometimes it seems that God is unfair and we have no relief from our pain. Remedies may bring relief for the moment, but often the comfort does not last. A personal relationship with Jesus Christ offers the hope we so desperately need during our most painful life experiences. If you are unsure of your relationship with God, then let that be the beginning point on your road to recovery, no matter what it is you have suffered. Take time to make your commitment to Jesus. Then, with His hope and help, you can find peace and comfort even in times of great suffering. (Taken from Billy Graham's Training Center Bible, NKJV. If you need further help understanding salvation and how to accept Jesus Christ as your Lord and Savior, please see the section at the end of this book called "The End: For Your Eyes Only.")They pulled into the hospital emergency entrance, and someone was waiting there with a wheelchair to take Jeanie in. By the time Ralph found a parking place and made his way back to the building, Jeanie had already been admitted. She stayed in the hospital for three days while they did everything they could for her, and then the doctors allowed Ralph to take her home. They had told him privately that her time was drawing to an end and there wasn't much more they could do for her. While she was in the hospital she had asked Ralph to go and purchase a cemetery plot. She had picked a spot on Route 61 so that every time Ralph, Stephanie, and Rodney drove by, they would remember her and so that she could see them often. On the way back to the house she made Ralph stop and show her where she would be laid to rest. By now this once very tough man had become an overly sensitive piece of mush. To drive into the cemetery and show his still living and beautiful wife where she would rest her body for eternity was more than he could handle. When they pulled up to the spot where her gravesite would be, she was ecstatic and filled with joy at the choice he had made. She loved the view and thought it was perfect. She wanted to get out and walk around a bit, so he helped her out of the car, and she threw her tiny arms around him and kissed his tear-soaked face, saying, "Thank you, honey, you did great ... I love you."

By June Jeanie was spending most of her time in bed, and the visits now from church friends had greatly increased. Ralph would help her into the living room so she could watch a program that had become a favorite of hers during her illness. Jeanie always said she just wanted to be near him, but the truth was that Ralph was spending most of his time in the office, next to her bed, making believe he had lots of office work to do. Jeanie insisted that Ralph go to work every day and assured him that she would be all right. Reluctantly Ralph would head up to Hal's, but Hal knew the time was getting close, so he kept his buddy real close to the house.

On June 10, as Ralph came over the hill and his house came into view, he could see an ambulance sitting in his driveway. With his heart racing he pulled in and jumped out running towards the house. When he entered the house there were three emergency medical technicians standing in the kitchen.

"What's going on?" He asked.

"Are you Mr. Walls?" One of them asked him.

"We received a call from your wife saying she needed help."

"Is she ok?" Before they could answer a voice came from the office.

"Ralph is that you?" Then Ralph rushed into the office.

"Are you alright?"

"I didn't know what to do; I am really hurting all over, and I can't take it any more. I'm sorry I caused so much trouble."

"You aren't causing any trouble; it's their job to help people."

"No, I'm causing trouble, they can't get the stretcher in here, and the hall is too narrow."

Now that made Ralph a little upset, so he turned to the squad and demanded, "Is that true, you can't get her out of here?"

"Well, sir, we need to get her on the bed and wheel her out to the truck."

Ralph now notices that he had run right past the stretcher bed outside the kitchen door in his hurry to get by Jeanie's side.

"Open the door and get ready," he said as he turned to where Jeanie was lying down and said, "Honey, I'm going to pick you up and carry you out, so don't be afraid."

"No, you'll hurt yourself." Jeanie replied. It was already too late; Ralph had already started to gently slide his hands under her frail body. She could feel every movement and would moan in pain. As he started to lift her she locked her hands around his neck to help hold her up. Ralph instantly felt the strain on his back, but he refused to stop. The emergency medical technicians were in rescue mode now as Ralph approached the door and laid her on the stretcher.

"We'll take her from here, sir."

"I'm going to be right behind you in the green car."

"Ok."

The ride to the hospital seemed to take forever. Ralph could see them through the rear windows working on her. For the last few months Ralph's prayers had changed from prayers of healing to prayers of mercy. *Please don't let her suffer*, seemed to be what he had been praying for quite some time now. The only part of her body that didn't have a lump from a tumor trying to push through the skin was her still beautiful face.

"She has suffered enough, Lord, please take her home!" It wasn't too long ago he was praying for God to take his life in trade for hers. He would say, "She enjoys life so much more than me; why her and not a worthless bum like me, Lord?"

After they got her settled in at the hospital, they eased her pain with a morphine drip. She told Ralph to go and get something to eat because he needed to take care of himself. After telling her he wasn't hungry and Jeanie replying that yes he was, he smiled, bent over the bed, gave her one of his patented juicy kisses, and then said, "I just love you to pieces." Jeanie responded, "I just love you to pieces too."

As he left the room he looked back and said, "Don't go anywhere, kid." She gave him one of her big smiles and he left. About an hour later Ralph returned to the room and walked over to the bed. "Hey, what happened" He noticed that they had brought her a dinner tray and her cup had spilled all over it. He started to wipe it up and glanced up at Jeanie to see why she hadn't responded to him. She was just staring at him.

"Are you ok, honey?" Jeanie gave no response. He moved closer to her and grabbed her shoulders.

"What's wrong, Jeanie, can you tell me?" Now he knew something had happened. He ran to the hall and yelled toward the nurses' station, "I think my wife just had a stroke, we could use some help here!!!"

Three people came running down the hall. Ralph was telling them that she wasn't responding to anything. They asked him to step back as they surrounded her bed and attended to her. Another doctor came in and told Ralph he should probably go down the hall to the waiting area and they would come and talk to him when they had some news.

An hour later they came to Ralph and said there wasn't too much more they could do for her and that she was resting comfortably. He asked if she was in any pain. They assured him she wasn't. Then he asked if he could see her.

"Sure, but she can't speak; whatever happened affected the right side of her body."

"Did she have a stroke?"

"We can't be sure yet, but by tomorrow we will know"

"So she will make it through the night?"

"She has a strong heart, and she should be ok for awhile. We will have more to tell you tomorrow."

"Thank you, sir." Then he went to her side.

"Hey, honey, you gave me a scare. How are you doing?" Jeanie was staring at Ralph with no emotion in her eyes. Ralph walked from one side of the bed to the other to see if her eyes were following him. He was relieved to know that they were. But the blank look was very uncomfortable for him. Not knowing if she could comprehend what was being said was terrible. He stayed at her side talking quietly to her until she fell asleep, and he knew he had to leave because visiting hours were well over. He was still in his work clothes, and he needed to wash and call all the family members yet that night. It was a very lonely and tearful ride home. It was dark and his eyes kept filling up making it hard for him to see the road. He kept thinking how it was five years and three months ago when the doctors first said she had from six weeks to six months to live. She was the strongest and toughest person he ever knew. She never quit her fight to live and always encouraged others when they were feeling sorry for her. As he drove past the spot where she had pointed out the flowers in the crags a couple of months ago, he realized that she had been a flower that God had put in his path along the way.

Wednesday morning Ralph was still calling family members to let them know of Jeanie's condition. He was in a hurry to leave because he wanted to make sure he was there when the doctors made their rounds. This way he could get some direct answers.

He arrived at the hospital at 8:30 and headed directly to Jeanie's floor. There were a lot of doctors standing in the hallway when he came around the corner, so he went straight to them. At this point Ralph didn't really care about proper etiquette, so he interrupted their conversation.

"Excuse me, I'm Ralph Walls, my wife Jeanie is in room 524 and I was wondering if you could tell me anything about her condition yet." One of the doctors commented, "Mr. Walls, we don't have the results of the test yet, but as soon as we do someone will come and talk to you." Then they continued their conversation with one another and walked away.

Under his breath Ralph muttered, "Thanks a lot." Then he went in to see Jeanie. He could see that a tray of food had been placed on the table next to her bed, but it looked like it hadn't been touched.

"Hi, honey, are you feeling better today?" Her face seemed to light up at hearing Ralph's voice. Knowing that he wasn't going to get a response he just continued to talk.

"Did you have anything to eat yet? It doesn't look like it. Would you like me to help you?" Her eyes went to the tray and then back to Ralph.

"Let's try some juice first." As he lifted it towards her mouth, she ever so slightly opened her mouth, allowing the straw to enter. When she had enough she pulled her head back. Ralph continued with some applesauce, but after a couple swallows she pulled away again. He sat in the room till noon talking to her, but she continued to nod off every now and then. It was ok; he just sat and watched her while he reminisced about the past. A nurse came in and asked if they could bring him a tray of food. Ralph said, "No, thank you, I think I'll stretch my legs and go down to the cafeteria to eat. While Jeanie was sleeping he left the room and went downstairs for some lunch. When he returned an hour later there were doctors standing around Jeanie's bed talking. As he approached them they started to leave the room. Ralph asked, "Can someone please tell me what's going on?" One of the doctors put his arm out behind Ralph and started to guide him towards the door.

"Mr. Walls, let's step outside."

"Sure ..."

"Mr. Walls, your wife is dying. Her body is starting to shut down."

"So how long does she have?"

"It's hard to say. She will more then likely slip into a coma first."

"How long will she be in a coma?"

"It could be an hour or it could be two weeks. You never can know."

"Did she have a stroke yesterday?"

"No, we think it was probably a tumor pressing against a nerve or nerves. She has lost most of her functions on her right side. Mr. Walls, there is nothing more we can do for her, and it would be best to take her home. Have you made contact with Hospice yet?"

"No ..."

"We can help you set that up, and we will have an ambulance set up for tomorrow to take her home."

"Is there anything else I will need to know to take care of her?"

"I'll send someone up to give you instructions, but basically just keep her comfortable. I'm so sorry for what you're going through, Mr. Walls."

"Thank you, Doctor."

With that the doctor put his hand on Ralph's shoulder briefly, then turned and walked away. Ralph stayed with Jeanie the rest of the day. That night he let the children know that he was bringing her home tomorrow. Ralph's mother called and said she was coming out to help him for as long as he needed her. The next day Ralph went to the hospital and told the ambulance drivers he would be following them back to the house. Once at home they pulled up to the back of the house and carried her into the office. Stephanie had already arrived at the house to help her dad and to hear all the instructions that Hospice would provide for them that day. With Jeanie resting in her bed, Stephanie and her dad went into the kitchen to talk. They talked about making sure everyone had been contacted, and who they should call when the inevitable happened. Stephanie was the strong one, just like her mother. She could tell this was starting to take a toll on her dad. She suggested that he go up to Hal's for a while, and that she would stay there and wait for the hospice representative. Stephanie told him not to worry, and that she wouldn't be alone. Rhoda and Elaine were going to come over to visit, too. He finally agreed and left the house. Hal and Sandy were just what Ralph needed, two friends who cared and were always there in times of need. Ralph really couldn't do much that day; he just mainly wanted to be around them. Hal always expressed his love for Sandy. He'd say something cute, and Sandy would turn and give a silly look or comment. On this particular day, watching them tease like this would make Ralph's eyes well up with tears, because Jeanie would always do the same thing, but now she was showing no emotion of any kind, just a blank stare.

When Ralph arrived back home that day, there were four cars in the driveway, so he knew everyone was still there. As he stepped onto the porch, Stephanie came out of the door all teary eyed, saying, "Oh dad, I didn't know you were home."

"What's happening?" Ralph asked, his voice full of concern over Stephanie's teary face.

"We all wanted to know if Mom knew what we were saying and could remember who we are. It's hard to tell with her just looking at you with that blank stare. So Rhoda and Elaine made a chart with names on one side and who they were on the other."

"So how did it go?"

"Here's the chart." She then showed her dad a chart with the following names on it: Ralph, Stephanie, Rodney,

Evelyn, and Carol. On the other side they had the following: husband, daughter, son, mother, best friend.

"So how did she do?"

"She did great!"

"So why are you crying?" Stephanie started to cry a little harder.

"When we asked her who her best friend was she pointed to your name."

Ralph couldn't even swallow; his throat was tightening up so much as his eyes filled up with tears. This was the nicest gift she could have ever left him with. The thought that flashed through his mind was from many years ago during one of their explosive fights when she had shouted to him, *you haven't got a friend in the world*, but now they were best friends. Just then two other teary faces came out from behind the door where they had been listening.

"What's wrong with everyone?" Ralph tried to say laughingly through his tears.

"You guys are too much." They all hugged one another for a moment and shared a little laugh of relief. Ralph wiped his face and went in to see his Jeanie. The hospice lady was standing there doing something, but Ralph had only one thing on his mind. In a nanosecond he was next to her bed planting, you guessed it, one of those patented kisses on her lips.

"Hi, honey, I missed you." Jeanie just lay there with her expressionless face staring at him.

"You must be Mr. Walls."

"I hope so, after that kiss." Ralph said jokingly. The nurse started to explain what she had done and that she had already shown Stephanie everything. She then asked Ralph if he could help her carry her bag out to the car. Ralph knew that she really didn't need help, but that she just wanted to talk to him away from Jeanie.

"I'm going now, Mrs. Walls, but I'll stop back by in a couple of days. Bye-bye." Out on the porch she stopped for a moment and then turned back to Ralph and said, "Your wife is in the final days now, Mr. Walls, and it won't be too long. If you need anything at all, just call this number no matter what time it is." Then she handed him a card and said, "You take care now, and I'll be praying for you all." Ralph said thank you and she turned and left.

Stephanie had received a call that afternoon from Jeanie's brother, Herb, who was at the shore with his wife Linda and his mother, Evelyn. She told Ralph that they said they would come up Sunday afternoon. As Stephanie was saying goodbye, Ralph's mother pulled into the driveway with her little dog, Toby. As she got out of the car, she was already talking, "It only took me two and a half hours. I kept telling Toby that we were going to see Ralph and Jeanie, and he stood up the whole way looking out the window." Then she put his little leash on him and walked him to the grass so he could bless the place. Then when she thinks he's done enough blessing, she yanks him and heads for Ralph and Stephanie.

"Here, let me give you a big hug," Mrs. Walls said as poor Toby was getting his neck stretched out while her arms reached to hug them.

"Is Jeanie here?" She asked.

"Yes, we've been home about two hours ..."

"Oh good, I was afraid to ask, because you hadn't said anything."

"Lets go in and see her; she's probably thinking we all left her." They headed into the house and noticed that Jeanie was sleeping, so they lowered their voices and went into the kitchen to talk. Twenty minutes later Stephanie said she had to run, but that she would be back tomorrow.

By Sunday Ralph's mother felt like she could take care of Jeanie for a couple of hours, so that he could go to church and teach his Sunday school class. That afternoon Herb and Linda arrived from the shore. When they entered Jeanie's room, the expressions on their faces revealed how shocked they were at her appearance; she had deteriorated quite a bit since the last time they had seen her. Fighting back the tears, Evelyn placed her hand on Jeanie's shoulder and spoke softly to her. She only said a few sentences and then turned suddenly and exited the room. Herb reached over and grabbed his sister's hand and said, "Jeanie, I just want to tell you how proud I am of you. You're the best sister anyone could ever have asked for. I know I wasn't always the best brother, and I'm sorry if I ever hurt you in any way. Please forgive me. You will always be the greatest. We're not going to see each other for a little while now, but we will be together again, I promise. I love you so much." Then he leaned down and kissed her check and said goodbye. By the time Herb had finished saying goodbye, no one could speak. Evelyn was still on the porch crying and Stephanie stopped to comfort her. Herb, Linda, Ralph and Stephanie walked out into the backyard and just talked, crying and reminiscing of the days gone by. No one knows for sure what Jeanie was thinking while she lay there listening, but everyone noticed that her eyes would go from one person to the next as Herb was talking. Jeanie had often told Ralph how she never heard her mother say I love you and I'm proud of you, and how she had hoped to hear those words one day. Later that night the phone rang; Ralph answered, and it was his mother-in-law trying to talk through her sobs. She was saying how she wanted to tell Jeanie something today, but she couldn't get the words to come out because she didn't want Jeanie to see her crying. She said she was so ashamed of herself and wanted Ralph to tell her. Ralph said, "Why don't you tell her yourself?" So he took the phone over to Jeanie's side, pushed the speaker button, then told Jeanie that it was her mother on the phone and she wanted to talk to her. Through her sobs Evelyn said,

"Jeanie, I'm sorry I didn't tell you this when I was there, but I love you and I always have. You have made me very proud to call you my daughter. I'm sorry I didn't tell you this sooner, Jeanie; please forgive me. You are very special to me, and I love you. Bye-bye." By the time she had finished you could hardly understand her through the sobbing. Ralph tried to say goodbye, but she had already hung up. Jeanie was still expressionless. He would never know if she heard or understood what her mother said.

Jeanie had only been able to get jello and apple juice down for the last week. Everyday Ralph would line up three small glasses of grape and apple juice along with ginger ale for her to drink, and each day less and less was being finished. By the following Saturday she was down to just a couple of sips a day. About midmorning she was in extreme pain; the morphine machine wasn't working properly and there was nothing they could do to relieve her suffering. Two hours later someone came and fixed it, and she began to rest comfortably again. Even the little dog Toby knew something was wrong. He had been sleeping each day by Jeanie's feet and watching her every move. Sunday Ralph checked on her to see how she was doing, and then decided he would go to church. When he came back home that afternoon and walked to the entrance of the office, Jeanie looked directly at him and gave him the biggest smile he had ever seen. He almost cried with joy as he walked to her side, leaned down, and put both his hands on her cheeks. Her face seemed lost in his hands as he gently kissed her lips.

"Now that's my Jeanie, where have you been? I've missed your smiling face."

As fast as it came, it was gone. Never to be seen again. Ralph spent the rest of the day in the office reading to her and talking to her. When she would nod off he would quietly leave. When the day had ended, Ralph and his mother went to their rooms to sleep. He usually was a pretty sound sleeper, but for some unknown reason he felt the urge to go back downstairs and check on Jeanie. He had only been in bed twenty minutes, and it was now 11:45 pm. When he got to Jeanie's side and checked her, he noticed that she needed to be changed. By then his mother had heard him and was down to help. With everything all better he leaned over to kiss her and noticed her eyes were not moving. He tried to get her to blink, but she didn't, and then he felt her pulse rate in her neck and noticed it was very rapid.

"I think she has slipped into a coma." He said to his mother.

"What should we do?" She asked

Remembering what the doctor said, that it could be twenty minutes or two weeks once she slipped into a coma, he said, "Nothing."

Then he got down on his knees next to her bed and whispered in her ear, "Jeanie, I am so proud of you. You are the most incredible person I have ever known. You're my hero, and I love you so much. But now it's time to let go. Look ahead of you, Jesus is standing there with His arms stretched out waiting for you. Go to Him. I'm going to miss you a lot, but I'll be along a little later. Let go now, honey. It's time to stop fighting. Go to Jesus." Then he kissed her, turned off the light, and they walked to the foot of the stairs and paused.

"I don't know why, Mom, but I feel that she just left us." He turned around, walked back into the room, and she was gone. He looked up at the ceiling above her bed and raised his hands above his head, reaching out for her as he said, "I love you to pieces."

18

TWO OLIVE TREES

Early Monday morning Ralph called the funeral home and told them that his wife had passed away at 12:12 in the morning. They said they would be down in a couple of hours. He then called the children to let them know of their mother's passing. Stephanie wanted to come right over to help and be a part of the meeting with the funeral director. Her mother had told her, well in advance of her death, what dress she was to be buried in, so Stephanie knew exactly what things needed to be given to the director when he arrived. She arrived before they did, so she had some time to spend alone with her mom, saying her goodbyes. Their pastor, Alva, and his wife, Laura, were away in Bolivia visiting their daughter, Joanna, her husband, Tony, and their children, who worked for New Tribes Mission. Alva had been coming to visit two times a week until they left for South America, and he had become very close to Jeanie. But Ralph and Stephanie thought they shouldn't bother him, so they made arrangements with Scott Fetterolf to handle the service. But someone must've called Bolivia anyway and told Alva of Jeanie's passing, and Alva immediately started to make the arrangements to take an earlier flight home. Less than a day before the funeral a very tired Alva arrived at home. Everything had been prepared for the service thinking Scott would officiate, but Scott graciously stepped aside so Alva could do the eulogy. Friends and family from all over came to pay their respects to the family and say their goodbyes to Jeanie. Rodney, Herb, Merv, Tim, David, and Mark were the pallbearers. When the service began, Alva welcomed everyone and prayed, and then he turned the microphone over to Ralph.

"I, Ralph, take thee Jeanie to be my wedded wife … to have and to hold, from this day forward … for better, for worse, for richer, for poorer … in sickness and in health … to love and to cherish … till death do us part. I made that promise on August 31, 1968. It wasn't till January 11, 1980, when I realized I had failed. I asked for forgiveness and we recommitted our vows to one another. While we were working on our marriage, we came across this little reading that we both enjoyed, and I would like to share it with you today. It's called "Not 'I' But 'Us'." Ralph turned the page and began to read.

> 'While we were walking along the beach one day an object caught my eye and captured my imagination. When I first saw it lying there, I thought it was a dead tree whose trunk had been sawn off and whose roots had been abandoned on the shore where they were now sand covered and sun scorched. But as I stooped over the mass of roots, I noticed that this was the remains not of one tree, but two. I could see where both trunks had once grown and where the roots of both trees had wound themselves around the roots of the other to form a solid, underground bond, which could not be severed even in death. I tried to imagine how those had looked when they were growing in the nearby olive grove. Above ground they must have

> started life like any other two olive trees, growing through the sapling stage until they became sturdy, strong and well rooted. But although above ground they retained their individuality, each shaping itself to the space provided for its growth, underneath the ground something quite different was happening. These two trees were pushing their roots first towards each other and then around each other. Far from strangling each other with this intertwining of their lives, they gave one another an anchor, a security. And eventually they became, not two, but one — yet they continued to be two as well.' (*Marriage on the Mend,* by Joyce Huggett.)

"On July 24, 1950, a baby girl was born in Lancaster, Pennsylvania to the proud parents Mervin and Evelyn Rohrer. To all of us here she is called different things. To one she is called daughter, to two she is called mother, to four she is called sister, one calls her daughter-in law, some call her cousin, some call her niece, one calls her sister-in-law, some call her aunt, and many called her friend. I call her Jeanie; she is my wife and the love of my life. No matter what you called her, we are all here today for one reason, and that is to say good-bye and to thank God for all she has meant to each of us."

"Each and every one of us has some special memories of Jeanie tucked away inside of us that we will cherish all the rest of our lives. Who can ever forget that smile or that playful frown? The way she laughed ... and the way she cried. The way she could cheer you up when you were feeling down. The way she could always find good in the things that seemed bad. Who will ever forget her strength and her determination, or her generosity and her faith in God?"

"The things I'll remember the most are the way her hand fit in mine, the touch of her lips, the smell of her hair, her smile, her voice, the way we held each other, the adventures we shared together … making up and falling in love. I'll remember her for giving me two children and the joy they bring to my life."

"Today we share the loss of someone special and mourn in her passing, but yet we are rejoicing in the fact that Jeanie is home with the Lord. She is not suffering anymore. There is no more pain, not even the memory of it for her, and for that I rejoice. Today and in the days to come I know there will be things that remind me of something special we did together. Some will make me smile; most will make me cry. Cry … only because we will not be doing them together anymore."

"When we suffer the loss of a loved one, we sometimes only think about our own loss, but I know that most of you here are grieving for the family. For Stephanie who can no longer pick up the phone and say, 'Hi Mom, just called to see how you're doing.' Or Rodney playing back his answering machine hearing his mother's voice saying, 'Hi Rod, it's just Mom, haven't heard from you in awhile, how's everything going? Give me a call back. Love you, bye.'"

"These things are all sad, but Stephanie, Rodney, and I all know one thing: we will all be together again with Jeanie in heaven. How do we know this? Because of our faith in God and His promise to us. Most of us don't think about dying until someone we care for passes on. Jeanie didn't fear dying; she was only saddened by the thought of leaving loved ones behind. So today while we are here thinking about the end of an earthly life, Jeanie wanted to make sure you all knew about an eternal life. In the hymns we sing and the message that's shared today, we pray that you will listen and consider where you will spend eternity. May God bless you for coming today!"

If you want to know more about heaven, read the following scriptures:
Heaven is a place. (Psalm 33:13-15)
Heaven has been prepared by God for us. (Hebrews 11:10)
Heaven's inhabitants. (Luke 15:10)
Heaven's activities. (Revelation 7:9-12)
God's assurances. (2 Corinthians 5:6-8)
Heaven's access. (Philippians 3:20)
(The Billy Graham Training Center Bible, NKJV.)

After the service, the funeral precession went to All Saints Cemetery where Jeanie was laid to rest. Never was the shortness of life so apparent to Ralph as when he stood in front of the gravestone that had his name etched on it next to Jeanie's. He had thought about death before, but just to see his name inscribed in stone meant death was inevitable.

* * * * *

Mike was attending Colorado State University in Fort Collins, Colorado, to obtain his Master's Degree. He thought it would be good, financially, to purchase a house and rent rooms to fellow students. The closing was set for June 27th. On June 24th Betty's good friend, Jeanie Walls, from Pennsylvania, passed away after a long battle with ovarian cancer. Betty had to be with Mike at the closing and was unable to change plans at the last minute to attend her funeral.

* * * * *

The days and weeks that followed were filled with sadness and loneliness for Ralph. So he made up his mind that he was going to get through this by staying very busy. He had asked the Lord to keep him busy, and the Lord answered his prayer. The phone was ringing off the hook. Hal had supplied him with work while he was not able to focus on running a business, but now he needed to get back to the grind of being self-employed.

The medical bills had really piled up over the last five years, and the fact that he had not been running his own business, but had just been someone else's employee during a good part of that time period, had pretty much taken a toll on their bank account. Ralph had said from the first time he heard that Jeanie had cancer that he didn't care if it took every red cent they had to fight it, she was more important to him than all the money in the world. But now he needed to pay off the leftover hospital bills and try to make enough to live on.

Stephanie had told her father that she was going to quit her banking job and begin working for him. He thought that to be a little strange, because she loved her job at the bank and especially the relationships she had with her girlfriends who worked there. Then he thought that maybe she just wanted to keep an eye on him. Why would she give up a nice, clean job at the bank to go to work on a dirty construction site? It just didn't make sense, but he agreed to it, and with all the calls he was getting he sure could use the help. Rod went back to Allentown where he still worked days at a video store and played keyboard nights in the band. Ralph's mother was back in Clinton Township with her faithful companion, Toby. She still took care of all the grass cutting on the property, but would let Glenn help with shrubbery trimming and general maintenance. Things were starting to settle into some kind of normalcy for everyone now.

On the outside Ralph seemed to be doing fine; he continued teaching a men's class at church, and he never missed a Wednesday evening Bible study and prayer meeting. He was also serving on the board of elders. But inside he was hurting. He was angry with God. He wanted to know how a loving God could allow someone to suffer the way Jeanie had. The humiliation and pain she had endured was inconceivable to him. *Why should anyone be allowed to die in such a manner? It just wasn't fair that she was taken home first. She loved and appreciated life far more than I ever did,* he thought.

Ralph's prayer time each day was now a struggle for him. While Jeanie was alive he sometimes found that he would be lost in prayer for over an hour at a time. Now he couldn't even focus on prayer for two minutes without being bitter towards God. He was so angry and bitter at God that he never really grieved the loss of his wife. He hadn't even shed a tear at the service the day she was buried. He mentioned it to a few of his friends, and they told him things such as, you have been grieving for over five years already. He didn't feel that was a sufficient answer, and thought maybe he was holding back, but why? He missed her so. At night before bed he would go into the closet and smell her clothes; he even took her pillow to bed with him until it no longer had any of her smell left.

About six weeks after her death, as Ralph was driving to work one day while verbally expressing his anger at God, with tears streaming down his face he said, "How could You be so cruel and unloving? Why did she have to suffer like that? You're supposed to be a kind and loving God. If I had an enemy I wouldn't even wish that on them." Then without a second of hesitation there came a response, not an audible voice, but of thoughts flashing though his mind, thoughts that weren't his own. *How dare you question Me? You don't have any idea what My purposes are. Do you know how many people Jeanie has reached in the last five years? Doctors, nurses, patients.* Then Ralph had flashbacks of the times he walked in on Jeanie sharing her faith while getting chemo, or sharing with a patient in the next bed. He even remembered standing outside her door one day listening to her share with a nurse. Then the strangest thought came to him; he suddenly remembered the old story about Johnny Appleseed.

Johnny Appleseed was a practical nurseryman. He realized that there was a real need and an opportunity for service in supplying seeds and seedlings. For the most part, moving ahead of the pioneers, Johnny started many nurseries throughout the Midwest by planting seeds that he had bought from cider mills in Pennsylvania. In order to assure the stability of the newly established homesteads, the law required each settler to plant fifty apple trees the first year. Because of the poor transportation that existed in the interior in those days, apples were a practical necessity in the early settlers' diets. John Chapman, or Johnny Appleseed, owned many tracts of land throughout Ohio and Indiana. He used this land to plant apple seeds, transplant seedlings, and set out orchards. He sold and gave trees to the pioneer settlers. John Chapman spread religion as well as apples. A deeply religious man, John Chapman became a self-appointed missionary for the Church of the New Jerusalem, a Christian church based on the biblical interpretations of Emanuel Swedenborg, a Swedish scientist and theologian. John shared his religious tracts and his Bible with the settlers who listened to him. His love for his neighbor made him accepted as a peacemaker between the Indians and the settlers. Just short of his seventy-fifth birthday, Johnny Appleseed died on March 18, 1845 in Fort Wayne, Indiana, after more than 50 years of travel. His path through the East and Midwest is today dotted with many monuments to the memory of this man who fulfilled the biblical requirements to "do justly, to love mercy, and to walk humbly with His God." (Credit to Leominster Historical Commission.)

Johnny Appleseed went across the country planting seeds. But as far as Ralph knew, he didn't live to see all the fruits of his labors. Then he thought, *That's what Jeanie was doing; she was planting the seeds of faith in all those people she came in contact with. She didn't get to see the results of her efforts, but she was doing what God had called her here to do.* Ralph was ashamed for his verbal assault on God and asked for forgiveness right then and there. *Who are we to question the mind of God,* he thought. We only see the here and now; we can never know the future. God didn't cause her illness, but He took her illness and used it for His honor and glory. In her illness she was serving God's purpose. During her illness she was showing her faith in God and her trust in Him no matter what the outcome. By revealing his anger and bitterness toward God and asking for forgiveness, Ralph had opened the door for the grieving and healing to begin. Ralph was completely taken aback when he heard the Lord speak to him, and he drove straight to the cemetery to say goodbye to Jeanie and let the grieving begin. Ralph didn't go to work that day; instead he spent the day in quiet solitude, walking, driving, and talking with his Lord. By the end of the day he was at peace with himself and God. That's not to say there wouldn't be more days of sadness or tears, because there were lots of things in the days ahead that brought back special memories of Jeanie. A special song, movie, hymn, flowers, pictures and especially the holidays could all trigger memories of joyful times spent together.

For more information on grief and grieving, read the following scriptures:

1. Grieving is a healthy process. (Revelation 21:4)
2. For the Christian, death is not the end of life. (John 11:25, 26)
3. We can find comfort in grief. (2 Corinthians 1:3, 4)

Grieving is an intense emotional process caused by personal loss. It involves acute sorrow, deep sadness, suffering, pain, and anguish. You can grieve the death of a loved one, or you can grieve losses brought about by changes or disappointments in your life. Grief is a difficult, lonely experience. Grief is not predictable—not everyone experiences it in the same way. Also, many times, especially after an overwhelming loss, a person may feel he or she has recovered to some extent only to be visited again by intense grief. There is no timeframe for ending a grieving process. In fact, in some cases, aspects of grief will always be present, but in a less intense form. (The Billy Graham Training Center Bible, NKJV.)

* * * * *

Betty was getting tired of being a landlord and decided to sell the properties. By the end of 1997, she had sold seven of her rental properties.

Kari spent a week with Betty in September. They had a good time going to the beach and shopping together. This was a very special time for the two of them to spend together. Kari was Betty's oldest granddaughter and growing up so fast. They had time to get to know each other and to share and reminisce about her Pop Pop. This turned out to be a time of healing together that they both had needed.

September 15, was Betty's Mother's ninetieth birthday, and the children had a birthday celebration for her, inviting friends, family, and former neighbors that she hadn't seen for a while. Her mind was still very good and she remembered most of the people at her party. Her eyes were giving her a lot of problems, but this didn't hinder her from getting around. It was a very special time for everyone. Elizabeth Herr was still very sharp and enjoyed all the family and friends, and she had lots of questions for them all. She had always been an avid writer, corresponding so frequently with her children that she was already pretty up-to-date with what was going on in their lives. But everyone could tell that she loved having the whole family with her for her birthday, and catching up on what they were doing now was important to her.

* * * * *

In the weeks and months that followed Jeanie's passing, Ralph had a lot of decisions to make. The main decision he wrestled with was whether he should stay way out there in the Mahantongo Valley. He loved being surrounded by all those beautiful farms, but it was pretty far from the church and Stephanie's house. Plus, they had subdivided the property into five lots, including the one the house sat on. The remaining lots wouldn't be an issue; they could just sit there until he was ready to build on them or sell them. He had just finished remodeling the house and was anxious to start another project, other than his daytime work. It would be nice to move closer to church and family and find an old house to fix up while he was living in it. Since he was now living alone, he wouldn't have to worry about the mess every day. So after weighing all his options he decided that's what he was going to do. First he would find an older home in need of updating, purchase it, then put his house up for sale. Within a month's time he had purchased a house in Marion Heights about four miles from the church.

* * * * *

On November 13, 1997, Betty flew with CJ from St. Louis airport to JFK airport in a TWA 747. This was CJ's first trip in a 747 and Captain Wally Moran gave them special attention. Wally knew CJ's grandfather, Gid, and had flown with him many times. Captain Moran even invited them to sit in First Class on the top deck. This was really exciting for CJ. When they arrived at JFK, a TWA employee named

Jamie met them and showed them around the hangar and training center. Al, a 747 Flight Instructor, gave CJ an hour of instruction in the 747 Simulator. Now CJ was on "Cloud Nine"! Next they were escorted to the office and CJ was given a lithograph of the TWA 747. Soon they were on a plane back to St. Louis. It had been an exciting day filled with a lot of firsts.

* * * * *

Stephanie was still working at the bank in Ringtown, but she had decided that in the spring she would come to work for her father. In November, on Black Friday, the bank was robbed while she was working there. No one was hurt and the robber got away, but he was eventually caught, a month later, when he tried to rob another branch in Girardville. Going through that experience made it even easier to plan on leaving the bank to work for her father soon.

Christmas was a difficult time. This would be the first time in 33 years (counting four years of dating) that Ralph celebrated Christmas without Jeanie. It just didn't feel the same without all those special touches that she had always added to the holidays. For years it had been a standard joke about "tree trauma time." How Ralph had hated traipsing through the Christmas tree lot for hours on end trying to find the perfect tree for Jeanie, only to come back to the first tree they looked at three hours ago. Ralph's plan was to just pick the ugliest one on the lot, because he said, no one else is going to take it and he felt sorry for it, so let's give it a home and dress it up for its funeral. But that was only the beginning of the tree trauma; the rest was hauling it home, trimming it up to fit the stand, then dragging it into the house with pine needles all over the place, standing it up, and finally decorating it. The decorating part was not his cup of tea; stringing the lights was a whole other story, but we won't go there.

After years of complaining, they had all agreed that an artificial tree was the answer. Things went a little better with the artificial tree, but right now Ralph knew he would give anything to hear her saying, "Just stop your complaining and enjoy the season." This year there wasn't any tree, there were no decorations around the house, no Santa Claus collection sitting out. But the family still got together at Stephanie's home for dinner and to exchange gifts. Then Herb and Linda had the entire family over which was a very special time for everyone.

* * * * *

Wil was tiring of the regional manager job and decided to try his skills as a Grease Monkey franchisee, so he and Karla bought two Grease Monkey locations in St. Charles, Missouri. This meant another move, but they found a nice house on a little lake that needed some cosmetic attention. There was even a little paddleboat to go with it. Their house was near a community pool, and this gave the children a chance to take swimming lessons, and it wasn't long before CJ was on the swim team.

19

IS THIS A DATE?

Springtime had come again, and with it came so many fond memories of gardening with Jeanie. Ralph had decided over the winter, however, that he wouldn't be putting a garden in this spring, but instead he would just put out a few tomato plants. He had decided this would be a good time to put the house up for sale, so he hammered a sign in the yard anticipating that it would take quite some time to sell. However, in no time at all he had a buyer, but they didn't want to close until sometime in August. This was a good thing, actually, because he still had to get at least one room livable in the Marion Heights house while he renovated it. That whole prospect didn't look too promising, because since he was so busy with work, he didn't have much time to spend on it. The most important job right now was getting a jobsite ready to build on before Stephanie came to work for him. A friend had asked Ralph to build an addition onto their house in Mt. Carmel. The problem was that it was sitting between row houses, with only one tiny access road in. And they wanted a three-story addition put on! A lot of this job would have to be done by hand, without equipment. Plus, some materials would be handled three times or more just to get them up to the third story. This was going to be quite a job for a father and daughter team. Stephanie was not afraid of work, and she soon proved to be one of the best employees Ralph ever had. The job went smoothly and Ralph had one of the best experiences of his life working with his daughter. He had really needed this time to be with her and get to know her in a closer way as the young adult she had become. They even spent part of the day on Sundays together going to church, and then he would take her out to dinner afterwards. Ralph had decided shortly after Jeanie's death that he was going to change his eating habits. He had always been a big eater; Jeanie had always said he needed three meals a day. Well, Ralph didn't quite agree with that; he had always said there are people in other countries who barely have enough for one meal, and he was curious to try eating that way as well. Now that he was on his own he had his chance, and this was what he did. (This is not recommended for anyone else without checking with a doctor or nutritionist first.) Ralph decided that for 30 days he would only eat one main meal a day. He decided it would be the evening meal and that it had to be eaten before 6:30 pm. He would eat nothing for the rest of the evening except ten unsalted peanuts. This little bit of protein would kick-start his metabolism and burn calories while he slept. The first few days were the hardest, especially sitting in front of the TV at night, so he had some raw broccoli and cauliflower to munch on if the urge was too great (no dressing). When he said one meal a day, he meant as much as he could eat with no restrictions, including dessert. When he started this 30-day diet he weighed in at 218 pounds. Thirty days later he had lost 45 pounds and weighed 173 pounds. Needless to say he needed a whole new wardrobe. People who used to tell him he had arms like Popeye (from hanging drywall all his life) couldn't believe what he looked like. "What happened? Where's the rest of you?" They would ask. Ralph felt good and healthy, but a lot of people were becoming concerned, thinking he was depressed or ill. He assured everyone that he was not ill or depressed and not to worry.

* * * * *

In June Betty felt it was time for another family vacation, and she made reservations for a week at Lake Chelan, Washington. First they spent a few days on the Olympia Peninsula seeing the Seattle Space Needle, and then they took a ferry over to spend a day on Victoria Island. Kari wanted to be able to tell her friends that she was in Canada over the summer.

Mike found a trail that they could hike two miles to the Pacific Ocean. It was a steep trail down to the ocean and they found hermit crabs, starfish, and sea urchins by the big rocks and tidal pools. Other areas they visited were the Quinault Rain Forest, Mt. St. Helens, and Mt. Rainer before arriving at Manson on Lake Chelan.

From Manson there were several day trips: the Boeing factory in Everett; Leavenworth, a Bavarian town; the Grand Coulee Dam; and Stehekin, a little town on the north end of Lake Chelan. You can only get there by floatplane or boat. There was also time for swimming, playing games, and watching movies, and Mike did a lot of biking. He had his dog, Koot, along with him, and Kalicia loved that dog. Sometimes they weren't sure who was taking whom for a walk! They were about the same size! Soon it was time to go back home and face the workforce. Before they all parted, however, Karla and Mike asked their mother how she was doing coping on her own. She responded by saying;

"Pretty good, I guess."

"Have you considered dating anyone yet?" They asked

"Well, some men have asked me out, but I haven't accepted any offers yet."

"Would you?"

"Sure, if the right one calls."

"Do you have anyone in mind?" Mike asked.

"I really haven't thought about it," Betty responded.

"What about Ralph Walls?" Mike asked, coaxing his mom a little.

"He hasn't called me, but I was thinking of calling him to see how he is doing; it's getting close to one year since Jeanie's death." No more was said on the subject, and they all left and went their separate ways.

* * * * *

June 23, 1998, marked the one-year anniversary of Jeanie's death. It was a beautiful day outside, almost as if in her honor, and Ralph went and visited the gravesite and spent a little time there. That evening he was sitting at his desk when the phone rang.

"Hello?"

"Hello, Ralph, this is Betty!" As soon as she said "hello," Ralph recognized her voice.

"Hi, Betty, how are you? It's so good to hear your voice."

"I'm fine; the question is, how are you doing?"

"Oh, I'm doing ok; today was the anniversary of Jeanie's death, but I'm ok."

"I knew it was, that's why I called. I remember the first year anniversary of Gid's death, and I really appreciated all the calls I got from friends checking up on me, and so I thought I would do the same for you."

"I really appreciate that, Betty, thank you."

"Our group isn't going to Spruce Lake this year, but I'll be in Lancaster County that week visiting with friends and family."Suddenly Ralph remembered what Jeanie had said to him about Betty being good for him, and so he thought,

Go for it, Ralph, seize the moment! So he asked Betty, "Could I come down and take you out to dinner and maybe a movie?"

"That would be great, Ralph!"

"OK, why don't we plan on it?"

"Great, I'll give you a call the week before to let you know when and where I will be once I get into town."

"Sounds like a plan to me, Betty; I'll be waiting to hear from you."

"Great. Well, I better let you go now. It was nice talking to you, Ralph."

"Same here, Betty, Thanks for calling. Bye."

"Bye."

Up until this point Ralph hadn't even thought about going out with another woman. *Was this a date or just two old friends getting together?* He wondered. It was probably three weeks away and he was already thinking frantically, *what do I say, what do we talk about? If we talk about our spouses surely there will be some tears, and then what do I do? This is just too much to think about; I need to relax and not worry about such silly things.* The next day at work things were going great, the jobs were all coming together well and they were accomplishing a lot. Then at one point Ralph remembered his phone call from Betty the night before, and so he said to Stephanie, "Guess who I got a call from last night?"

"I give up, who?"

"Betty Miller."

"Really? What did she say?" Stephanie was showing a lot of excitement.

"She just called to see how I was doing. She said she had remembered it was the one-year anniversary of Jeanie's death, and she wanted to see how I was doing."

"What did you tell her?"

"I said I was doing fine."

"Did she say anything else, Dad?" Stephanie was smiling a little, trying to pull more details out of him.

"No, not really."

Ralph hadn't stopped working while this conversation was going on, but Stephanie had stopped right away and was staring at him. She knew he was holding out on her and that there must be some juicy details he hadn't shared yet!

Ralph continued trying to look busy as he said in an offhand manner, "Oh yeah, there was one other thing.""This is like pulling teeth, would you get on with it, Dad?!?"

"What's your hurry?"

"Just tell me the rest of it! I know you're holding back!"

"There's nothing to tell."

"You just said there was one more thing."

"Oh yeah, I forgot ...quit interrupting me and I'll tell you."

"I don't know how Mom put up with you, just finish the story already."

"I would if you would let me. Let's see, where was I? Oh, yeah, she told me she was going to be here in Pennsylvania in July, and we decided to get together for an evening."

"You've got to be kidding." Stephanie was smiling from ear to ear now.

"No, I'm not kidding, and why are you smiling?"

"No reason, just ... you're going on a date!"

"It's not a date, just two friends getting together."

"It's a date. It's a date. It's a date. My Dad is going on a date with Betty Miller."

Stephanie must have sung that phrase a dozen times.

"Say what you want, it's not a date."

On the weekend of July 10th Ralph and a group of men had gone to Philadelphia for a Promise Keepers weekend. Ralph didn't get home until late Sunday evening, and when he got home he could tell by the voicemail messages that Betty had been calling for the last two nights, and on the last call she had seemed a little down in her voice. Even though it was late, he decided to call.

"Hello, Betty, this is Ralph."

"Oh, hi, Ralph!"

"I'm sorry to be calling so late, but I was away all weekend at a Promise Keepers event in Philadelphia, and I just walked in the door and saw your calls. I hope I didn't wake you."

"Oh no, you didn't wake me. I'm glad you called; I just wanted to know if you still wanted to get together.'

"I sure do."

"Great. I will be arriving on the seventeenth and I will be spending the night at Fred and Reba Umbles' house. Have you met them?"

"I'm not sure."

They made their plans for the upcoming week and Betty gave him directions to the Umbels' house, and then they said goodnight.

Stephanie was enjoying this immensely. In the three weeks that had passed since Ralph told her about his upcoming date with Betty, everywhere Ralph looked at work Stephanie had drawn a heart with Betty's and her Dad's initials in it. This was starting to get him a little nervous. Two nights before the big date night, as Ralph was leaving the prayer meeting at church, he paused outside with his two buddies Hal and Bob and asked them for prayer first and advice second. Big mistake! They had a field day teasing him about his date, and of course he kept insisting it wasn't a date. What he really wanted to know was this: what do I do if she starts to cry? This made his two friends laugh even harder. Hal said, "You'll know what to do when it happens, trust me."

On Friday, July 17, Ralph got up and went to work just like always, with the only difference being the big smirk on Stephanie's face as they worked together all day long. She could tell her father was a little apprehensive about his date that night, so she behaved herself a little bit. She did, however, make him promise that he would call her first thing Saturday morning with an update. He finally agreed just so she would be quiet about it. Since he had to drive to Lancaster to meet Betty, he left work early that day to allow enough time to go home, get cleaned up, and make the two-hour drive. The directions were right on the money, and he pulled into the Umbels' driveway with time to spare, early, of course, in his usual style! As he was getting out of the car, there was this fine-looking lady walking toward him with a smile that wouldn't quit.

"Hello, Ralph, it's so good to see you," she said as she walked toward him.

"Hello, Betty, it's so good to see you too."

They embraced each other in the driveway.

"Did you have any trouble with my directions?"

"No, not at all, they were right on the money."

"Let's go in the house, I want you to meet Fred and Reba."

"Ok, sure thing."

As they walked to the house Ralph told Betty how great she looked and she commented, "You don't look too bad either."

Once inside the house the introductions were made, and they all sat in the living room for a few minutes and chatted. Right off the bat, Ralph knew he liked her friends. They were very kind and considerate, and he could tell they cared deeply for Betty. Fred had a great sense of humor, which made Ralph feel more relaxed. At first Ralph thought this would be the great inquisition to check him out and see if he passed their inspection, to make sure it was safe for Betty to go out with him, and if it was, they did it in a manner that was not recognizable to Ralph. Just before they got up to leave, Ralph thought he'd ask the question, so he turned to Betty and said,

"So, is this a date?"

"What do you want it to be?" Betty asked, with that killer smile on her face.

Without hesitation Ralph replied, "It's a date."

"Good, that's what I thought, too."

Things were already heading where Ralph had never thought they would. He was going on a date with Betty Miller. He had not been on a date with another women in over thirty years. He was sure this was just a one-time thing, because there must be fifty guys knocking on her door in Sarasota waiting for the chance to take her out. But he encouraged himself by thinking, *Nevertheless, it's a date, so tonight she's all mine*. Time was flying by so they said goodbye to Fred and Reba and left for a restaurant. This was Betty's stomping ground, and Ralph had no idea where to go, so he left all the decisions up to her. As it turned out she already knew where they would be dining that evening. She took him to a restaurant that had once been an old farmhouse and was adjacent to her Mother's family farm. They had a great time, and if you had asked him what he had eaten that night he couldn't have told you, he was too busy listening to every word she had to say. Of course, that was when he wasn't drooling in his soup. During the main course of the meal Betty said, "You know what today is, don't you?"

"No, I can't say I do."

"Today is the anniversary of Gid's accident."

Ralph was totally embarrassed.

"Oh my, I'm so sorry, I didn't even think about what the day was."

"It's ok, don't worry."

"So, why are you out with me? Don't you want to be with family?"

"Because I can't think of anyone else I'd rather spend this night with than you."

If any line ever could melt Ralph's heart that was the line. He didn't know what to say, and if he had tried he probably wouldn't have been able to speak. They just sat there all teary-eyed for the next few minutes. With the meal over, they went for a walk around the lake just talking and enjoying each other's company. A little later they decided to go to a movie and then back to Fred and Reba's house where they sat in the living room and talked some more.

With the evening coming to an end, they got up and walked back to Ralph's car, and on the way Betty asked Ralph if he would be interested in escorting her to a wedding the following Saturday. Ralph said he would love to, and Betty said she would call during the week with all the details.

They hugged and said goodbye, and Ralph began the two-hour drive home, which passed by in a happy blur of good memories of the evening. It was just thirteen months ago when Ralph said he had no more love to give and would probably never even consider another woman in his life again. Now as he drove home his mind was racing. *What just happened? Why is my stomach in knots, like a teenager on a first date?* It was the same feeling he had when he first started dating Jeanie. *What's wrong with me? I'm an old man, why am I having these feelings? Is this normal to be like this?* After he got home it didn't diminish; he tossed and turned all night long, and at one point he just got up and went to the Lord in prayer, looking for help. *If this is ok, Lord, to have these feelings so soon already for another woman, please let me know!* The next morning Ralph got up totally exhausted. He had spent a good part of the night thinking about Jeanie and feeling as though he was betraying her by thinking about another woman. He was determined to get his mind on something else. Saturday was always a busy day, with laundry, about two acres of grass to cut, groceries to buy, and finishing up his Sunday school lesson for tomorrow. Everything was going fine until about mid-afternoon when he remembered he was supposed to call Stephanie. He really didn't want to because he knew she would have a thousand questions, but he did anyway because he had promised her he would call.

"Hello?"

"Hi, Steph, it's me."

"It's about time, where are you calling from?"

"Home, where else would I be calling from?"

"Well, it's so late I figured maybe you stayed over there and spent the day together."

"No, I came home last night."

"So how did it go?"

"Great."

"So what does great mean?"

"We went to dinner and a movie, and then I came home."

"That's it?"

"What did you expect?"

"You didn't talk or anything?"

"Of course we talked, and oh yeah, she asked me if I would like to take her to a wedding next weekend."

"Really?"

"Really."

Now Stephanie was jumping up and down and cheering.

"Why are you all excited?"

"You know why, Dad."

"No, I don't know why."

"Because of what Mom said."

"What did your mom say?" Ralph remembered what Jeanie had said to him about Betty, and he'd given his wise-crack reply of how she was a princess and he was a frog, but he had no idea that Jeanie might have said anything to Stephanie as well.

"Mom asked me to pray for you and Betty."

"Your mom asked you to pray for Betty and me?"

"That's not all, Dad; Kayleen and Aunt Millie and I have been praying for you two for over a year."

A cold sweat had just come over Ralph at hearing those words.

"You have got to be kidding me ..."

"No, its true. Now are you *sure* there isn't anymore you want to tell me?" Stephanie coaxed with a smile in her voice.

"Well, let's see, I couldn't sleep at all last night, because I was thinking about Betty. I've got knots in my stomach, and I think I have feelings for her." Now Stephanie was really cheering.

"I think there must be a higher power working here. If you guys have been praying for over a year, I don't stand a chance."

"Probably not." Stephanie stated triumphantly through her laughter.

"I don't want to wait till next week; do you think it would be alright to send her flowers or something?"

"Of course, send her flowers."

"Ok, I better get right to it before she leaves the Umbles' house. Bye."

"Bye, Dad, and lots of luck."

"Thanks."

Ralph was frantically thumbing through the phone book looking for the number to call Trail Gardens, the nursery where he got all his flowers, plants, and landscaping supplies. Finally he had the number and dialed it with quick jabs on the phone keypad. "Hello, Trail Gardens."

"Hi, do you deliver flowers?"

"Yes, we do, but I'm afraid we are closed. I was just going out the door when I heard the phone, so I came back to answer it."

"Oh, well, I'm sorry to bother you."

"Was it something special you needed?"

"Well, since you asked, I just saw an old friend last night and her husband was on TWA flight 800 when it went down. I had dinner with her and just wanted to let her know what a great time I had with her."

"Sir, I will get those flowers to her tonight."

"You will?"

"Yes, I will, I promise."

"Thank you so much."

The lady took down all the information from Ralph and then asked, "What would you like me to put on the card?"

"Just put, thanks for a great evening, Ralph."

"Sir?"

"Yes?"

"I hope everything works out for you two."

"Thank you!" Ralph hung up the phone with a very good feeling about this.

That evening at the Umble house, flowers were delivered to their guest, Betty, who was totally surprised by the delivery. The following morning Betty left the Umbles' home and went to Mechanics Grove church where her mother and sister Ruth were attending Sunday services. When the service was over they all headed for their biannual visit to Charter Hall in Maryland, where the rest of the family would be. Now Betty wasn't about to leave her flowers behind, so she was carrying them with her when she arrived at Charter Hall and quickly displayed them on a table so all could enjoy. Well, it didn't take long before her brother Carl noticed the card on them and started to inquire about this note that said, "Thanks for the great evening."

"What's this great evening all about? And who is this Ralph?" He had a lot of fun ribbing his sister about the "great evening" all week. It was just like when they were teenagers! After she got settled in and she thought things were calmed down, she decided to call Ralph and thank him for the flowers and tell him about all the trouble he had caused her by writing what he did on the card. Now the family, led by Carl, of course, had been quietly waiting for Betty to make her call.

"Hello?"

"Hello, Ralph, this is Betty." The second Betty had said hello, the whole family called out from the background, "Hello, Ralph!"

By now Betty was laughing and trying to quiet them down so she could hear Ralph on the other end. Ralph could easily hear all the goings-on in the background, and he quickly figured out that they were happily teasing Betty just as Stephanie had done to him. After a minute Betty finally got them to quiet down so she could speak.

"First of all, thank you so much for the flowers, Ralph, that was so sweet, and they're very pretty."

"You're welcome; I just wanted you to know that it was a very special night for me, so thank *you*."

"It was special for me, too. I want to apologize for all the noise here; my family has been teasing me since I got here with the flowers. They all want to know about this great evening and who Ralph is."

"Sorry about that."

"Oh no, it's all in good fun, they just get a little carried away sometimes."

They continued to talk for a few minutes, and then Ralph asked if he could have the phone number there so he could call her another time. Betty gave him the number but reminded him of the possibility that any one of her family members could answer it. He told her he knew what she meant and laughed. They said goodbye and hung up.

Just talking to Betty on the phone had strengthened his interest in pursuing this further. He was constantly going to prayer about this whole situation, seeking wisdom on what was the right thing to do. It came to him that he should be totally honest with her and just tell her exactly what he was feeling. This way if it was just one-sided he would be the only one who would get hurt and look like the village idiot. He had sensed that Betty seemed a little interested, but he doubted himself, thinking he might be misreading the signals. Betty was always very friendly and outgoing with everyone, so he could be wrong. All this was so sudden; how could these feelings be for real? But he kept coming back to the fact that three people had been praying for both of them for over a year, and he could still remember that night when Jeanie pulled him close to her and said, "when I'm gone, please consider Betty." *You only hear about things like this happening to other people, not me,* he thought.

Late the next evening Betty called to give Ralph all the information about the wedding. The wedding was going to be in Meadville, Pennsylvania. She said she would drive to Ralph's house on Friday and they could leave from there. Ralph decided that the time had come to share his heart with her, and so Ralph dove in and said, "Betty there is something I want to tell you, but I want you to know that no matter what your response is, you will always be one of my best friends, and you can always count on me for anything."

OK, now that I've said that, I've got to keep on going, Ralph thought. So he took a deep breath and said, "Betty, the other night when I left you at the Umbles' house and started my drive home, my stomach was in knots, and I felt like a teenager on his first date. When I got home that night and tried to sleep, I couldn't stop thinking about you. I have these feelings for you and figured I better tell you up front."

There was a momentary silence. Ralph thought his heart would beat out of his chest as he waited for Betty to respond.

"How do you feel about these feelings?" Betty asked.

"I like them." Ralph replied.

"Me too."

This was the response Ralph was hoping to hear. "So now what do we do?"

"We just take one day at a time and spend more time together."

"Sounds good to me. I can't wait till Friday when I can see you again, Betty."

"Me too!"

With that settled they said their goodbyes and hung up. Ralph was elated; he didn't know what to do first, but being the kind of guy who likes to keep busy, he thought, *why not keep a diary of every day, starting with Friday night.* So that's what he did, he wanted to capture every thought and feeling he had on paper so he could always remember them. That evening before bed, he committed it to the Lord, "Lord, if this relationship between Betty and me is of You, then may it be so, but if it isn't, let us know right away before someone gets hurt." The remainder of the week couldn't pass by fast enough, but thanks to telephones, they stayed in touch almost every night.

Friday, July 24th, Betty called on her cell phone as she got close to the house, and Ralph was watching from the porch as she came down the road and pulled in the driveway. When he reached the car, he asked her if he could kiss her and she responded, "Please do." They embraced and walked to the house. Ralph was expecting a quick visit from his friends, Tony and Joanna Murrin, who were home on leave from their mission work in Bolivia. He knew it took six hours to get to the wedding, but they had lots of time to kill, and he didn't want to miss the chance to see the Murrins. They arrived right on time and Ralph introduced them to Betty. Tony's a pilot for New Tribes and was really interested in hearing about Gid's story. They only had a short time to visit before Ralph and Betty needed to leave for the wedding.

Even though it was a six-hour ride, the time went quickly. They talked and shared the entire trip. There were tears and laughter; it was a time they needed to get to know each other on a much closer level. By the time they arrived at their destination, they were feeling quite close and very comfortable with each other. A lot of the Spruce Lake Gang were there and were quickly introduced to Ralph. The wedding wasn't until Saturday, but the whole gang had planned to go out to dinner that evening. After dinner they all made plans to go to Joe and Sharon Bradshaw's home (Sharon was Carl and Shirley Grace's daughter) to wrap the cookware set they had chosen as wedding gifts for Ann and Pat. This was the first time Ralph had met Joe and Sharon. In the short time he spent with them, he came to the conclusion that they were the ideal Christian parents. The way they related with their three children was like he had never seen or known before. It wasn't until later on that he found out that Joe was a youth pastor in a local church. Ralph left that night very impressed by the entire Bradshaw family, and before he left he told Joe this.

Back at the motels everyone was getting ready to go to their rooms. Ralph hated to have to say goodnight so soon, so they went for a short walk. When they got back and were talking outside of Betty's room, John Kauffman came out to get something from his car. They heard later that his wife, Marie, scolded him for spying, saying to him, "Would you let them be?" as John peeked out the door.

They said their goodnights and parted. The next day everyone had breakfast together, and soon it was time to go to the wedding. The wedding was for Lois's daughter, Ann, who was marrying Patrick Bywater. It was a beautiful wedding and the fellowship with everyone was terrific. After the wedding they all went back to Joe and Sharon's house to visit. Ralph wasn't used to all the sitting he had been doing for the last two days, so the two of them took a long, slow walk, enjoying each other's company and talking together. By the time the day was over they pretty much knew they would be spending a lot more time with each other. On this second night together it was even harder to say goodnight and head to their separate rooms, but they knew they would have the long ride home tomorrow morning to enjoy each other once again.

After breakfast they all said goodbye and headed home. Betty had some great friends and Ralph enjoyed getting to know them better. On the drive home the questions turned to the "what if" game, which included the subject of marriage. Remember these were just "what if" questions, but in six hours' time they were home and talking about scheduling two flights, one for August 7 to Harrisburg, Pennsylvania, and the second to Sarasota on August 18–they had now entered the realm of commuter dating, but the distance didn't matter. With some time still left before Betty had to leave, they went into the living room and watched a video that Ralph had filmed of his last visit to Florida. The video was of Gid and Betty and Ralph and Jeanie at the Renaissance Fair in Sarasota. There were lots of memorable things on the tape, but the one they enjoyed the most was when Gid was pulled out of the audience and put on stage to act out a drama. Gid was to play the villain, and every time it came to Gid's part to act sinister, the audience would roar with laughter. Needless to say Gid didn't make a very good villain, because he couldn't act mean if he tried, and this made it all the funnier.

That afternoon as Betty headed back to Lancaster County, Ralph stood there watching as the tail lights disappeared over the horizon and thought to himself, *I was alone for thirteen months, but never lonely, and now here I stand only two minutes after Betty has left, and suddenly I'm feeling very lonely.*

20

THE PRINCESS AND THE FROG

It was only the 26th of July, and that meant thirteen whole days had to pass before they would see each other again. This wasn't going to be easy, but Ralph knew he had plenty of work to do and had to give it his full attention. At least that's what he thought; the next two weeks at work Ralph drove Stephanie crazy talking about Betty. She was beginning to think, *what have I done by praying for this man? Have I created a crazy man or what?* Ralph did manage to do all the necessary work that needed to be done. On August 2, Evelyn had the Rohrer family reunion at her house, and this gave Ralph the opportunity to take Herb aside and tell him about Betty. Herb's response took Ralph by surprise when he said, "I kind of thought you two would wind up together," and he said he wished them both the best. Ralph asked Herb if he could tell his mother and the rest of the family. A few days later Stephanie said she had gotten a call from her grandmother wanting to know all about Dad and Betty. Stephanie told her that everything Herb had told her was true. Evelyn responded by saying she was very happy for them both. Ralph had already told Rodney about dating

Betty, and now with the whole family knowing, he was wondering what Betty's children were thinking.

Betty was spending a week with her grandson CJ in Sarasota, and on one of those days they went parasailing and had a blast. This was a very special time for Betty, because she had not forgotten the comment her grandson had made shortly after Gid's death. She had been concerned how CJ was coping with the loss, and this week was very beneficial to both of them. They spent a great deal of time talking and just having fun together. Betty and Ralph had been calling each other practically every night, which helped pass the time while they were apart. The day of Betty's arrival was just around the corner, and Ralph had some special surprises for her. One was a little juvenile, but he figured it was the thought that went into it that counted. One night while sitting there in his almost empty house, an idea came to him to write a fairy tale about a princess and a frog, so he sat down on the floor in the living room and began to write. He wanted to make it a true story about the four of their lives, but still make it sound like a fairy tale, so that's what he did.

On Friday, August 7, Betty arrived at the house right on schedule, and this time there was no need to ask how they should greet one another, because they were in love. Even though the closing of the sale of the house was just two weeks away, Ralph had left some furniture there so they could spend the weekend there. He had left a couch, two beds and the kitchen set for them to use, planning that on Monday after Betty left he would move the rest to the storage garage and start living in the Marion Heights house permanently. After they spent a long time saying hello in the driveway with lots of hugs and kisses, eventually they went into the house where Ralph led Betty into the living room. Ralph asked her to sit on the sofa while he went to get something for her, saying, "Don't go anywhere, I'll be right back!" Now Ralph had already told Betty the story about Jeanie's last request and how Stephanie was asked to pray for both of them, so she knew Ralph considered himself a frog and her a princess. When Ralph came back into the room carrying what looked like a book, she had no idea what he was up to.

"Betty, the other night after we talked on the phone, an idea came to me, so I put it down on paper."

"What is it about?"

"It's a story about four people; now it's a little juvenile, but it's from the heart, and it's for you. It's called the Princess and the Frog." Ralph began to read it to Betty.

"To Betty, with all my love.
In memory of Gid Miller and Jean Walls:
May we never forget the part they played in making us who we are today.
Love, Ralph (the frog)

Once upon a time in a place not so far away there lived a princess. She was very beautiful and kind and was married to a prince who could fly. He could fly anywhere and everywhere and took people to their destinations and back, always safely. He too was very kind and friendly.

In another part of that same kingdom there lived a frog that was a carpenter. He also had a beautiful bride and she was very friendly too. They all lived a long time in different parts of the kingdom. But one day, the frog's bride decided to leave. This made the carpenter frog very upset. So he decided he'd just let her go; there's other frogs in the pond. But he was still very sad and began to cry. It just so happened that very day the princess was in that part of the kingdom and heard the frog crying, so she, being very kind, stopped to help. She talked to the frog for quite some time and convinced him that the proper thing to do would be to win his bride back. The frog thanked her and the princess put him back in the pond where he swam off with new determination. And he did win back his bride, and their love grew stronger than ever. But then after eight years the frog and his bride got some bad news. The bride had a terrible illness and didn't have long to live. They said about six months. But she was strong and fought hard. And four years later she was still alive.

Meanwhile, at the other end of the kingdom the princess and the prince were praying for the frog's bride. One evening, however, the prince was flying over the sea when his wings were broken and he crashed and was no more. The princess mourned the death of her prince. The whole kingdom mourned with her; even the frog and his bride came to comfort her.

Back at the other end of the kingdom the frog's bride grew weary and died after another year. But before she died she pulled her husband in close to her mouth and whispered, "The princess would be perfect for you when I am gone; please consider her." The frog replied, "Sure, honey, sure," knowing full well there could never be a princess and a frog together as husband and wife.

The princess mourned her lost prince for two years and the carpenter frog had mourned the loss of his bride for one year. The princess called the frog many times to see how he was doing. He replied "Fine" each time. She even invited him to visit her in her kingdom, but the frog was always too busy to go. Then one day the princess was in the frog's part of the kingdom and asked him to come and see her! He remembered how she had helped him so many years ago, and so finally he said yes. What was supposed to be a night of visiting a dear friend became much more when his eyes beheld her. And suddenly he remembered his bride's dying wish. *This could never be*, he thought, *a princess and a frog*. So he erased it from his mind. They had a lovely evening together, and the princess asked the frog if he would escort her to a wedding the following weekend. He was shocked, but he answered that he would be glad to. On the way home that night the frog sensed this was more than just friendship he was feeling. Could she be reaching out to him this time or was he reading this all wrong? He felt saddened to think she might have needed him all this time and he hadn't seen it. The frog made a vow that he would come right out and tell her how he felt about her. Two nights later he got his chance and told her, and she seemed happy. *How could this be*, the frog wondered. *I'm just a frog and she's a princess. It could never work*, he thought, but still the excitement grew in him as the anticipated weekend drew near. It was a long way to the wedding celebration so they had a lot of time to spend talking. The frog had a hard time keeping his eyes on the road ahead because of her beauty and the way she talked and laughed and even cried when she talked about her prince. The frog just wanted to hug her and hold her in his arms, but he was still uncertain if he should, for she was a princess and he was just a frog. When they got to their destination, however, the frog got up his courage and asked the princess if he could hold her hand, and to his surprise she said, "by all means, please do." And later that evening, before they were to retire to their separate rooms, he even asked her if he could kiss her goodnight and again she replied, "Please do." That night the frog couldn't fall asleep. That day was so incredible he kept playing it over and over again in his mind and asking himself, *how could this be?* The rest of the weekend went just as well. They talked, laughed, cried, shared, held hands, and yes, they even kissed some more, and by the end of that weekend the frog, who was just a carpenter, was hopelessly in love with the princess. This is not the end of the story. Nor is it the beginning of the end. This is just the end of the beginning. Because everybody knows fairy tales always have happy endings."

When Ralph had completed the reading, he noticed that Betty was touched by the story, so he handed her the book and then they sat and talked for a while about their spouses, who they both missed. Later on that day Ralph gave Betty a necklace with a frog charm on it, which she immediately had him clasp around her neck . The weekend went by too quickly, and before they knew it Betty was flying back to Florida. Then in two weeks Ralph had the closing on the house and moved into the Marion Heights house he was going to renovate. In the months to follow Ralph was making trips to Sarasota every two weeks, and he got to meet a lot of Betty's close friends. He even attended her church, Bahia Vista Mennonite, and met her pastor, Barry Loop. That time of year in Florida is hot, so Betty always made sure she moved Ralph from one air conditioned place to another quickly so he would want to keep coming back, she said. He assured her that the heat wasn't about to stop him from coming back. On September 7, Ralph and Betty met with Barry and Sue and walked three miles along the shore of Siesta Key Beach. This was a great time for Ralph to share his life story with Barry and get to know the man who would be marrying them. Barry was a terrific man, in Ralph's opinion; he had a heart for the lost. It was his passion to reach those who were without Christ, and Ralph admired his devotion to his calling.

On Sunday the 13th Betty called from Florida with some bad news; Ella Mae had been diagnosed with a brain tumor, and more tests were going to be done on Thursday to determine what steps needed to be taken. John Kaufman had gone into the hospital that same week also. She asked Ralph to keep them and their families in prayer.

On Thursday at 3:30 am Ralph left for the airport to meet up later that day with Betty and travel to Denver, Colorado, where they would drive to Steamboat Springs to visit Mike for a couple of days. The main reason for this trip was because Mike had told his mom that Ralph had to ask him for her hand in marriage before they could marry. In all Ralph took four flights that day. They were together for two of them, and the flight in St. Louis was delayed by two hours. It had been a long day by the time they reached their hotel that evening. The next day they met up with Mike and had a great time with him and his faithful companion, Koot (a black Labrador retriever). Mike had done a research project near Dinosaur, Colorado, and wanted to take them to some old Indian grounds that most people never get to see. They stopped along the way to pick up some hoagies, and then they continued on to where they would begin their hike. It was an outstanding and very interesting day of adventure. And yes, Ralph did ask Mike if he could marry his mother, and Mike enthusiastically gave the go-ahead. While in Colorado they made another stop at Betty's cousin Edith's house to spend the night. Edith loved to have fun and had prepared a little quiz for Ralph to take, just to see if he met the right criteria to be Betty's husband. It was a lot of fun and Ralph made sure he had some good answers for her. The next day they were back on a plane to fly to St. Louis to eventually meet up with Karla and her family. Karla picked them up at the airport and took them back to her home to meet the children and Wil. The children had been well informed about the frog fairytale, which Ralph could tell by the gifts they had made for them when they arrived. This particular day was Karla's birthday, so that evening they had a party. One of the gifts she got was a video camera. The children quickly put it to use. They had their Mema (Betty) and Ralph act out getting a tooth pulled in the dentist office. Ralph was the patient and really screamed every time Mema yanked on the tooth she was supposed to be pulling out. When she finally got it out Ralph talked really funny which made the children laugh even harder. When they had completed their movie they wanted to view it on the TV. The whole family sat around enjoying what the children had created. After the movie, Jake the cat walked into the room, and Ralph wanted to show the children how his family had played with their cat when Rodney and Stephanie were little. He asked them if they had a paper grocery bag, then he made a small hole in the bottom of it, just big enough for his finger to fit in. Then he placed the bag on the floor with the large open end facing the cat. Then he stuck his finger in the little hole in the other end and wiggled it so the cat would notice it. Every time the cat saw the wiggling finger it would squat down and go through a little wiggling motion just before lunging full speed into the bag. The idea is to be faster than the cat and get your finger out in time. Once the cat was in the bag it most often stayed there, watching the hole. Then the real fun would begin. You try getting the cat's attention by wiggling something in front of the small hole, and before long the cat's paw slams through the little hole trying to grab what it just saw. The children loved it and had a lot of fun getting Jake to charge into the bag, most of the time moving the bag a couple of feet with every charge. Betty and Ralph spent a couple of days there letting Ralph get to know everyone, and he enjoyed it thoroughly. The time eventually came when Ralph and Betty had to say their reluctant goodbyes to the family, and so Karla drove them back to the airport. When they arrived there and were unloading the bags, Karla turned to Ralph and said, "thank you for making my mother so very happy." Ralph could hardly speak as they hugged goodbye. That had really meant a lot to him. On the flight back to Florida, they spent a lot of time talking and reliving the past week's experiences. Ralph told Betty that he thought her family was great and couldn't wait to be a part of it. Once back in Florida they met with Randy Spalding to go over the music for the wedding, and then they went back to the house to work on the wedding invitation list.

The 3rd of October Ralph picked Betty up at the airport in Philadelphia and they left for Lancaster to spend the evening there before driving over to meet Betty's mother and sisters the next day. The next morning after they had breakfast, they decided to surprise Fred and Reba by showing up at their church, the Calvary Independent Church. They were indeed surprised and it was real special to see them, especially since they were the first friends of Betty's that Ralph had met the night of their first date. After the service they drove over to the Mennonite Home to visit with Betty's mother, Elizabeth. They could tell she was pleased to see them when they walked into the room by the smile on her face. She treated Ralph like he was already part of the family or had been for years. They stayed quite a while showing her pictures of the grandchildren and where Ralph had lived. She was even able to tell them how Jeanie's family, the Rohrer's, were related to them. They had a real pleasant time visiting with Betty's mother. The next stop was to visit Betty's sisters, Lydia and Ruth, and their husbands Keith and Don. Ruth prepared a great meal for them, and after they were finished they all took a drive over to look at their new home. The rest of the week went well, and on one particularly fun day they drove up to Lake Jean and hiked all the waterfalls. They stopped at the house Ralph was renovating and spent some time with Stephanie. Stephanie and Betty got along great together and enjoyed the time just talking. Stephanie especially enjoyed telling Betty the events leading up to her dad's and Betty's first date and the days that followed. They had a lot of fun laughing about Ralph's concerns at that time, all his "what if's" and "should I's." Ralph just sat there letting them have their fun at his expense. The time passed by too quickly, and before they knew it, Wednesday the 7th was there and once again it was time for them to say goodbye. Standing there at the airport watching the plane disappear from view was very difficult for Ralph. It was easier when he was the one leaving; it just didn't feel right standing there as she left. Plus, the idea of going back to an empty house didn't feel right either. They had just spent a week together and the thought of being alone made his stomach feel funny. All he kept thinking was, January 2nd is a long way off, how will I ever make it till then? That evening Ralph went to the Bible study and prayer meeting and then rushed home anticipating a call from Betty saying she had arrived home safely. There was always plenty to do in the house while waiting for the call. But once Ralph was cleaned up for the evening he just didn't feel like getting involved in a messy job, so most of the time he would just go up to his room, put on some tapes to listen to and write in his dairies until Betty called. Finally, after what seemed like he had waited an eternity to hear her voice again, at 9:30 that evening Betty called saying she had arrived home safely. They didn't talk too long that night since they had just been together that morning, but it was still calming for Ralph to hear her voice.

By October 15, Ralph was back in the air to Sarasota, and once he was there they hit the pavement running. They had a number of things already lined up to do. First of all the new car was ready to pick up, and then on the way back from there they had to stop and pick up the free sample of their wedding cake to take home and try. The next day they were up early and walked three miles with Betty's walking buddies Verda and Joy. Every day after the walk they would go in and have their fruit. While it was still a cool seventy-five degrees Ralph would go out and pull weeds in the flowerbeds for an hour or until his shirt was drenched. Betty would be working at the desk trying to stay ahead of the mail. By about 9:00 am they would meet in the kitchen and start breakfast, and on this particular day they had granola pancakes. This was pretty much the routine every day. They had decided that once they were married they would live together in Florida, and the heat was the only thing Ralph was concerned about getting used to. Since Ralph had told her he wouldn't take her from her friends and church, it was a natural given that he would be moving to Sarasota. His children were both elated about that. Ralph figured they just wanted to get him out of their state, but they insisted that this way they would have a reason to come to Florida and a place to stay when they got there! After breakfast they had to get cleaned up and run a few more errands concerning the wedding, and the final errand of the day was to be their wedding portrait on the beach. By Thursday, Ralph was heading back to Harrisburg and Betty was getting on a plane to go to St. Louis and spend a few days with the grandchildren while Wil and Karla went to Colorado to look for a new home close to where Wil would be working.

On the 26th Ralph started his last scheduled job as a contractor in Pennsylvania, work that he would be doing for his friends Woody and Pam Williams. It was a siding and window job and wouldn't take that long to do. When their job was completed, he planned to spend the remainder of his days in Pennsylvania working on the house he was living in. Since he had moved into that house he'd had to eat all his meals out, because he hadn't installed a kitchen yet, and this would be his main focus once the Williams job was finished. The next day Ralph ordered the cabinets and the countertops. Back in Florida Betty was expecting a visit from her long-time girlfriends, Mim Martin, Ann Miller, Lucy Frey, and Mim Mylin. They had a full week of activities planned for their visit with Betty and even helped with some of the wedding preparations.

The flights back and forth continued in November, and the plans for the wedding had pretty much been all taken care of. On Thanksgiving Day Ralph's mother, Norma, had reserved a dinning room at the Holiday Inn in Clinton, New Jersey, for Ralph's entire extended family to get together and meet Betty, and as expected, it went very well. The next day they started making plans for their second wedding reception. This one would be for all their Pennsylvania friends who couldn't make it to Florida. That evening two of Betty's brothers were going to be passing through town, so they planned on meeting them for dinner in Danville. So at 5:00 pm in Danville, Ralph got to meet some more of the family: Betty's older brother Henry and his wife Carol; her brother, Carl and his wife Carolyn; and their daughter, Lori, and son, Tim, and his wife Christy. Ralph really had a good time with her family and knew he would enjoy getting to know them better in the future. Two days later, Ralph got a call from the cabinet company saying that his cabinets never got made. This was a full four and a half weeks after he had ordered them, so needless to say he wasn't very happy about this. It was a good thing Betty was there to calm and comfort him.

At 4:00 am on December 8, 1998, Stephanie picked up her dad at his house in Marion Heights and drove him to the airport. When they arrived they hugged and said their goodbyes, and Stephanie told him she would see him again soon on the 26th. This was to be Ralph's last departure from Harrisburg, Pennsylvania for the year. From now until January 2 he would be spending his time in Florida, helping Betty get ready for Christmas and their big day. At least, he would *try* to help and not get in the way! It wasn't that long ago that he had resigned himself to the fact that he would be spending his remaining years as a single person, and now, here he was about to get on a plane to go to his soon upcoming wedding. How could things have changed so suddenly? After Jeanie had died, someone who was trying to comfort him had said to him, "God has someone out there that He has in mind for you to love." Ralph could still clearly remember saying to that person, "I have no more love to give; I've lost it all." Now, in twenty-five days' time he would be pledging his love to a wonderful women named Betty Miller. From the first moment he saw her in July 1998, he had been head over heels in love with her. *That just doesn't happen for real,* he thought, *I'm afraid to pinch myself for fear I might wake up from a dream.* As he sat in the airport, he couldn't help but think about the two who had lost their lives, which had to happen to even make it possible for him and Betty to be together. It was almost too much to fathom. It saddened him to think about the shortness of their lives and how much they both enjoyed and cherished life. They both had left their marks on the lives of countless others, and for that they would never be forgotten. As he sat in the airport waiting to board the plane that would take him to a new direction in his life, he began to write all these things in his journal. *What has God got in store for Betty and me,* he thought. *Why has God allowed this turn in my journey of life? Is there a purpose that he has for me in His plans? And if so, will I know?* All he knew was that if this was God's will for his life, he would need to trust Him and allow His spirit to speak to his heart. The time had come for boarding the plane, and as he looked back he realized the next time he stepped down in this airport he would have a new bride and a new direction in life. In a few hours he would be in Sarasota, where someone very special was waiting for him, and for now that was the only thing on his mind. The plane didn't even have enough people to put one person in each row. The captain came on the loudspeaker and said they were flying at 20,000 feet and to take a look at the sunrise. It was absolutely gorgeous, and it made that day even more special. The plane touched down in Cincinnati for a layover, and at 8:50 Ralph was on the next plane ready to continue his way to Sarasota. There were only 37 people on that flight and he wondered where they were all going and what stories they had to tell. He had been writing in his journal since 6:00 am that morning and had even shared his story about the lives of four special people. It happened when three ladies behind the ticket counter asked him why he was there so early and traveling to Sarasota. *Well,* he thought, *since there is no one else in line and they have asked, I'll tell them the story.* When he was done, there were three ladies standing there with soaking-wet hankies, wiping their eyes. He told them someday he hoped to write a book about it, and they asked if he had a title yet. He told them that he had one in mind but that he wasn't disclosing it yet. Then they asked how they would know if he wrote it. Ralph told them he would make sure it was in a lot of airports, and that he would personally bring it to this one. The last entry Ralph wrote in his diary that day was, "It's 9:10 and we are leaving the ground, and even when we land I'll still be flying high."

Watching old movies had always been one of Ralph's favorite things to do, and the way lovers greeted each other in airports was something he thought only ever happened in movies. That is, he thought this until that day in Sarasota International Airport. Walking through the terminal with bags in his hands as his eyes were scanning the crowd for Betty … well, it just felt like an old movie, especially when he dropped his bags straight to the ground to wrap his arms around her and sweep her off the floor in a loving embrace.

21

RINGING BELLS

The next few days they were up and running; Betty had everything scheduled down to the minute. There was the dress fitting, and then the meeting with Randy at church to make sure the music was right, and then off to Frank's, a craft store, for Christmas supplies, then a dentist appointment, then on to the photographer's to pick up their photos, then to the wedding supply store to drop off the information for printing the wedding programs, then to see the limousine company, and finally, decorating the house for Christmas! On the evening of the 12th Ralph and Betty were invited by Harold and Kathy Kornhaus to go out on the boat with them to watch the annual Christmas boat parade. It was quite a sight, seeing all those boats decorated with lights and other Christmas decorations. They had also invited another couple along, Glen and Marilyn Denlinger, who helped to make this night a very special one indeed. Glen was the executive director of the Charis Center, which is a Christian organization that does family counseling. It was just a great evening, and the parade made the perfect entrance to the beginning of the Christmas season. The only thing missing for Ralph was the snow. Somehow the warm temperatures and the lack of snow were making it feel like the Fourth of July instead of Christmas. Time was moving by rapidly, and before long it was time for the families to start arriving. On the 23rd at exactly 10:00 pm, Wil and Karla and the children pulled into the driveway. Wil said it had taken 17 hours of driving time, and they were exhausted, but they all stayed up talking till 11:30 pm. Now that the family was there, Ralph had to be extra careful with his displays of affection for Betty in front of the children and since they were camped all over the place, and trying to sneak a goodnight kiss seemed impossible. He finally gave up and retreated to his room depressed. He thought everyone was asleep when he heard a soft knock on his door. He got up to answer it, and there stood Betty with the same idea. He pulled her into the room and they started to laugh because of their sneaking around. He tried to get her to stop laughing so he could kiss her, and just then there was a knock on the door. It was Karla wondering what was going on in there. Betty left in a hurry laughing even harder, and Ralph stood there thinking, *There are nine days left until January 2nd … this is going to be a long nine days.* On the 24th Ralph and Betty drove to the Tampa Airport to pick up Mike, whose flight was coming in at 10:45 that evening.

Friday the 25th Ralph and Betty exchanged their Christmas gifts, while Wil, Karla, and the children went to spend the day with his family who were also in Florida at that time. On the 26th Ralph and Betty made the Christmas dinner and then celebrated Christmas with her family. At 7:00 that evening Betty's brother Pete arrived with his wife Dawn and their sons Kyle and Brendan. This was the first time Ralph had met Pete and his family. Ralph told Betty afterwards he wished Pete lived closer, since he shared the same love for the outdoors that he did. On Sunday, the 27th, getting ready for church was a little difficult. CJ was asleep in the family room, Mike was in the living room, and Kari was sleeping on the floor in Betty's room guarding her from

Ralph. The one good thing was that at church they let him sit next to Betty just for the hour service. The 2nd couldn't come quick enough! The rest of the week was filled with lots of busyness, going here, waiting there, the final fitting for the girls, last minute gifts for all those in the bridal party, and family visits, so that by the time is was the day before the wedding, Ralph and Betty were totally wiped out. When the day of the rehearsal dinner came it meant they had only one more day of this hectic pace, and then they could relax together on an island somewhere, the location of which they weren't disclosing to anyone.

The rehearsal was beautiful and very emotional. The dinner afterwards, which was prepared by David and Dorothy Yoder, was for those in the wedding party and all their out-of-town guests. Their friend Dave Christner filmed the entire event for them. After the dinner Ralph stood and invited people to share things, good or bad about Betty and himself with everyone, sort of as a roast, if you will. Ralph reminded all of them, though, that he got to be the last to speak! There were some funny moments directed at both of them, as well as some moments that were really touching. Mostly though, everyone spoke words of encouragement and blessings for the two who had lost their first loves, only to find new love with each other. When everyone was done speaking, Betty asked Ralph to read "The Princess and the Frog," and then they thanked everyone for coming. The visiting went on for over an hour, and then it was time to go home and rest up for the big day.

Wedding day!!! The day began with all the guys taking Ralph out for his last meal, as a single man, that is. They enjoyed a huge buffet meal at what was once the Der Dutchman Restaurant. The girls all scurried off for their hair appointments. The wedding was to take place at Bahia Vista Mennonite Church at 2:30 pm. Dale Beachey was assigned the task of keeping watch on Ralph in a small room that was on one side of the church while Betty was getting ready on the other side. This was no easy job. Ralph was determined to see Betty one more time before the big moment. He did break free and made it all the way to the door of the room where Betty was sequestered, but on the other side was a more determined woman named Verda Beachey who was not about to let him in. The attempt was fun though, and everyone had a good laugh about it, even if it did fail to achieve the desired results of Ralph sneaking one last kiss from Betty!

People had begun to file into the sanctuary, and everyone behind the scenes could hear the selected music being played and sung by Randy and Laura Spalding. The big moment finally arrived, and Kari was the first to walk down the aisle followed by her brother CJ. It was time for Ralph to take his place. He entered the sanctuary and was escorted to the front by his son Rodney and daughter Stephanie. Next was supposed to be their flower girl, Kalicia, but all the bribing in the world wasn't going to get her to walk down the aisle that day. All but three were gathered up front with Pastor Barry Loop. Then the music changed, and Betty entered the Sanctuary escorted by her son, Mike, and daughter, Karla. The back of the sanctuary is all glass and at that hour of the morning the light coming through the balcony and rear doors was so intense that all Ralph could see was the silhouette of Betty and a brilliant glow around her head. It truly looked like an angel was coming down the aisle toward him. When she was within twenty feet of him he could finally see that it was indeed Betty.

Everyone was in his or her place, and the service began. Betty had been telling Ralph that she was going to need help, because she would be too nervous, but as it turned out Ralph was the one who was nervous and Betty had to calm him down by giving him a little wink. The service was going fine and then it was time for their friend, Mike Christner, to sing the song they had picked for him to sing to them. The song was, "I Will Marry My Best Friend," written and arranged by Steve Ragsdale:

I will marry my best friend
And our love will never end
From beginnings humbly sown
A lasting love has grown
Though maybe not at first sight
But in times revealing light
We found the love we were dreaming of
And were lost in love's delight

I will marry my best friend
The one who knows my heart
The one who holds my hand
When the times are hard
What began as a prayer
Has become reality
Friends for life, we'll be husband and wife
And our love will be complete

God has brought us here
To this holy place
And as we make our vows
We seek His face

I will marry my best friend
And a new life will begin
Friends for life, we'll be husband and wife
And our love will never end.

Indeed they had become best friends, and as Ralph looked at Betty while Mike was singing, his eyes welled up with tears thinking of all the events in their lives that had taken place in order to bring them to this point in time. God didn't cause those tragedies to happen, but He did take their pain and suffering and use it for His honor and glory. The song says, "What began as a prayer has become reality." As Ralph stood there gazing into Betty's loving eyes, he couldn't help but think about how Jeanie had asked Stephanie to pray for Betty and him to be together, and that Stephanie did pray this for over a year. And then he remembered how his mother-in-law had prayed for him for over thirteen years that he would come to know Christ. God had been there throughout his life, putting His people in Ralph's path, but it took thirty-four years for Ralph to notice Him.

Why would God want me? Of what earthly good am I? How did I get so lucky to be standing here next to this precious, godly woman, getting a second chance at life? If You, Lord, have a godly purpose for this union, then how will I know? I love her with all my heart and soul, but why me, Lord? She could have had anyone she wanted, so why, Lord, am I standing here about to take her hand in marriage and not someone else? She does deserve better; reveal Yourself to me Lord, and show me how I can serve You. These thoughts were flashing through his mind as he stood there about to say his marriage vows to Betty. He had done this once before in his life, and at that time he'd had no idea what he was really saying, but now these words held great value and meaning. He was promising before God, Betty, family, and their friends to stand by her and love her no matter what, for all the days of his life.

With their vows said they were pronounced husband and wife. A kiss followed and they turned to face their families and friends, and then they were introduced for the first time as Ralph and Betty Walls. Betty was handed a bouquet of roses and as they started down the isle they paused for Betty to give Ralph's mother, Norma, a rose. After the greetings they returned to the front of the sanctuary for all the different pictures to be taken. Then they were off in the limo to the reception at Laurel Oaks Country Club, where the family had a few surprises waiting for them. Wil was the master of ceremonies, and on his cue, as Ralph and Betty entered the banquet hall, the song, "Another One Bites the Dust" began to play. The second prank they had up their sleeve was when Mike was giving the toast. They had filled Ralph's glass with three miniature frogs, and the grandkids couldn't wait to see what would happen when Ralph picked up his glass. Ralph had already noticed them, but he figured he would have some fun making believe he didn't see them. As he tipped his glass up to start to drink, Kalicia became very worried that he was going to drink the frogs. Kalicia was hanging on her Mema's arm trying to get her to stop Ralph. Mema came to the rescue, and she grabbed Ralph's arm just in time to save those pretty little frogs from certain disaster. They were then given to Kalicia to take care of.

The reception was a great time to get to visit with everyone. There were some jokesters in the crowd like Henry, Carl, and Bob, but all in good fun. Their theme for the whole wedding had been "The Power of Love," which was a popular Celine Dion song at the time. They had played her album so much that they wore it out and needed to buy another. Ralph had even written a letter to a talk show host who seemed to be good friends with Celine, telling her the Princess and the Frog story, and asking her if she could get Celine to come and sing at their wedding. Well, she didn't show up, but Ralph worked her into it anyway. When it became time for the garter ceremony, Ralph and Betty had decided they were too old for that kind of carrying on. Instead he had her come to the center of the room and sit in a chair while he knelt in front of her and read the words to another Celine song.

"The Color of My Love"

I'll paint my mood in shades of blue
Paint my soul to be with you
I'll sketch your lips in shaded tones
Draw your mouth to my own

I'll draw your arms around my waist
And then all doubt I shall erase
I'll paint the rain that softly lands on
Your wind-blown hair

I'll trace a hand to wipe your tears
A look to calm your fears
A silhouette of dark and light
While we hold each other oh so tight

I'll paint a sun to warm your heart
Swearing that we'll never part
That's the colour of my love

I'll paint the truth
Show how I feel
Try to make you completely real

I'll use a brush so light and fine
To draw you close and make you mine

I'll paint the truth
Show how I feel
Try to make you completely real
I'll use a brush so light and fine
To draw you close and make you mine

I'll draw a sun to warm your heart
Swearing that we'll never part
That's the colour of my love

I'll draw the years all passing by
So much to learn so much to try

And with this ring our life will start
Swearing that we'll never part
I offer what you cannot buy
Devoted love until we die.
(Written by David Foster and Arthur Janov)

After the reading they danced their first dance to "The Power of Love," and then all were asked to join in. When the evening was completed, Betty had one little surprise left. She went into the lobby where she sat on the couch and asked the photographer to get a picture of Ralph giving her a foot massage. Ralph couldn't wait, but when he started to lift her foot up to his lap he noticed an ankle bracelet with a frog dangling from it. She had worn it the entire day without him noticing it, and everyone had a good laugh as well as it made for a great picture. The newlyweds scurried off to an undisclosed hotel in Tampa to spend the night, then the following day were off to St. Lucia in the Caribbean where they would spend a week at the Jalousie Hilton Resort and Spa. It was nestled in between the two Piton Mountains and was a very relaxing time for them both.

With the honeymoon over it was time to get back to work. When their feet hit the ground in Florida, they took off running. They had three days to get everything accomplished before they would be on a plane again heading back to Pennsylvania. Stephanie had planned a reception for family and friends who were not able to make it to Florida for the wedding. At last count she had 140 people coming to the Bethany Bible Fellowship Church for the Sunday afternoon reception. Ralph and Betty had scheduled an early morning flight for Thursday and would be spending a week working on the house in Marion Heights. But now the task ahead of them was getting everything back in order at their Sarasota home after having such a houseful of visitors, including three children! For one thing they had all the Christmas decorations to take down and all the wedding gifts to put away, a pile of mail to contend with, plus all the other little things that were daily occurrences. The most important thing, though, was that they were husband and wife and they had each other. It was difficult just passing each other in the house; tasks that should have taken minutes to perform started to take a little longer, but that was perfectly fine to the new couple, because that little show of affection while passing was worth it. The work eventually got completed. Thursday's flight was on time and they touched down in Harrisburg around noon. Stephanie picked them up at the airport and drove them back to the house, where Ralph had left his vehicles. Ralph hadn't even put the bags down and he was already planning what he wanted to work on first. Betty and Stephanie convinced him to slow down a little and relax. He did, kind of, for the moment, but just being there had his mind racing with all the projects that were left to do to make this house complete. The girls didn't want to hear about it; they just wanted to sit, talk and look at the pictures of the honeymoon. Ralph finally gave in since he saw that he was getting nowhere, being outnumbered by two women. But by Friday morning they were ready to start work. The kitchen cabinets had been delivered when Ralph was leaving for Florida, back in December, so they were still boxed and sitting on the floor. The kitchen now became the number one priority, that is, when they could free up their hands to do the work. Betty needed work clothes, and Ralph found a pair of bib overalls of Jeanie's that looked like they had never been worn. Betty loved them and Ralph did too, so this became a photo opportunity. Ralph mentioned that she was the best looking cabinet installer he had ever seen. Later on that day they did get the cabinets installed and even got the sink hooked up with running water. Now with a totally functioning kitchen they needed to buy groceries to put in it, and finally it would seem like a completely livable house, though it was by no means fully renovated yet. They still had the entire ground floor to work on, but that could be done at a later date. For now the two upstairs floors were all they needed to make this house a home.

The annual Christmas get together with the Miller family was scheduled for Saturday in Lancaster. So, bright and early that morning, Ralph and Betty drove the two-hour trip to Bird-in-Hand Restaurant where Betty had rented a dining room for their gathering. This family gathering was real special for Ralph. They all treated him like he was a family member, like he had always been one of their own, and that meant a lot to him. It actually turned out to be a sort of surprise party for Ralph and Betty, as wedding gifts showed up along with Christmas gifts. Gid's mother would always give Ralph a kiss like he was her own son. Whenever he left after visiting with them, he always felt blessed for knowing them.

While in Lancaster they stopped to visit Betty's mother. She also made Ralph feel like he was one of her own family, giving him a big welcome kiss and a hug. She was always eager to know what was going on in everyone's life, and she thoroughly enjoyed looking at all the pictures of the places they had been and where they were living. She had the presence of a very godly woman about her, and it was evident that she was very strong in her faith. She was 92 years old at that time but still looked younger than her years, and Ralph remarked that now he knew from whom Betty got her looks and especially that great big smile.

Sunday was a lot of fun. Going to Sunday school and church at Bethany felt really special to them both. Stephanie had done an extraordinary job of putting together the reception and had made every little detail perfect. Ralph was asked to read the Princess and the Frog story, which he just so happened to bring along. Of course, there is always one in every crowd who has to call your attention to details, and this time it was Brian, who was cracking up at some of the wording and wanted Ralph to explain it. It was all in fun and everyone had a great time as usual. The week went fast and before long they headed back to Florida. This time they were driving Ralph's van back with some things packed in it.

During the month of February, Stephanie called to give Ralph and Betty some good news. She had finally gotten pregnant and was expecting her first child in September. Betty commented it must have been the Florida water, but Ralph thought kind of differently about it. Stephanie had been through so much the past three years, with all the stress of her mother's illness and eventual death, and then the uncertainty about what her father was going to do with the rest of his life, and then striving to honor her mother's dying request to pray about her dad and Betty getting together. She had carried a great deal of the family's burdens when Jeanie had died, being the oldest and the only daughter. No wonder she couldn't get pregnant. But once she could relax knowing her father was in good hands, it happened. Ralph was elated, but then his next thought would be, *now if Rodney would ask Peggy to marry him before she wakes up and changes her mind about him, we'll be all set!*

The weeks and months ahead were filled with trips to Pennsylvania. Working on finishing the house was a major concern for Ralph. He made a couple of trips up for a week or more by himself, but he didn't like being away from his Betty for too long. He had also come to the conclusion that he wanted to sell that property. They just didn't need the worry of having an extra home on their minds. So as soon as the work was complete, the house went on the market.

July was a real busy month. Ralph and Betty had started to build a home on one of the Miller's Field subdivision lots. This was going to be just a speculative venture property to sell. They thought they would try their hand at a modular home and already had the foundation built. It had been scheduled for the modular home to be set onto the foundation on the 30th of the month. CJ was going to come and help them build the adjoining garage once the house was in place. His mother Karla and both his sisters were already visiting their cousins in Lancaster and were planning to come over for a couple of days to visit them also. On the 22nd Ralph and Betty invited Stephanie to join them along with Karla and her children for a farewell brunch before Karla headed back to Colorado.

The family had conspired together to throw a surprise baby shower for Stephanie. That night Ralph and Betty were technically supposed to be taking Karla and the girls to the airport, but they really weren't, because they had a mob of people hiding at the house waiting to surprise Stephanie. Ralph had dreamed up a plausible excuse for getting her to come over to their house. The Marion Heights house was on the market, so Ralph called Stephanie and told her that someone wanted to come and look at the house just as they were leaving for the airport. Ralph told Stephanie that he hoped this wasn't too inconvenient for her, because he had already promised the prospective buyer that she could come over and show the house to him in Ralph's absence. Stephanie wasn't too happy about this, because she still had her dirty clothes on from working all day and was just about to rest her legs. But being the great daughter she is, she said she would do it. The expression on her face as she opened the door was priceless. It was the first time anyone had ever tricked her. The next day Stephanie was going to the shore with her cousin, Kayleen, to rest, which she jokingly said she really needed now after getting the shock of her life with their surprise! But the baby shower was a great success, and she received many wonderful gifts.

On July 23rd the annual weekend retreat to Spruce Lake was taking place. Most of the Spruce Lake gang was there. At night they always opened up the snack shop and everyone would gather for ice cream. Ralph had just finished his ice cream and was standing on the deck when someone came running from the office looking for Ralph Walls.

"I'm Ralph."

"Your daughter just called, and we have some bad news for you..."As soon as Ralph heard those words his body went ice cold, and he could feel himself getting weak as he thought frantically, *Oh no, not the baby...*

"Hal Snyder died this evening. I'm sorry to have to give you this news. Your daughter asked that you call her at the shore." Betty grabbed Ralph knowing that he was not taking this well. Ralph slowly walked to the car to get his cell phone and called Stephanie. Betty was by his side all the way, and she was thinking how they had just seen him in Florida a couple of months ago while he and Sandy were at their Bradenton condo. They had gotten together to visit and play games and Hal was just filled with life, laughing and joking around. This was just so unexpected.

Ralph got to the car, found his cell phone, and called Stephanie.

"Hi Steph, what happened?"

"I just got the call from Mark at home. Rhoda called to say that Hal had a massive heart attack and was gone instantly." Ralph could hardly speak as he looked over at Betty and shook his head sadly. His eyes were two big pools of water.

"Was he alone?"

"I think they said Sandy was right there with him when it happened."

"Steph, I can't talk now, but Betty and I will be back in town Sunday afternoon. I got to go now." Stephanie knew her father was taking this badly and literally couldn't talk right then, and that's why he'd said a hurried goodbye. This man had meant so much to Ralph from the day he first met him, and now he was gone. He was there for him through Jeanie's ordeal with her fight against cancer. He had supplied Ralph with work when he couldn't think about anything except the well being of his wife. Betty was rubbing Ralph's back and saying poor Sandy, and Ralph had to think how he had said that same phrase when seeing Betty at Gid's memorial service. They both knew how it felt to lose a spouse and all the grief and suffering that the family would go through. It just brought back so many memories for them both that it made it all the more tragic. The Spruce Lake gang wanted to know all about this man, which in a way helped Ralph that first evening to cope with the loss of his dear friend. Hal died the day before what would have been Jeanie's 49th birthday, and he was only 59. The service for Hal was held on the 28th of July. The church was packed and people were standing outside while the service went on. It was a powerful service to honor a godly man who had touched the lives of many. A young lady whom Hal had lead to the Lord stood upstairs on a tiny balcony out of everyone's view and sang the following song by Ray Boltz:

"Thank You"

I dreamed I went to heaven and you were there with me.
We walked upon the streets of gold beside the crystal sea
We heard the angels singing then someone called your name
I turned and saw this young man and he was smiling as he came

And he said, friend you may not know me now
And then he said, but wait.
You used to teach my Sunday school when I was only eight
And every week you would say a prayer
Before the class would start
And one day when you said that prayer I asked Jesus in my heart

Thank you for giving to the Lord, I am a life that was changed

Thank you for giving to the Lord, I am so glad you gave.

And then another man stood before you and said
remember the time
A missionary came to your church, his picture made you
cry
You didn't have much money but you gave it anyway
Jesus took the gift you gave and that's why I am here today

Thank you for giving to the Lord, I am a life that was
changed
Thank you for giving to the Lord, I am so glad you gave.

One by one they came as far as the eye could see
Each life somehow touched by your generosity
Little things that you had done and sacrifices made
Unnoticed on the earth in heaven now proclaim

And I know now up in heaven your not suppose to cry
But I am almost sure there were tears in your eyes
As Jesus took your hand and you stood before the Lord
He said my child look around you great is your reward

Thank you for giving to the Lord, I am a life that was
changed
Thank you for giving to the Lord I am so glad you gave.

Everyone was amazed that she had been able to make it through that song without choking up, as there wasn't a dry eye in the church. It was the most fitting tribute that ever could have been given to this godly man. It almost seemed as if this song had been written just for him.

The following scripture was read at Hal's funeral, and it certainly deserves to be quoted again here:

I have fought the good fight, I have finished the race, I have kept the faith. Finally there is laid up for me the crown of righteousness, which the Lord, the righteous Judge, will give to me on that Day, and not just to me only but also to all who have loved his appearing (2 Timothy 4: 7-8 NKJV).

It was a strange feeling going back to work that week knowing that he would never hear his dear friend's voice again, saying, "Hey, buddy, how are you doing?" But he knew Hal would want him to carry on and be strong in his faith.

CJ had arrived to help out with the garage addition on the modular home, and they were back to work on the house. The first job Betty and CJ tackled was tarring the foundation while Ralph was getting the materials for the construction of the garage. When he returned there was a real good photo op for him of CJ. Ralph asked him if he was standing in the bucket of tar on purpose while he was doing the foundation coating. He must have had it planned, because his Mema took him out and bought him new sneakers later. It was great having him there, and that summer he learned at lot about framing a house. He turned out to be quite skilled and fearless on the roofs. His Mema just held her breath every time he would go whizzing by her.

* * * * *

Two weeks had passed since Hal's death, and one day Betty received a phone call from Marie Kaufman with some more bad news. Their dear friend, Ella May Lehman, had died the day before. Her son Kevin had stopped by the house and heard the mower running out back, and when he looked he found his mother slumped over on it. This was another tragic loss of such a vibrant and active Christian friend. With five deaths in such a short time span — Shirley, Gid, Jeanie, Hal, and now Ella Mae — it was almost too much to bear at one time. Ralph, Betty, and CJ drove to Ohio to support Jay and his family during this time of their devastating loss. The service was held at the Kidron Mennonite Church where many turned out to honor the memory of this dynamic lady of God. There were many testimonials given and words of comfort and praise offered to the family at that time.

* * * * *

With the new house completed and the Marion Heights house on the market for sale, it was time to head back to Florida to pick up the pieces after another summer filled with terrible losses. They knew both their friends were in a better place, where there was no more suffering or pain, but just knowing that they wouldn't see them any more was painful. But because of their faith in God they had comfort and peace, knowing that they would be together again with those that went before them.

* * * * *

You may remember at one point in this book I mentioned how much I love old movies – yes, I am that infamous Ralph Walls of the story, in case you hadn't guessed it by now!

One of my favorite old movies is "It's a Wonderful Life." If you've seen it, you'll remember how the angel was sent to show George Bailey that his life did have meaning after all, and that it was a good thing he had been born. The angel came to take him back in time and show him exactly what it would have been like if he had never been born. The angel, Clarence, showed George all the people that his life had touched, and Clarence also showed him what it would have been like if George had never existed. George was shocked to see how just one individual and their actions could affect so many people's lives, whether for good or bad (as in the case of Mr. Potter). In this case all their lives would have been tragically worse without him. In the end George Bailey changes his mind and doesn't jump off the bridge. The last scene of the movie shows him gathered with all his family and friends, celebrating Christmas, when he hears a bell tinkling on the Christmas tree. You see, the angel had been sent here on a mission, and if he successfully completed it, he would earn his wings. George smiled when he heard the bell tinkling and he reminded his little daughter that whenever you heard bells ringing, that meant another angel had earned his wings.

Why am I telling you this story? Because a little boy of ten was told that when he turned twelve his Pop Pop would teach him how to fly an airplane. The day before his tenth birthday, his beloved Pop Pop was killed in a plane crash. This little boy told his Mema he hated his birthday and never wanted to celebrate any more birthdays again.

On July 18, 2002, sixteen-year-old C. J. Esh took his first solo flight. I stood there with the rest of the family filming and snapping pictures. When he touched down on the ground again, we all ran over to congratulate him. As we approached the plane I asked, "Am I the only one crying?" His mother turned and looked at me and didn't say a word. I could see by the streaks of tears and expression of joy and her face that she was overwhelmed. At that precise moment, I was sure I could hear bells ringing, and when I looked skyward I could see his Pop Pop, Gid Miller, ringing them with a big smile on his face.

EPILOGUE

The title *Flowers in the Crags* was chosen for this book because it had such an impact on my life. The day I traveled to the hospital with my wife and she startled me with that phrase, I think it was a wake-up call for me. I had never seen my wife complain about pain before, so on that particular day, when she said she was hurting and in pain, I knew it was for real. Then when her whole attitude and countenance changed upon seeing those flowers on that dangerous hillside tucked into those crags, I instantly thought God had placed them there for such a time as this. Those little flowers had taken her eyes off of her own painful situation and turned them toward something beautiful that God, in all His wisdom and glory, had created and put in her path. I started in the beginning of this book by using a phrase from Scripture: *The road to life is narrow, and few are those who find it.* I believe that narrow road is the road to eternal life with Jesus Christ. It's the road less traveled, because it's narrow. This thing called life is a journey, and this journey has a destination. I will talk about that destination in a moment. But first let's take a look at our journey through life. I truly believe there is a purpose to our lives; we weren't just put here to aimlessly wander this great planet of ours. I believe that our great Creator, God, has a reason for each and every one of us here. The Bible says we are here to honor and glorify Him. Do we? How many of us here on this planet take time to honor and glorify Him? I traveled my journey of life, living for myself for thirty-four years before I realized that I didn't have to travel alone — that there was a God who loved me and wanted me to become one of His children. He cared about my life, and even though I was the scum of the earth, He still loved me. Throughout my journey in life, He had placed all kinds of people in my path who knew the way that led to eternal life, but I had failed to notice them. But He never gave up on me; He continued to pursue me until finally, one day the blinders fell off my eyes and I saw the truth. Those people were the flowers in the crags along the treacherous journey of my life. They were tucked down into the crags, the times in my life when I was hurting, lost, and even being tempted; they were there along the road of life showing me the way to eternal life.

This book is a feeble attempt to pay tribute to those precious ones who were the flowers in the crags for many people. Some have gone on ahead of us to their reward, but there are still many here among us. If you are a child of God's, brighten up someone's day today, and be a flower in the crags for them. If you're not sure where you are in your journey of life, slow down; take time to see what God has planted just for you along the way.

THE END OF THE BEGINNING: FINDING THE NARROW ROAD
(FOR YOUR EYES ONLY)

You're probably wondering what this is all about – THE END OF THE BEGINNING. What does that mean, anyway, and why is he still writing? The End: at some point in their life, everyone will have to face those two words one day. Yes, life is going to come to an end. The question is do you know where you will spend eternity when the end comes? I'm sure you understand that there are only two choices. The Bible is pretty explicit about that. You also probably know that they both start with the letter **"H."** You know what both those words are, don't you? That's right, Heaven and Hell. Why am I telling you this? Because as a believer I have been instructed to do so. No, God didn't come down here one night and sit in my living room and chat with me, and reveal to me some amazing truth, but what He did do was to come into my heart. Wait a minute you say, you're starting to freak me out.

Do you see those other words at the top of the page? That's right, the ones in the parentheses that say "for your eyes only." That's just what it means; if you don't want to hear anymore of this, then this is a good place for you to bail out, but if you want to hear more, then this is for your eyes only. You see, we have a loving God; He loves each and every one of us no matter what we have done. Yes, He *loves us*, but He *hates our sin*. He loves us so much that he sent His Son to pay the penalty for our sins by dying on the cross. God is willing to throw away all your sins, forgive you of them, and not remember them. Ok, you say, what's the catch? Listen very carefully, because this is the hard part. You must believe in Him. And exactly who is this "Him"? It is His Son, Jesus Christ. Do you want proof? Then, if you have a Bible turn to John 3:16, or you can just read it right here.

For God so loved the world that He gave His only begotten Son, that whoever believes in Him should not perish but have everlasting life.

So you ask, how do I get to have this assurance that I will go to heaven and not hell? If you believe that Jesus Christ is the Son of God and that He died on the cross for your sins, then you need to tell Him you believe in Him. The best way is to go to Him in prayer. It's real easy, but it must be sincere and come from your heart. You probably remember how I prayed three times before I felt the presence of God in my life. Let me say this first. That isn't always the case. Many people have sincerely prayed a prayer of repentance and salvation and have never had any flash of light or something dramatic happen, but they still were truly saved and had become new creatures in Jesus Christ. In my case, I think the first two times I was just saying the words without making them real in my heart. After I cried out to God in the third prayer, it was real, and I could finally see all that I had been guilty of being erased from God's memory. Sometimes when I think about that, I see a VCR tape being rewound while I'm watching it, right before my eyes. In Psalm 139: 23-24 it says: *Search me, O God, and know my heart; Try me, and know my anxieties; and see if there is any wicked way in me, And lead me in the way everlasting.*

In a sense, that's what I think God was doing for me that day. He took my life on tape and rewound it right back to the beginning. Not so I could start life over, but I think He was saying to me, this is a new beginning, let's start here, and this time put Me in the center of your life. It was years before I figured out that's what was happening to me that day when I sincerely asked Him into my heart. He promises in Hebrews 8: 12: *For I will be merciful to their unrighteousness, and their sins and their lawless deeds I will remember no more.*

He erased my sins, and He remembers them no more. I became a new creature in Christ. How do I know this? For one thing, the old me never felt remorse for anything wrong I said or did to anyone. Oh sure, I *knew* right from wrong, but I never thought it was a big deal if I said something hurtful to someone; I figured they would just get over it. I never felt guilty for having a bad thought. *What could that possibly hurt?* I reasoned. *It's my brain, I can put what I want in it, and no one needs to know.* The only problem with that reasoning is this: when you ask Christ into your heart, His Spirit comes to dwell in you. That probably sounds a little strange; so let's take a closer look at that.

When you ask Christ into your heart, His Spirit takes up residence there. He moves in. Now when you have a bad thought or say something bad or even look at something you probably shouldn't be looking at, you will be convicted of your sin because God's Spirit is pure and Holy. In other words, your wrongdoing will be brought to your attention. Whereas previously that same thing would have slid right by and you wouldn't have even given it a second thought. But now since God's Spirit is living in you, it flashes up a warning sign. That is called conviction. His Spirit is pure and Holy, and once we become born again it takes up residence in our sinful bodies, and good and evil can't reside in the same body. The Bible tells us you can't serve two masters. Luke 16:13: "*No servant can serve two masters; for either he will hate the one and love the other, or else he will be loyal to the one and despise the other. You cannot serve God and mammon.*"

Let me make another point here. Just because you have made that commitment of asking Christ into your heart does not mean from that point on you will be a perfect human specimen walking around not committing sin anymore. You and I are a work in progress; we are working toward the goal of becoming more Christlike in our daily walk. There was only one perfect individual who walked the face of this earth, and that was Jesus when He was here in His earthly body. We will not reach that state until the end, when He takes us home to be with Him for all eternity. That is His promise to us if we are His on the Day of Judgment. We will spend all eternity with Him. That day will come when we all will stand before Him and have to give an account of ourselves. From what I have read in the Bible, it's not going to be very pretty for those who don't know Him. He is going to say to those who know Him, "Well done, my good and faithful servant," and to those who don't, He is going to say, "Go away from me, for I never knew you." I have also read that those He sends away will say, but I did all those good deeds for you and I went to church for forty years and gave money every week, and He will say to them, "But I never knew you." They never asked Him into their lives; they never made that personal commitment to serving Him. They will be sent to the Lake of Torment (Hell).

Did you ever stop to think what hell would be like? The Bible gives some descriptions of it, but let me give you something that sticks in my mind. When I was a child we lived in an old farmhouse with the bedrooms upstairs. There was no air conditioning then and we didn't even own a fan. I'll bet there wasn't any insulation in the attic either. The month of

August was always the hottest of all the months, and trying to sleep upstairs in my room was unbearable. I would toss and turn all night long, never getting comfortable and never falling asleep. By morning I would be totally exhausted from not receiving the rest I needed. To me that was hell. Now multiply that by a million and it might still not be as bad as hell. God's Word says that in hell there *will be weeping and gnashing of teeth*. It sounds like a terrible place to have to spend all of eternity.

You may be wondering how someone can go to church their whole lives, and put money in the offering plate, and still, once they face judgment God says to them, "Depart from Me, I never knew you." How can this be? The answer is simple and straightforward – they have not made a personal commitment to Christ. They have sat there all those years not *really* hearing the Word of God. The Bible talks about people's hearts becoming hardened. If a heart has become hardened to the truth, then the truth just can't penetrate it. Others might sit in a church where the truth is not revealed. How can that be, you ask again. Not every church teaches or preaches the truth about salvation. The true church of Jesus Christ will teach and preach that Jesus Christ is the only way to God. There is no other way. We are all sinners, and there must be forgiveness for sin. There are a lot of churches out there steeped in traditions. Everything is done with the mindset of, "This is how our fathers did it and their fathers before them, so we are going to continue to do it this way." Traditions won't get you in the door of heaven. Signs and symbols won't do it either. Praying to the saints will not do it either. The Bible is very clear on the fact that there is only one way to the Father, and that is through the shed blood of Jesus Christ, His Son. His blood was shed to cover our sins, yours and mine. If you saw the movie, "The Passion of the Christ," you witnessed the brutal beating our Lord took on our behalf. Yes, He took that beating *on our behalf.*

Every lash, every blow, was in payment for the sins we have committed and are yet going to commit.

In the scene of that movie where it shows the hand of a Roman soldier driving the nails into Christ on the cross—that could be all our hands driving those nails. It was because of us that He went to the cross. He was the only perfect sacrifice that could be made on our behalf. The Son of God did that for you and for me. Our God does not wish for one of His children to be lost. He loves us all.

I've written a lot of extra words to the body of this book, and it is going to cost me some extra money, but every penny is worth it to me if even one soul comes to know Christ. But when you compare that small cost to what it cost Jesus to go to the cross because of His love for you and me, it's nothing. The shame and humiliation that He took upon Himself for us is priceless. If you have read this all the way through and you want to know Jesus as your personal Savior, then you must ask Him into your heart. You must admit to Him that you realize you are a sinner and ask for His forgiveness. If you don't know Him and you want to start your relationship with Him right now, I'll help you. If you are in a place where you feel comfortable and can talk to Him in private, without being distracted by anyone or anything else, then start by saying this prayer:

Father, I recognize that I am a sinner and that I have been living only for myself. I realize that is wrong, and I need You in my life. I understand that Your Son, Jesus Christ went to the cross and gave His life on my behalf, to pay the price for my sins. I am asking for your forgiveness for those sins. Come into my life, Lord, and make me a new creature in You. I ask this in the precious name of Jesus Christ, my Lord and my Savior, Amen.

If you prayed that prayer from your heart, you are a new creature in Christ. You have been born again! You are now part of the family of God. Welcome to the family! One of the first things you need to do is to tell someone the good news. It's not going to be easy — remember, I was teased and criticized for my new beliefs. As a believer we are instructed to pass the good news on. Maybe you have a family member or friend that you would like to make sure will be in eternity with you, so take the time to share God's truth with them. Second, if you have a Bible, start to read it. I would suggest starting in the New Testament. Third, take all your cares and concerns to the Lord in prayer. Do you realize His line is always open; there is no such thing as a busy signal with God? You can reach Him anytime and anywhere. Go to Him often in prayer; make it a habit. It's one of the best habits you could ever have. Always start off by calling Him 'Father,' because that is what He is, He is your heavenly Father. Be respectful, but don't be afraid to share your heart with Him. He wants to hear all you have to say.

Another important thing to do is to find a good Bible preaching church. I realized that you're never too old for Sunday school, either. It's not just for children. It's nice when you can be fed from the Word of God a couple of times on Sundays. It has been a real pleasure sharing the Word of God with you in this book, and it certainly would be nice if I could meet you while I'm still here walking this earth. I know, however, that if we don't meet here, we will be together when the roll is called up yonder. Blessings! And may the peace of God be with you always.

The End of the Beginning!

UPDATES

1999........Carl Grace married Fern Schmucker
1999........Stephanie gave birth to Madeline Jean Broda
2001........Rodney and Peggy were married
2002........Jay Lehman married Emma Shrock
2002........Betty's Mother Elizabeth Herr passed away at 94
2002........CJ took solo flight
2002........Ralph and Betty mission trip to Haiti
2002........Stephanie gave birth to Alexandra Lyn Broda
2003........CJ got his PVT. License
2003........Karla and CJ mission trip to Papua New Guinea
2004........CJ got his Instrument Rating
2004........Joe Bradshaw became associate pastor at Bahia Vista Menno.
2004........Ralph and Betty mission trip to Hungary
2004........Kari mission trip to London
2005........CJ got his Commercial License
2005........Kari mission trip to Guatemala
2005........Karla and Kalicia mission trip to Czech Republic
2005........CJ became a Certified Flight Instructor
2006........CJ Received his Multi Engine Rating

2006........Gid's mother, Arie Miller, passed away on May 6, 2006

Upon her death Arie Miller was 90 years old, and she was survived by seven daughters, 51 grandchildren, and 178 great-grandchildren.

Gid and Betty wedding day April 22, 1961

Gid's Meyers 200

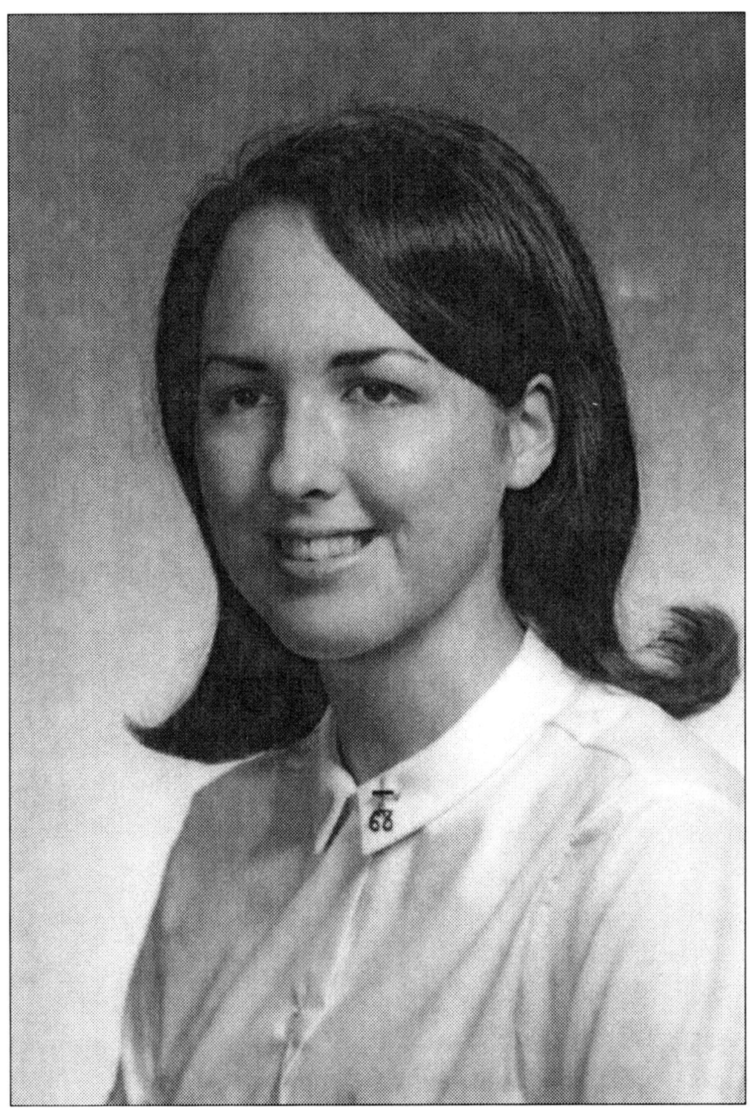

Jeanie high school graduation 1968

Ralph and Jeanie prom engagement 1968

Ralph after basic training

Gid and Betty 1994

Ralph and Jeanie in Bermuda 1975

Ralph, Jeanie, Stephanie and Rodney 1979

Gid Miller TWA Captain 1981

Kari, Kalicia, CJ, Gid, Betty, Mike, Karla, and Wil 1995

Last photo of Gid with grandchildren

Jeanie waving goodbye seven months before her death

Ralph and Betty wedding day 1999

Combined family 2002
Kalicia, Maddie, Lexi, Kari,
Stephanie, Peggy,
CJ, Karla, Betty, Rod,
Wil, Mark, Mike, Ralph

LaVergne, TN USA
06 December 2009
166105LV00002B/8/A

9 781602 660823